Life in Christmas Letters

A Story of Friendship, Love and Loyalty

Theresa McKenna

Dedication

This book is dedicated to my husband, Dan, who has filled my life with love, joy and memories beyond my hopes or dreams. My life is blessed because of you. Thank you for encouraging me to write this story.

Preface

This story has several layers wrapped in a Christmas theme. First, it is a love letter to my family: my husband, Dan, and two sons, Kevin and Carter. Secondly, it's a story about how relationships enrich our lives and that life is a collection of memories, big and small. Lastly, the book is about resilience and growth as well as a light commentary on working mother's issues. My goal is to tell a story that fills your heart with laughter and love all year round.

PART ONE

What is *more*?
June 1999 – December 2001

Chapter One

Life … what is it … really? Get up, go to work, come home for a couple of hours of free time or family time … press repeat … forever? If those are the major activities in life, what makes a good life? These are common questions people ask themselves from time to time, or maybe all the time. In the years after college, Teddy asked herself these questions with a bit more frequency. At thirty-one, she surmised that life was really just creating a collection of memories – an invisible scrapbook filled with carefully culled happy moments.

This conclusion didn't seem quite right in light of her Catholic upbringing and her continued spiritual beliefs. But if life could be defined as a collection of memories, Teddy began to consider if she would be pleased with her personal collection when the end came. Was her life on track to be a good life? Would it get high marks from the imaginary panel of life judges? These were her thoughts when she was optimistic about life.

Other times, she found it all pointless. As her parents aged, this became quite an acute opinion. Her mom and dad seemed to simply go through the motions of everything they thought to be a good life – kids, grandkids, church, gardens, woodworking, cooking. The list of time-filling but somewhat empty activities was long in their lives. But their lives seemed void of any true meaning, which Teddy had come to define as meaningful relationships. None of their children genuinely cared for them. They were more in the obligation category than people any of them sought to spend time with. Maybe a few of their fifteen grandchildren enjoyed their short visits with them, but that list was sparse too.

So, what was the point of life? To make relationships and memories that you can't take with you to whatever may be on the other side? Was it all a treadmill of drudgery until it stopped? Teddy felt this way often. Sometimes when things were hard in her life, she would lie in bed wishing to be whisked away, not to some tropical island, but to the nothingness she supposed was more than likely on the other side of life. Were these suicidal thoughts she sometimes wondered? Probably not, just someone wallowing in what nowadays is cheekily referred to as "first-world problems." She wanted a so-called good life. But was she creating one?

Teddy, whose childhood nickname was intended to shorten her awkward given name of Theodora and to give her a "boy" name to blend with her four older brothers, was not a sentimental or emotional person. Theodora DeGarmo. Quite a name. She often described herself as more of a guy than a girl. She was hardworking and career minded. Practical and tactical, she created and attacked to-do lists in her professional life with the precision and accuracy of a sharpshooter. She was a one woman show of getting things accomplished. "Taking care of business" – "TCB" – was her personal motto.

But as the years wore on and she realized that working at a job she felt no passion for was grating on her. Corporate life was highly overrated, not nearly as glamorous as it was positioned to her in the '80s. Politics. Incompetent coworkers. Arrogant executives. No tangible purpose. Teddy dreamed of being a teacher from an early age. She played teacher in front of her chalkboard in the basement of her childhood home for hours. Her poor little friends, always relegated to being her students. Clomping around in her mother's high heels imitating Mrs. Drake and Mrs. Roush was heaven to Teddy.

Teddy's straight A's in high school, however, put her on a path not towards teaching, but towards business. She couldn't possibly count the number of people who told her, "You're too smart to become a teacher," or "There's no money in teaching; you can do better, Teddy." And it was the '80s when business was king, and girls were told they could have it all. And having it all was defined as having a job that men had. Hooray, congratulations girls! What a prize.

Due to her unfulfilling experience in the corporate world, Teddy came to long for the meaning that she believed a traditional family could provide. She now looked back at some aspects of her family upbringing as fulfilling instead of debilitating. Maybe she did want a family after all. Maybe that is what was missing. And, of course, in her mind she would be a much better parent than her own and raise children who would of course adore her. She certainly knew that her collection of memories so far was not all that fulfilling. Travel got old much quicker than she ever imagined. She knew that her life was good if measured by possessions, comfort and fun. That feeling that there had to be more to life seemed to become naggingly constant.

What is *more*, though? Deep down, she knew that what

she was doing and where she was headed was not her true definition of a good life. She concluded that *more* was marriage and children. That was the fix. She was certain. She had done her homework, her self-reflection. Family was the answer.

But first, where did this execution-oriented, high achieving person come from? Teddy had heard whispers around the house during her childhood that she was a "blessing," the Catholic code word for an unplanned pregnancy – an oops. She realized she did not quite fit in her family at a very early age when she understood that her brothers were significantly older than she was. Her oldest brother was seventeen years her senior and the youngest was nine. They were not siblings. They were uncles.

"If I wasn't a girl, my parents would have given me away," Teddy would tell children on the playground. Teddy was seemingly born with the notion that she didn't quite belong and rightfully so, as her mother told a teenage Teddy that she cried every day when she was pregnant with her. The reason for these tears, her mother explained, was that at thirty-seven in the late 1960s she was too old to be pregnant again, with her youngest of four children in late elementary school and her oldest a high school senior.

Revealingly, Teddy always defined herself as a

"mistake," which led to a lifelong pursuit of proving her worth. Teddy chose to cope with her nagging feeling of being a mistake by pleasing people and striving to be the best at everything, following all the rules set out for a good girl in the 1970s and 1980s. She committed never to cause trouble like her older brothers were so often inclined to do. One moved across the country breaking her parents' hearts. Another had drug and alcohol problems. Another got married at eighteen to his pregnant girlfriend, and another lived in the basement until he was twenty-eight, spending all of his money on booze at bars.

If she helped her mother with chores, absorbed her mother's venom about her unhappy marriage that spewed nightly while they prepared dinner and washed the dishes and excelled in the classroom and at the piano, her parents would have to love her, right? Teddy was going to redeem it all so that she could justify her existence.

Teddy's life operating model of rule following perfectionism caused stress that she was unaware of until well into adulthood. When she looked back at her childhood, she saw that she was constantly striving for a finish line that awarded her a gold medal that would make people like her.

Teddy's unfulfilling relationship with her family hinged upon the feeling of all give and no get, especially emotionally.

She certainly received the necessities of a clean home, clothes, food and money for education, but she never felt the emotional connection that she desired, despite her efforts. Teddy visited all her brothers at some point or another at their various homes across the country once she graduated from college and had a job to fund travel. None ever bothered to visit her. This disconnection is where Teddy's ambivalence towards having a family of her own most certainly emanated.

Despite her upbringing and never wanting a husband and family before, Teddy now had complete conviction that marriage and children would be the only things that could fill her void. So, she set a new course and aimed her intensity on personal endeavors. It was scary because Teddy had never been particularly successful when it came to men. But, in true Teddy style, she set a goal, took action and, of course, achieved success.

Chapter Two

It was hot and humid. It was July in Houston, after all. Summer 1999 had been an unexpectedly terrific one for Teddy. She met a promising man. This was quite a big deal as Teddy came to Houston from her home state of Ohio just a year earlier for a job but not knowing a soul in her newly adopted home. She was happy to be trading in four seasons for the forever summer of the south. Teddy had a strange optimism about her future in Houston. She had no idea why or where the feeling was coming from, but it was there, that feeling that it was all going to work out.

Perhaps a Christmas miracle happened in June when she met whom she thought was *the guy*. The brochure she was reviewing about a tax service that her accounting firm was launching – not exactly the most riveting topic. She stared in a daze at her computer screen while she daydreamed about him. Surprisingly, Teddy just didn't care. Checking things off her to do list was a favorite pastime and admired skill. Daydreaming about boys was not a Teddy-like thing to do. But this man was so promising, and she had come to the realization that the job she moved to Texas for was not a great use of her time or talents. So why not daydream about a boy? Teddy couldn't recall ever doing something like this with any frequency, even as a teenager. Of course, maybe that's because she didn't go out on a date until she was a senior in high school.

Earlier that summer, she made last-minute plans to stop by a work happy hour for just one drink to be what is now known as a "wingman" for a work friend interested in dating the event's host.

"Oh, come on Teddy, just one drink," begged Jenny.

"Jenny, it's been such a long week. I am tired," replied Teddy emphatically.

"Seriously, it can be just one drink. Just one, one, one," said Jenny repeating the word "one" with a different pitch with each repetition.

"Seriously me? Seriously you! Admit you just want to go because you want to spend more time with James … who is married, married, married," mocked Teddy matching Jenny's previous pitch changes.

"How many times have I told you he is just a friend. I think he's funny. But if we want to bring men into this, then we can. How are you going to find that 'Notre Dame boy' you've set your sights on if you don't go out?"

"Oh yes, just a friend. Silly me. Well, I admit you got me on not finding a man in my apartment. Believe me, I have checked, and none are hiding in there who want to be the father of my children. There are lots of men hiding in there, sure, but it's the fatherhood thing that makes them run every time!"

Jenny won. Teddy went to the happy hour with her friend. It was there that she met this promising man.

His name was Colin, and thankfully he did not work at her accounting firm. Instead, his college friend, Timothy O'Malley, who was on assignment in Houston from the firm's Chicago office, extended Colin a last-minute invitation to the happy hour, similar to Teddy's. O'Malley, the unintentional matchmaker was only still in Houston because Dallas thunderstorms cancelled his scheduled flight back home to

Chicago. Clearly, Teddy and Colin were meant to meet that night. Even Mother Nature was playing a hand in this match.

Their initial meeting was not notable for Teddy. No lightning bolts went through her. She did find Colin's job fascinating. In a short conversation she learned about the many jobs that support professional sports franchises.

"You work at the NBA team, the Rockets?" Teddy inquired somewhat skeptically after Colin introduced himself and where he worked.

"Yes, I am in media relations," Colin replied.

"So, that means you work with the media, but what, with the players or the ownership?" Teddy probed.

"Yes, so if a reporter wants access to a player or a coach, I arrange that and help them stay on message."

"Ah yes, those pesky messages," Teddy laughed being a marketing professional herself. "What about the owner, that little goofy guy who looks and sounds like Elmer Fudd?"

"No, the owner has a different PR/media team which deals with the business side of things. Sometimes there is crossover, but that would not be me who would lead that effort."

"Oh, interesting. I really never thought of jobs like this

at a sports team. I guess like everyone, we just see players and coaches and think that's it."

"Yeah, that is a common belief, but there are lots of mundane roles. Event planners, ticket sales, even accountants. Basically, anything a normal company has, we have but the jobs are just typically filled with twenty-five-year-olds who don't know what they are doing."

"Ha! Like yourself!"

"Yes, exactly like me," Colin laughed.

These were the types of conversations Teddy had with men because she asked questions as if she was Oprah in the middle of an interview. She was not a natural at the casual banter and hair toss laughter that expert flirters executed without thought.

Colin and Teddy's first touch came about because the obnoxious event host that Teddy's friend was pursuing was making fun of Teddy's large hands by forcing men in the group to compare their hand size to hers. The term "man hands" was used more than once during these comparisons, citing an episode of the '90s sitcom *Seinfeld* where an episode featured a woman who was attractive to the lead character except for her large "man hands," which turned him off.

"Hey O'Malley and O'Malley's friend, what's your name

again?" said James, the organizer of the happy hour.

"This is Colin, my college friend from Notre Dame, James," said Colin's friend, O'Malley, who was accustomed to being called by only his surname.

"O'Malley, put your hand up to Teddy's. Look at the size. I bet they are bigger than yours," screamed James who was clearly on his way to inebriation.

O'Malley put his hand up to Teddy's as reluctantly as she put her hand up his.

"Damn, yours are bigger, O'Malley. You must be quite a man," continued James. "Colin, step right up, you're next. Teddy, stop being shy get your hand up here."

Colin slowly raised his hand up to Teddy's. The look on his face seemingly telegraphed his lack of support for this little hazing ritual the event's obnoxious host had masterminded. It appeared he was complying out of courtesy to his friend not complicity with James. Teddy's hand was noticeably larger than Colin's. A jolt of embarrassment shot through her making her feel like a second grader again being told to stand in the back row with the boys for the First Communion group picture. Or the little girl who was encouraged to quit gymnastics at the age of six because she was already too tall. The humiliation and the anger from those scarring episodes ping ponged in her brain.

Teddy sharply pulled her hand away and said, "Ha, ha, you proved your point James, I am an Amazon. Can we be done now?"

Colin's bright blue eyes caught Teddy's. He mouthed the words "I'm sorry," as he scrunched up his face at the unfortunate situation that had unfolded.

"At least he was nice about her humiliation," she thought to herself. Obviously, her first touch with Colin did not send shockwaves through Teddy. "Always the large, ugly duckling instead of the tiny princess yet again," she thought sadly. Teddy examined her hands after the fun was had at her expense. Yes, her fingers were longer than average, but they enabled her to play the piano quite exceptionally as a child and teen. Her hands spanned more than an octave on the piano which is quite impressive for a female. They, however, seemed to represent her conundrum, being strong and skilled versus being viewed as tiny, feminine and, therefore, attractive to men.

Teddy always felt awkward and undesirable her entire life, always being the tallest girl in the class, sporting a dainty size ten shoe by eighth grade. Maybe this was another manifestation of her feeling like a mistake. In high school and college, it was always her friends who had boyfriends, never Teddy. Heck, her nickname was a male name, but it suited and stuck. It took years for her to realize she just might be a swan. But the conundrum always reared its ugly head when she was young. Smart, capable, strong and tall seemed to be boyfriend kryptonite.

Teddy's one drink and done gameplan was abandoned, but not for any particular reason. Going home to spend Friday night alone just didn't seem very appealing once she had made her way to the happy hour. She didn't have an active interest in anyone at the bar that night, but the lively atmosphere just seemed to take her in on that June evening. And Teddy was an expert at shaking things off so the embarrassment from the hand comparison fiasco was whisked out of her mind shortly after the conclusion of James' little game.

As the evening progressed, she learned that Colin and his friend went to the same college as she did, but six years after her. So, they were both younger men, breaking her self-imposed *"he's gotta be within five years of my age, older or younger"* rule. Teddy gave them no further thought, despite the appealing Notre Dame pedigree. She carried on chatting with various people in the crowd at the trendy Mexican restaurant's bar.

Not only was Teddy a strict rule follower, but she was

also an avid rule maker. She found rules gave her comfort and structure in all aspects of her life, so much so that she did not even realize that by adhering to her five years younger or older rule, she was dismissing having just met two very eligible men.

Drink after drink brought the group to nearly midnight when Teddy found herself stuck in a debate with a guy from her office. The young troll was the typical obnoxious, just-starting-out accounting professional who thought he was the king of business when he was truthfully the king of making copies. She doesn't even remember the guy's name. What she does remember is Colin intervening and telling him, "She clearly doesn't want to talk to you, so why don't you just go away?" To which, the troll scurried away. Colin's clear, bright blue eyes flared with intensity as he told the guy to take a hike. Teddy remembers those eyes clearly to this day.

Teddy was not familiar with gallant moves. Teddy typically took care of Teddy and everyone else. Being of larger stature didn't lend itself to men treating her like a damsel in distress. This display certainly got her attention and made an impression. She invited Colin to sit next to her. That's when love at second sight happened to her.

They drew together like magnets. After Colin sat next to Teddy, the others in the bar vaporized.

"Wow, thanks for handling that little gargoyle," Teddy said enthusiastically.

"Yeah, you seemed very bothered by him. Who is he?" replied Colin.

"He works at my firm. I don't know him. He's just an arrogant little first year who thinks he knows all. He was insulting the sales and marketing at the firm, which is the group I am in."

"Oh, interesting. We have similar careers then?"

"Yes, I guess. But your world is certainly a lot more glamorous than mine."

"Yes, looks glamorous on the outside and there are some fun things. It is my dream job, but it's not all glamor."

"Oh, come on, tell me an interesting story about something that happened."

"Well, remember earlier this year when Scottie Pippen got arrested for DUI, I had the pleasure of dealing with that starting at four in the morning and the media interest for that juicy story was crazy."

"Ugh, yeah, I don't do marketing after midnight," Teddy laughed. "I would not last in sports."

"By the way, sorry about that hand thing. James is an

ass, isn't he?" said Colin.

"Oh, thank you. You are kind. I am used to that kind of thing. I guess I appear as though I can take it. And James. Calling him an ass is being kind. He is married but keeps flirting with my friend Jenny – over there – who is too stupid not to flirt back."

"Geez. From what I've seen of your accounting firm people, they may be just as ridiculous as those who work in sports, both those on and off the court," Colin said laughing.

They continued their conversation, never moving from their seats to talk to anyone else until closing time. About what? Lots of things, including family, Notre Dame, jobs, dogs, cities they lived in.

"You won't believe this, but my dog is named O'Malley. I guess that's why the human O'Malley and I are such good friends," laughed Colin.

"How did you meet O'Malley the human?"

"He was in my dorm, but a year younger. I was a trainer for the football team, and he liked all the free Starter branded gear I got so he wanted to become one too. I helped him get the gig."

"Wow, what is a football trainer? I honestly do not

know what that is."

"You tape ankles and do minor medical care for the athletes," replied Colin. "I did it because it would help me get a job in sports after college, and it did."

"So, a waterboy, wearing the height of '90s fashion with Starter clothing?" teased Teddy.

"Something like that. My dog O'Malley is a twelve-year-old poodle. He was mine when I was young."

"Oh, so he is your family's dog?" Teddy clarified.

"Well, he started out that way, but I had to take him from my parents. Long story, but he lives with me now."

Teddy's heart was melting. A young guy who is taking care of an old poodle!

The conversation was effortless, and there was a genuine connection. As the clock approached closing time of two o'clock, Teddy took a bold approach and asked Colin out for the next night. Interestingly, Colin had to decline, admitting he had a date with someone else on Saturday night. Strangely, this didn't bother Teddy. She knew she would hear from Colin. She just simply knew.

Teddy would learn later that Colin felt love at first sight upon seeing her earlier that evening. He claims that her face just struck him. At that time, Teddy's dark hair was cut in a short bob that framed what Colin told her was an extraordinarily beautiful face. Her face was narrow, punctuated by dark brown eyes and full lips on fair complexioned skin. Although one hundred percent Italian, Teddy looked more French with her dark hair, fair skin, and refined features. At that time, Teddy was sporting large, chunky blonde highlights that framed her face in stark contrast to the rest of her dark hair. This was a Spice Girls look that became popular in the late '90s due to the popularity of the girl band and the most popular Spice Girl, Ginger Spice – AKA Geri Halliwell. Teddy's coworkers took to calling her Corporate Spice because of the trendy blonde streaks she sported in a nontrendy workplace.

That's another thing to know about Teddy. She was trendy yet classic, always finding a way to stay current in fashion, hair, and makeup, but in her own way. Despite not being a size zero, Teddy always looked fashionable and put together.

Colin was scruffy that night with several days' worth of stubble, not something Teddy particularly liked, but also didn't dislike on that festive evening. He was cute in a Matt Damon, boy-next-door sort of way. Teddy would later come to know that Colin was of Irish, English and Lithuanian heritage and that Colin's father had citizenship in the U.S. and in Ireland. That evening, he was the perfect package of adorable to her.

Their first date was on a Tuesday after having had long phone calls every day since meeting on that fabulous Friday night. Teddy later learned that Colin took her to his go-to first date restaurant recommended to him by Charles Barkley, the aging basketball superstar who was at that time on the Rockets to try to return them to the glory of their two championships early in the '90s. Given Charles's star status, Colin worked with him frequently, handling numerous public relations and media needs of the superstar. When Teddy learned months later that she got the standard first date treatment, she decided she couldn't mind, given it became her favorite restaurant and because not many people can say they got restaurant tips from a pro athlete who was a household name.

Teddy teased the entire summer, "I hope you are okay that we have to break up when I have my birthday in September because we'll be six years apart then. This must be a summer fling since you turned twenty-six in June and I will turn thirty-two in September. You are so lucky that you snuck in during this three-month window, aren't you?"

Despite Teddy's teasing all summer about their

inevitable breakup, they both knew that the five-year older/younger rule was going to be broken. They were in love.

Chapter Three

It seemed they were exactly what each other were seeking. Teddy's work colleagues – her only friends at that point due to her recent move to Houston – said that her list of qualities in a man was a bit too strict for her current location of Houston, Texas. That's because graduating from Notre Dame – a medium-sized Catholic university one thousand miles away in Indiana – was a requirement on Teddy's list! For her, now thirty-one, she realized that there were so many small yet important qualities she wanted in a partner that were typical of a "Notre Dame boy." But had she intentionally crafted criteria that would be impossible to fulfill? How would she find this needle-in-a-haystack guy in Houston? Heck, she never had any success with Notre Dame guys when she was in school there. It seemed complete madness to have this quality at the top of her "perfect man" wish list. For no concrete reason, Teddy felt an unfounded sense of calmness about her vision for her ideal man.

Colin had it all – not just Notre Dame but the other characteristics that she desired. He was funny, social and just fun to be around. His lack of seriousness, really just abject goofiness, was the perfect balance to her being a more pensive sort. His Notre Dame alumni status also checked the Catholic faith box, the desire for a family box and the love of sports box.

Colin was so secure in himself, not in a cocky way. He just embraced who he was, quirky and unique. A guy who couldn't play sports but was intellectually the smartest sports person Teddy ever met. Growing up with four brothers and being around Notre Dame's sports addicted culture allowed Teddy to discern between guys who just talked gibberish about sports and those who really understood and analyzed them. An unassuming guy, Colin was strong in his convictions in a tender way. Teddy guessed Colin's comfort with himself was because of his mother. She was the kind of mother who was big on emotionally connecting with her children.

Colin spoke of how he and his mother would take boat rides on a little lake near their house to just talk about life.

Teddy found this quite amazing. She could not recall her own mother talking about life with her, ever! Her mother just blabbered on about the daily infractions Teddy's father and her mother-in-law who lived next door had committed, never bothering to engage with her daughter about anything meaningful. And obviously Teddy's mother never realized that complaining to Teddy about her father and grandmother was not acceptable parenting, especially since this started when Teddy was five or six years old.

Her mother would say things like, "Can you believe that woman just walked straight into my house and brought me vegetables from the garden? As if I am not capable of picking my own vegetables or don't know what vegetables are ready to be picked. Does she think I am an idiot? That woman has been driving me crazy for twenty years." or "Oh, your father is over at your grandparents fixing something of course, so dinner will need to be later. They always come first, you know."

Teddy's response was always to agree with her mother. Absorb the poison and be her mother's tiny confidant.

Yes, her mother did crafts with Teddy and threw the softball with her, but was there any real connection? No. Her mother never gave her the sex talk and merely handed Teddy a pad when she got her first period. No discussion, just the material needs satisfied.

On the flipside, some of Colin's stories about the lack of cleanliness in their house, hand-me-down clothes that did not fit him at all and ants in cereal boxes made Teddy's head and heart hurt. Cleanliness and good food were next to godliness in her book. Despite the lack of emotional support, her parents were on every material detail. It was hard for Teddy to say which parenting style was superior, but her lack of emotional support from her parents certainly was not a positive in her development.

For Colin, he seemingly found Teddy perfect. She was smart, fun and had a simply beautiful face. Colin had shared with her that he declared himself a "face guy" when guy friends would talk about being a "boob guy" or an "butt guy." She was feminine but into sports more than the typical girl. Colin didn't know if that was due to her being raised in a family with boys or to attribute that characteristic to her going to Notre Dame with its sports culture. Either way, Teddy appeared to be his idea of perfection. He had made a concerted effort to enter the dating scene in the two years leading up to their meeting. However, despite his effort, no real connections were made, until now.

At this point in her life, Teddy was making a conscious effort to not be her worrisome, overeager self. She decided she needed to be light and carefree and see where that took her. It seemed to be working, as it brought her to Colin who helped encourage her lighter side, allowing her to enjoy life in a carefree way. And even break some rules. With Colin, Teddy let go of her weekday rule of bedtime by ten. With Colin, she was living like a twenty-year-old, staying out late on weekdays! Wild, rule breaker that she was.

To both Colin and Teddy, this relationship had much promise.

Then it happened. Of course. Colin's flaw presented itself after dinner in the month of August. Colin brought a CD of Christmas music to Teddy's upscale apartment. Since the first *A Very Special Christmas* album came out in 1987, pop Christmas songs were one of her favorite things, and the surprise of hearing them in August was comical and endearing to her. Others may have seen such a date as corny or pathetic. To Teddy it was creative, sweet and original. She loved Colin's offbeat sense of humor and fun-loving nature. It helped Teddy lighten herself. She also enjoyed Colin's encyclopedic knowledge of pop music, especially the '80s, her decade, having gone to high school and college completely in the '80s. What sort of crazy genius knows that Elvis Costello bet Shane MacGowan of the Irish band the Pogues that he couldn't write a Christmas song of any merit? To which Shane wrote "Fairytale of New York," one of the best, irreverent pop

Christmas songs ever written. Colin was that crazy genius.

"Another plus," she thought to herself. "A guy who loves Christmas and pop Christmas music. This is an unexpected bonus." Her reverie accompanied by Wham's "Last Christmas" was interrupted by Colin's question.

"So, what do you send at Christmas to people, like cards or what?" he asked casually.

"I just send cards, typically right after Thanksgiving," she replied. "Get 'em done and out!"

"Well, my parents always do a Christmas letter. They still do one each year," Colin said.

"Oh," Teddy replied, not seeing where this was headed.

"I started doing one of my own after college," he shared.

"Oh, really," Teddy said, trying to show as little emotion as possible.

But her mind swirled. "A Christmas letter. Oh my God. Could Colin really be one of those self-obsessed braggy people who go on and on about themselves in these insipid letters that they actually have the audacity of sending under the guise of wishing them a Merry Christmas?" she shrieked inside her head.

"Yeah, but I make mine funny," said Colin quickly, as if he could sense Teddy's unspoken discomfort.

"Well, I would be interested in reading yours ... probably not your parents," Teddy managed to say.

"Yeah, my parents do the typical letter. Very matter of fact about what they did during the year. I try to make mine a little different," said Colin.

"God, I hope so," Teddy thought to herself without overwhelming optimism. "But, c'mon. How different could his letters be? These types of letters were always snoozefests or bragfests ... or a combination of the two. Was this Colin's dealbreaker flaw?" She had not seen this one coming.

She put this extremely unfortunate disclosure to the back of her mind, and they continued to enjoy a fun-filled evening listening to Christmas songs on her ivory couch in her picture-perfect apartment in August. The first time Colin came to her apartment he asked in all seriousness, "Is this the model apartment or something?" In Teddy's magazine-esque surroundings, it was another idyllic evening, excluding the letter revelation.

At work the next day in her office overlooking Houston's new baseball park, Teddy's mind kept wandering to the Christmas letter, as she gazed out the window. She was getting more and more curious. Hopefully, tonight when she and Colin saw each other again, she could see an actual letter.

At lunch, she asked her friend about her views on Christmas letters, as they enjoyed vegetable dumplings from the "famous" dumpling lady in their building's food court.

"Jenny, Colin told me he writes a Christmas letter. He says his parents have done them for years. Do you think it's odd that a single guy does a Christmas letter? To be clear, this is a one-page letter detailing the year, not just a Hallmark card, or those photo cards people have started doing."

Jenny's face broadened with a devilish smile. She was seemingly relishing the notion of Colin having some sort of flaw. Jenny was a true "frenemy," if ever there was one. But it was Jenny's desperate desire to go to the happy hour where she met Colin, so maybe her frenemy status wasn't all bad.

"Well, I cannot say that I've ever heard of someone without a family writing one of those letters. And, I cannot say that I am a fan of them in general. Not sure I've ever read one all the way through," she chuckled. "Not overly thrilled with this intel on him, but more importantly, how do you feel about it?"

"I find it really bizarre to be completely honest, but I really am into him. He seems perfect. This little tidbit has just thrown me a bit. He claims he doesn't write the typical Christmas letter, so maybe this really isn't a sign that he is an axe murderer disguised as a nice, normal guy," she optimistically said to herself, as much as to Jenny.

Jenny laughed in response. Teddy took her laughter to mean there was nothing else that could be said about this bizarre topic. They finished their dumplings, smiled broadly at each other so they could check each other's teeth for remnants of spinach and made their way through the hustle and bustle of the food court to the elevators of their office building.

"Merry Christmas," said Jenny sarcastically as she exited the elevator two floors before Teddy's stop on the Sales and Marketing floor on seventeen.

Teddy grimaced at Jenny as she exited the elevator.

Chapter Four

That evening, Teddy headed to Colin's dingy mancave apartment, which was only a couple miles away from hers. While the fastest route was the freeway, Teddy opted for surface streets. She was in no rush, fearing that a crucial letdown was awaiting her.

"What if I hate these letters? How should I react? Should I hide my feelings? Why couldn't things just stay perfect? Why does nothing work out for me?" she mentally spiraled. She let out a long primal scream in the car, probably appearing insane to the driver next to her at the stoplight. Teddy always had to combat her innate defeatist attitude. It was true that things rarely came easily to her. Life had proven to her that she had to work hard for everything and anything.

Of course, that seemed to be true in matters of the heart as well, much to her dismay. No silver platters ever seemed to be sent her way. Her frustration seemed to be rooted in allowing herself to think that Colin may have been an uncommon silver platter moment in her life. And possibly being wrong.

Earlier in the day when she and Colin spoke on the phone, he said he was excited for her to read his letters. So, she knew it was going to happen tonight. She took advantage of the congested Houston streets to mentally prepare. Why was she letting a silly thing like a Christmas letter spook her? A neat freak, Teddy had been willing to overlook Colin's less than tidy accommodations. Deep down, she thought that a cleanliness flaw was fixable. But there was no instruction manual for fixing this Christmas letter madness.

She drew in a big breath while she waited in the shady courtyard of the aging apartment complex for Colin to answer his door. When she saw him, Teddy had the same elated feeling she had every time she saw him. She really was in love with him. She felt that he was in love with her too, despite those words yet to be exchanged. "Grow up," she thought, as Colin tenderly kissed her hello. Those blue eyes and the endearing crooked teeth of his smile always made her feel good.

"So, are we going to have the big read right away?"

asked Teddy, plunging headfirst into the topic that had been nagging at her all day. As a direct person, she always chose action over inaction. Tonight was no different. "Let's dive right into this," she thought bravely.

"Sure," Colin replied casually. He seemed to have no sense of her apprehension about the Christmas letters. "Can I get you a drink?"

"Yes! A beer is fine. Thanks." Teddy replied with perhaps a bit too much enthusiasm. Anything to numb the pain of what was coming.

What came next was quite the spectacle. Teddy was expecting a few pages in a pile. Instead, Colin presented her with a binder of letters. The binder had handwritten green and red calligraphy on the front declaring it "The McNamara Family Christmas Letters."

"Wow, the McNamara family took this stuff seriously," she thought. "Thank God I have this drink to get through this agony."

The binder began with the 1972 letter from his parents, the year before Colin was born. This outlined the story that Colin told Teddy at the bar the first night they met. His parents met when his father was in college and his mother was a high school senior. They even went to her senior prom. A college classmate of Colin's father was Colin's mother's brother. That is how his parents initially connected in the early 1960s. Colin's dad was very interested in his mother, but the feeling was not reciprocated. So, they went their separate ways for fifteen years after her prom. In that time, Colin's father married someone else and started a family. His mother wasn't interested in Colin's father at the time of her high school prom, because she had plans to become a nun and, apparently, her interest in Colin's father was not enough to make her stray from her post-high school plan. She joined the convent shortly after graduation and was a nun for more than a decade.

The pair were reunited upon Colin's father getting divorced. He became a single father to four children, and his mother left the convent in the very same year. These independent life changes brought the prom couple back together. Colin came on the scene pretty much nine months after they reunited.

When Colin told Teddy this story at the bar, it sounded like the plot of *The Sound of Music*. Reading the first Christmas letter reinforced how special Colin and his family were. Teddy's frostiness about the Christmas letters was thawing, a bit.

"Colin, your parents' story is really so amazing. I am

looking forward to meeting them," she said sincerely.

Teddy's parents were good people on the surface. However, they were not the kind of people with whom you could bond. Even things as nice sounding as a Sunday dinner ended up being tense or stilted. There was always some infraction committed against Teddy's paternal grandmother and grandfather who lived next door that caused drama. Or some misstep by one of her brothers like being late, that caused anxiety, inhibiting any real family connections.

It was not the stereotypical warm and outgoing Italian family. Maybe it was the stoic style of both her mother and father. Maybe it was because their marriage was not a particularly happy one with her father's parents being the third wheel, so they didn't create an emotionally engaging home. The McNamaras seemed different. Their story and their first letter signaled something deep. Something Teddy was missing.

"Can I skip ahead to your first letter, Colin?" Teddy inquired, after reading a few of his parents' works, including the one announcing Colin's birth.

"Sure," Colin replied, flipping the plastic sheathed pages of the binder, finding the 1995 letter. Teddy took a breath and started reading. The letter was humorous, self-deprecating and oh so Colin. Just adorable. The story of Colin's last days as a student at Notre Dame and his pursuit of his dream career in sports public relations was told in such a way that it couldn't help but keep the reader's attention and leave a warm feeling.

It wasn't the relationship dagger that Teddy feared. The letter solidified that she wanted a life with Colin.

Chapter Five

"Colin! This is not what I expected," Teddy said, elatedly. "It is really funny and refreshing. You know what it is?" After a lengthy pause that gave time for a growing smile to form on her face, Teddy declared, "It's genuine!"

"Yeah, I thought you might like it. I actually get compliments and people who say they look forward to my letters," said Colin with a huge smile on his face, his blue eyes smiling as well. "And a lot of people I know have started writing their own letters because of mine. Those haven't turned out so great though, so I am not sure I am a good influence," said Colin, always the joker.

"Okay, next letter, I need to see how the story of Colin

progresses," Teddy chirped excitedly.

The letters of 1996, 1997 and 1998 told the story of a young, single Colin living what is today often referred to as "his best life" doing his dream job of sports PR. Every year, he managed to make fairly normal life events fun, light and entertaining. His letters had a comedy writer's edge to them, well-crafted with playful wit. Teddy could see why people looked forward to the annual update. They were indeed great reads, and Colin was clearly a talented writer.

Upon reading his letters, Teddy was convinced that Colin would ultimately be a writer, not a PR guy. She did not share this view until later in their courtship when she gave him a leather-bound notebook for his birthday with his name on it so he could jot down notes for a future novel of some sort. Teddy enjoyed reading for as long as she could remember. The thought of being a novelist's wife intrigued her. Teddy was already imagining how she was going to change Colin when he became her husband – standard practice for most women in a serious relationship. Clearly, she was in love, and Colin was a keeper.

The letters, by omission, revealed the lack of love interests. Teddy knew he actively dated, but it appeared that nothing was notable enough to make the annual Christmas letter material cut. This matched what he had shared with her.

Facts lining up is always a nice occurrence when dating. Her observation made her wonder what would happen in his letter this December, the December of 1999 letter. Would she be referenced and, if so, would it just be a casual mention? A joke perhaps? Four months until Teddy would find out.

They spent the rest of the evening snuggled on Colin's grandmotherly-looking floral couch with his childhood dog, O'Malley. He was an odd little poodle that Colin confiscated from his parents after the dog was hit by a car. He felt the accident was his parents' fault with the dog running down the street, so he stripped them of their dog caring rights. Like the letters suggested and caring for a twelve-year-old poodle demonstrated, Colin was not a man of pretense. He was a deeply genuine person, one that would take on the responsibility of an old dog because he believed his parents were not doing an adequate job. As Colin mentioned, the dog O'Malley shared a surname with his friend Timothy, who was the reason they met that fateful night. Teddy sometimes wondered if this O'Malley coincidence was another sign of their destiny to be together.

The scorching Houston summer finally came to a close, as did their carefree summer. Colin's work with the Rockets started to ramp up towards the end of September. Teddy learned about media day and the media guide. As a fairly casual fan of all major sports, she never realized there was a specific day all the players and coaches spent time with reporters, which served to kick off the preseason. Now she did. She learned of the herculean effort of putting together the media guide, which was one of Colin's key responsibilities. This three-hundred-page almanac housed a litany of background information and statistics about the team that the media would use as reference all season long. This was back in the days of print only, so the detail and fact checking involved in such an endeavor was quite something.

Meanwhile, Teddy's job at her accounting firm chugged along. She was far more focused on this relationship than anything her boss could throw her way. Besides her job was a bit of a joke. She was an idea person, but marketing at an accounting firm was not a place where ideas were needed nor welcomed. She was sold on taking the job by her highly persuasive boss, Jeremy. Sales and Marketing was a new group at the firm, and he enticed her with the idea of building a department from the ground up at a well-regarded firm. There were many times when she wondered what she had gotten herself into because the reality was that no one besides Jeremy was interested in what the Sales and Marketing team could offer to the firm. The marketing function was only mildly recognizable to Teddy, who had ten years of experience in far more mature sales and marketing departments where her energy and ideas were acted upon.

In Teddy's mind, one of her best personal ideas was for satellite radio. She continues to this day to claim she had this idea years before it came out in the early 2000s. Her claim is she just didn't have the resources to make it happen, despite the laugh this gets from everyone she tells, and she tells more people than she probably should. On a big and small scale, her mind was always working.

At this job, at this time in her life, however, she was just marking time professionally. Her endless energy and thoughts were on her personal life. Since she met Colin, she had been in the habit of going out nearly every night of the week, either with Colin or friends. She hadn't had this busy of a social life since college ... and maybe not even then! And, as the basketball season began, she took advantage of inviting friends to attend as many games as possible with her. Colin got a pair of free tickets as a perk, but was it a perk given he was busy working on game nights? To Teddy, who was the beneficiary of the tickets, they were certainly a perk. But seeing Colin frantically running around courtside in a suit providing information to reporters was always an entertaining bonus on top of the original perk.

Teddy also took to staying at Colin's on his last night of

a road trip with the team so that she was there to greet him upon his arrival at times well past two in the morning. Team schedules and travel processes were a whole new world to Teddy. She never knew a member of the PR department traveled with the team on private jets and stayed in luxury hotels. Now she did. This life with Colin was a fun-filled whirlwind with sitcom-like situations at every turn. The serious Teddy never thought she would see a millionaire NBA player in a hotel elevator with half his head cornrowed and the other half an afro jutting out nearly a foot because he was late for practice and couldn't get his whole head braided in time. Such fun and frivolity made Teddy feel a lightness she had never felt before. She and Colin were in love and starting to talk about the future.

After Thanksgiving, Teddy awaited the creation of the Christmas letter. She no longer wondered if she would be mentioned. She was certain she would be. The question was how.

Christmas 1999

The last 12 months have been some of the best in my oh-so wonderful life! Both work and play have surpassed all expectations. I just hope I don't sicken you too much as I gush on with my highlights from this past year.

Christmas presents kept coming well into the new year, as the league lockout came to an end and the mini-season was salvaged. Six-time champ Scottie Pippen heard good things about me and decided to come to Houston to see if they were true. Upon realizing that I could not carry a team like Air Jordan, who lifted him to half a dozen titles, he headed out of town after just 50 games.

A memorable moment occurred in March, as the University of Texas at San Antonio unveiled a sculpture of my good friend Terrence Green, who passed away a year ago. The tribute was beautifully created by my father and continues to bring me good feelings. Back in Houston, I packed up all my belongings and moved … approximately 10 doors down. I still live in the same apartment complex, caught in some bizarre strip club checkmate. Yes, there are at least four strip clubs within walking distance.

My basketball perks also increased in the shortened season, as I accompanied the Rockets on several road trips and made solo journeys to the NBA Finals as well as the Draft. Vacation came sooner than expected with another early playoff exit, and the newfound freedom brought about the completely unexpected. A girlfriend entered the picture. Even more shocking, this was **my** *girlfriend. Pick yourself up off the floor and continue reading.*

Teddy – who is female – and I have been dating for over six months now. I promise to refrain from getting mushy here, but things do look promising. My dear late grandmother welcomed her with the poignant greeting, "Do you like beer? Good. You have that in common."

With Summer came a baseball odyssey to dream of. College roommates James, Steve and Fernando and I traveled 2,000 miles to six of the best ballparks in the game. The 10-day trek was the perfect mixture of camaraderie, home runs, hops and barley. My second summer trip landed me in Colorado, where Teddy and I escaped the heat to view the peaks. We also got the chance to join my brothers and old friends for an R.E.M. concert at Red Rocks.

A return to Houston coincided with another championship for our women's team, the Houston Comets. For me that's now three years, three rings and three games attended. Rockets roster activity also heated up around this time, as we experience another makeover by importing rookie Steve Francis and shipping Pippen. Before the hoops season started, I made my yearly stop at Notre Dame, where my Dad's Moose Krause sculpture was the latest in his takeover of campus, following the 1997 Frank Leahy unveiling. The football weekend was a perfect reunion for the McNamara family and for me and my classmates.

The new season has been one of expanded duties for me, as my boss spends more time at home with the arrival of his baby girl, McNamara. Now, who out there doesn't think I'm a good employee? The Rockets training camp and road schedule has kept me away from my apartment more than I could have imagined. But the travel has allowed me to visit family and friends thousands of miles away. Workwise, it's been an unforgettable experience with Francis making his debut and Charles Barkley bidding farewell, leaving the Rockets and the league.

This Christmas will be my first sans family, as Mom and Dad will be up north with Grandpa and the siblings will be staying put at their homes. But Teddy and I will be sure to enjoy the humid holidays in Houston. Here's wishing you the best this Christmas season.

Colin

So, there you have it. Very respectable mentions in his very funny letter. Teddy was pleased. She also realized that these letters serve as a mini diary of sorts. Perhaps a collection of memories. The letter brought back the year, well in her case, half year, in a way that even photos do not.

"So ... what do you think?" asked Colin, somewhat confidently. He knew it was a solid effort.

"I really love it, Colin. I like how I am mentioned, but it's not over the top, as I'm not that into sharing my life's details with a big group of people," she gushed. "You are a very gifted writer. I am in awe at how you turn the mundane into something funny, relatable and informative ... all at the same time."

"Thanks. I am so glad you like it. Doing them is important to me. I just really enjoy keeping in touch with people, I guess."

"I know, sweetie. I love that you love doing them. I see the appeal now, and I want to be part of them for a long, long time," Teddy whispered into Colin's ear.

They had been talking more and more about the future together. Things were coming together for both of them.

Teddy just couldn't get over how witty Colin's letters were. That line about his grandmother asking if she liked beer was completely true. No embellishment needed from the author. Because he couldn't include everything, Teddy thought about other highlights of the year. Tubing on the Guadalupe River came to mind. It is quite the Texas pastime and something Teddy had never done, nor heard of. What says summer and Texas more than floating down a brown river in an innertube tethered to another tube cradling a cooler of beer? She recalled the horrible sunburn her fair-skinned Colin got that day. The letter helped her savor what had turned out to be a wonderful year. Little memories that may have been forgotten were brought to the forefront whether they were mentioned in the letter or not. A memory prompt was apparently an unintended benefit of the letter, she surmised.

Their first full year together was 2000, when they rung in the new millennium in style at a party at Olympic track champion and legend Carl Lewis's restaurant hosted by NBA superstar Charles Barkley, a six-foot-six, two-hundred-eighty-pound hulk with an even larger personality. Teddy was never a celebrity chaser or even that interested in them, but she had to admit, these glitzy things were fun, and she chose to take it all in. That night will always provide Teddy with the priceless memory of Colin forcing his body between hers and Charles's when Charles decided he was going to lean in for a kiss with Teddy. Colin at six feet and one hundred and eighty pounds fighting with the tenacity of a little terrier to ensure the big dog didn't touch his prize was comical. Colin told Teddy afterwards, "I mean I was not going to let him kiss you. You never know where on earth Charles' mouth has been!"

She and Colin were fully committed and began talking seriously about marriage in March, which is when they booked the Basilica of the Sacred Heart at the University of

Notre Dame for the ceremony. The Basilica is the dream wedding venue for virtually all Notre Dame graduates. It's a jaw-droppingly beautiful cathedral that looks like it belongs in Europe, not Indiana. Colin and Teddy decided that a wedding in Houston had no real meaning to anyone and that Notre Dame would provide a perfect middle ground for both families.

Teddy called the Basilica one morning that March of 2000 while at her desk at work, not working, just to get information about wedding reservations, she told herself slyly. The woman on the other end of the phone line, promptly said, "Well, if you are looking for 2001 reservations, we have only two dates with two timeslots open, so you better call your fiancé right now and then call me right back."

Teddy hung up the phone in disbelief. 2001 ceremony dates were already taken, save for two August slots nine o'clock in the morning.

"Well, I guess we're not getting married at ND then," she thought to herself. "How could she contact Colin, who had not yet proposed, and tell him we needed to book at date now if we wanted a 2001 wedding at the Basilica?" Teddy decided to call Colin and bring it up as a joke. That seemed like a safe strategy so as not to look like a complete lunatic.

As she dialed her office phone, she inhaled. Hoping she did not misplay this conversation and come off looking like a fool.

"Hey Colin, how are you?" she asked casually but didn't wait for an answer. Her nervousness flung her forward in her monologue. "You will never believe this, it's sooooo funny! I called ND about the wedding reservation processes and the lady told me they have two dates, and two timeslots open for 2001 and that if we wanted one, we needed to call back right away! Can you even believe it? How funny is this?" she rattled off without taking a breath.

Colin paused and then sternly replied, "That is not funny at all."

"Are you serious? What do you mean, Colin?" Teddy asked urgently.

"Well, I mean, shouldn't we take one? I mean, well, we've talked about getting engaged this year, and we both want this. So, let's not let the order of events get in the way," he replied emphatically.

"Okay, so you want me to call back and get us booked? Even though we are not engaged," stated Teddy to ensure she heard what she knew she heard.

"Yes, what are the dates?"

"August fourth, the nine o'clock time slot and August eleventh, also at nine o'clock," Teddy said.

"I vote for August eleventh, since we met on June eleventh. What do you think?" Colin asked.

"I really cannot believe this. You really want to do this?" Teddy asked, beaming to her reflection in the computer screen.

"Yes, Teddy, I love you, and we want this, so we need to do what needs to be done, however unorthodox. Just don't mention to the lady that we aren't actually engaged."

"Okay, August eleventh, 2001, will be the day. See you bright and early on that day, nine o'clock. Don't be late," Teddy joked.

They hung up the phone. Teddy could not believe it. This was happening. She dialed the phone and reached the testy lady at the Basilica and made the reservation for August eleventh, 2001, at nine o'clock.

Teddy sat back thinking about how lucky she felt. Colin was a tremendous guy. He was a guy, but a guy with so much feeling and depth. He wasn't a player or a macho guy. He was just like their relationship: deep and genuine. Her good fortune was more than she could believe. How did she become the girl marrying a Notre Dame guy and marrying him there, in that beautiful church? She honestly always felt a little out of place at ND. She, who never had a date there, couldn't believe she was the *she* getting married there!

The wonderful adventures of this year were, of course, captured in the annual Christmas letter. Although Teddy had come to enjoy the letters, this year she would be featured. She was a need-to-know kind of girl and telling family and friends that she and Colin had taken several trips together while unmarried felt awkward for her. Although certainly not perfect or lilywhite, Teddy preferred to project an above reproach image and telling the world about her personal life was a bit uncomfortable. But alas, the Christmas letter was happening no matter what. And she was in love, so she decided to just go with it. Besides, it was still Colin's letter. It wasn't going to her friends or family yet.

Christmas 2000

As I write to you this Christmas, The Magical McNamara Tour of 2000 is coming to a close. Teddy and I have enjoyed many adventures over the last twelve months. Here's a look at the highlights.

Y2K didn't treat the Rockets well, as they posted their first losing season in over a decade. But the PR department scored big by successfully campaigning for Steve Francis as the league's Rookie of the Year. I produced mountains of statistical support to try and make him look like the Second Coming in sneakers. I was then rewarded for my efforts with a promotion to manager of communications.

Summertime gave Teddy and I a chance to take several weekend treks across Texas. We headed to San Antonio for my niece's baptism and grandfather's birthday, to Dallas for a reunion with my old roommate Fernando and to Austin for a stay with O'Malley – not the dog, but a recently relocated Notre Dame friend who was instrumental in Teddy and I getting together. While on the subject, O'Malley the dog is as feisty as ever in his thirteenth year, accompanying us on every Texas trip.

After the Texas tour, Teddy and I set our sights a little farther. Together we embarked on a two-week trip to England, France and Ireland. A weekend in London started the fun, then we chunneled to Paris for a day before spending a week on the Emerald Isle. Here I took a turn at the wheel, concentrating on staying on the other side of the road, as we traversed from castles to singing pubs.

Ireland had many highs, but none as majestic as the afternoon of July 6 at the Cliffs of Moher. High atop a ledge on the island's west coast, I offered Teddy a diamond Claddagh ring and asked her to be my wife. Fearing I'd either push or jump, she accepted. Our wedding is scheduled for the summer at our alma mater, Notre Dame.

Soon after our engagement, Teddy and I celebrated the

news with both sets of parents. We connected with my mom and dad at the end of our Ireland trip and then visited her parents in Ohio upon our return stateside. With a wedding to organize, Teddy and I journeyed to South Bend in July and September to hammer out the details for the big event. Being a true ND couple, we used the second wedding-planning weekend as an opportunity to catch the Irish play Nebraska.

Six months of travel for fun segued into another Rockets season, during which I travel for work. Of course, charter flights and Four Seasons nights ease the hardship of life on the road. This Rockets season has started on an extremely positive note and not just because of improvement on the court. The famous November election of Bush vs. Gore, with its hanging chads drama, also contained a local referendum for a new arena, which passed overwhelmingly to ensure that the words "Louisville" and "Rockets" never link together.

This holiday season has Teddy and I on the move again. Imagine that. For Thanksgiving, we went tropical with some fun in Miami. Then came a jaunt to New York, where visits to Rockefeller Center and Tavern on the Green helped to get two Texans in the Christmas spirit. In a few days, Teddy and I will be enjoying Christmas and New Year's with my family in San Antonio.

All the best wherever you may be this Christmas season!

Colin

Teddy thought it was another great letter. The only detail she wished could have made the cut was the fact that Colin gave her a Ring Pop as well as an engagement ring on the Cliffs of Moher. When they discussed rings, Teddy always said that a Ring Pop would be just fine. So, Colin complied with her wishes by leaving a cherry-flavored candy ring for her on the seat of their rental car to show that he had indeed listened. Teddy had quite a laugh when she opened the car door minutes after Colin's proposal. She was quite glad that she had the beautiful diamond Claddagh ring as her real engagement ring but appreciated the hilarity of the Ring Pop.

She treasured the real Claddagh ring. It was so perfect and unique. A Claddagh ring is a traditional Irish ring featuring a heart with a crown representing love and loyalty, respectively, held by two hands representing friendship. Friendship, love and loyalty. That said it all about Teddy and Colin. It became their theme for not only the wedding but their lives together.

For Teddy, the letter sparked a flood of memories not even mentioned. All the socializing they did, of course, was not letter material. Her thirties had become a renaissance period for going out and staying out late. It was not uncommon for she and Colin to stay out until two in the morning and sleep in until past one in the afternoon. These were habits she had long since given up prior to meeting Colin, but she was just in love with all the fun that he brought to her life.

With 2001 ahead, Teddy and Colin focused on their wedding and grown-up things like getting a house. Teddy and Colin agreed that starting a family would be priority number one given her age, so getting settled into their first house was as important as the wedding planning.

The wedding planning, although fun, was stressful for Teddy. Colin really wanted the big white wedding more than Teddy. He had so many friends he wanted as groomsmen it caused silent stress for Teddy. She had lots of acquaintances and work friends but was not someone who kept in contact or had longstanding friends. Without the ease of social media and cellphones, staying connected after college was difficult and expensive. So, filling out a bridal party of six was a challenge for her. She ended up with a friend who was more Colin's friend than hers to fill out the six. And not having a sister or true best friend presented challenges for the maid of honor role. She went with her sister-in-law, which annoyed her mother who always seemed to have a feud going with someone in the family.

In addition, her family was so disconnected. Nothing like Colin's family, which appeared so close at the time. The thought of her socially awkward, motley crew of a family gathered in one place for the first time since her brother Jason's wedding more than fifteen years prior was anxiety-inducing. She kept it inside because she wanted to continue to be the positive, fun-loving Teddy whom Colin had come to love. Being the perfect couple and having the perfect wedding could not be accomplished by being a fretful bride, so Teddy forced herself to do what she did best: grind through it and make it happen.

Needless to say, it was a busy and eventful year. Moving into a new house was followed by a new job for Teddy then the wedding/honeymoon double-shot and, shortly after, Teddy getting pregnant with their first child. The pregnancy fact was not shared in the Christmas letter, but it was the pinnacle of a quite thrilling year for both Colin and Teddy. It was all coming together. It was storybook by anyone's definition.

It was difficult not to share the good news of Teddy's pregnancy just two months after the wedding, but they followed the doctor's advice not to share until twelve weeks. In Teddy's mind, professional guidance equated to a rule, therefore, she would dutifully follow, even to the point of not telling her parents or in-laws. Colin and Teddy were elated. Teddy, especially. As a modern woman, years are spent trying to not get pregnant, then a switch is seemingly flipped and the worrying about potentially having trouble getting pregnant immediately begins, especially over thirty. Teddy was eternally grateful that something this important and completely out of her control went easily.

Thankfully this year, Colin didn't feel the need to write a prank letter for his boss. The 1999 letter had two versions. The version that everyone received, the non-insane version, and an insane version written for Colin's boss, Tom. Although he was Colin's boss, Tom was more like a college roommate to Colin. Propriety was not the defining characteristic of their relationship. Colin's version of the 1999 letter for Tom included a reference to "unbelievable bedroom activity with Teddy" as well as a mention of his "prick boss, Tom." The prank worked because Tom said to Colin, "I cannot believe you put that stuff in your Christmas letter." A triumphant Colin will always have this prank as a win in his relationship scoresheet with Tom.

Christmas 2001

Sometimes a year has so many highlights that it's hard to believe it all fit on one calendar. The past dozen months have contained countless lifechanging moments for the McNamara household. After all, before this year, we weren't even really a household.

The main event for us this past year took place at

Notre Dame on the eleventh of August, when we became Mr. and Mrs. McNamara in the company of family and friends. The event exceeded all expectations, as we were blessed with perfect weather and a beautiful ceremony. Our Fighting Irish roots were frighteningly evident when the limo driver's first stop after leaving the Basilica was Notre Dame Stadium for a photo with the bride and groom in front of the locker room's famous "Play Like a Champion Today" sign. The wedding celebration stretched into a daylong marathon, as the Mass led into a brunch, happy hour, dinner and dancing. Wanting the night to truly last forever, we capped off twenty-two hours of activity with some late-night carousing at the Linebacker Lounge.

Following a few weeks of recovery, we carried out the Irish wedding theme to its fullest extent with a trip to the Land of Leprechauns for our honeymoon. A backdrop of castles and pubs provided us with a relaxing setting to enjoy our first days as husband and wife. We kicked off the trip with a three-night stay at Ballynahinch Castle and then spent a week exploring the West Coast of Ireland. We even made it back to the Cliffs of Moher, where we were engaged a year earlier, but newly built fences to battle Mad Cow Disease and ferocious winds kept us from recreating our special moment on the ledge.

The year featured not only a marriage and a honeymoon, but also the introduction of a new home. Our neighborhood makes you nostalgic for yesteryear, as it seems like nothing has changed here over the last half century. Our home is nestled nicely between the Cleavers and the Cunninghams. Having a house has also helped with our hospitality. We've hosted a few parties and welcomed a number of overnight guests, including both sets of parents. The new addition to our life has already gained a special place in our hearts, and we look forward to raising a family here in the years to come.

In the work world, Teddy said goodbye to LMC after two years, as she took a job in marketing with Omni Energy. She is currently gearing up for when electric deregulation hits Houston early next year. Meanwhile, Colin continues to work in PR with the Rockets, who this summer parted ways with Hakeem Olajuwon after almost two record-setting decades by the legendary center. This trade made Colin one of the elder statesmen in the Rockets travelling party, as not a player remains from when he first arrived.

We also managed to take a few short trips this past year. During a June weekend, we did the requisite bachelor/bachelorette parties, as Teddy got wild in New Orleans while Colin opted for a more subdued Chicago.

Consequently, Colin got to live it up one more time a few nights before the wedding at the lively bachelor options available in South Bend. And, of course, it wouldn't be a year without a few trips to San Antonio, including a return for Colin's 10th high school reunion. We also participated in this fall's Bob Davie Farewell Tour, witnessing Irish losses to Michigan State and A&M to give the school its first 0-3 start ever. We're anxiously awaiting next season and a new chapter in ND football.

These days, we're just enjoying life on the homefront. Our dog O'Malley sure likes this change in pace, as he has a little more company while he sleeps his days away. Colin handles yard work and odd jobs outside, while Teddy keeps the inside of our home immaculate. Call us an old married couple if you must. But at least do it behind our backs. Here's wishing you a wonderful Christmas!

Colin and Teddy

Teddy thought it was a great letter, as she typically did. Her only critique was that she didn't understand how Colin could have left out the story of the dress. Teddy selected a particularly large wedding gown. She justified the princess-like dress because it matched the majesty and scale of the Basilica at Notre Dame. Unlike her, Teddy didn't think multiple steps ahead to how this massive dress would be transported to Indiana from Texas. Much drama ensued when Teddy realized she had no plan in place to bring the dress on an airplane. Like a typical bridezilla, Teddy burst into tears at the realization that she had no plan for dress transport.

Like a true knight in shining armor, Colin saved the day by arranging for the airline to take the dress as freight, not luggage due to the size. All that was left was to get the dress to the airport. They packed the massive dress in a wardrobe moving box to keep it from being completely smashed and wrinkled. However, neither of their cars could transport a box of that size. So, Colin's friend, Roger, who was the mascot for the Rockets, was called upon to help. The mascot, Clutch, who was a large gray bear, had a "Clutchmobile" which was in fact a van with flashing lights and sirens with paintings of the mascot on each side. So, the trio put the gigantic box in the back of the "Clutchmobile" and headed to the airport where Colin and Teddy paid a large sum to have the box included as cargo on their flight. Driving to the airport with a large teddy bear's head painted on the side of a van absolutely seemed letter-worthy.

The other memory that didn't quite get its due treatment in the letter was the wedding afterparty. The letter described it as "late-night carousing." This unorthodox wedding afterparty included virtually everyone aged fifty and under in attendance at the reception, including the bride and groom. It was a wild scene of dancing and drinking at the college dive bar which lasted until four in the morning. It was a night no one in attendance will ever forget, except the many whose memories are fuzzy or blacked out completely!

Colin, rightfully so, left out the gory details of the night at the 'Backer in his reflection on this big day. A mass audience didn't need to hear about the debauchery. It was hard for Teddy to accept that all the silly things in their lives could not make the cut, but she felt the letter perfectly captured the wonderful start to their lives together.

PART TWO

What is *going on?*
September – December 2021

Chapter Six

"Hello," said Teddy brightly, who only answered the phone because it was an international number, and Colin was in London on a business trip. She expected to hear his voice on the other end when she picked up. She had that jolt of excitement she always got when he called her, even after more than twenty years of marriage.

"Hello, ma'am, is this Theodora McNamara?" asked the voice on the other end in a thick English accent.

"Yes, this is she," answered Teddy politely.

"Mrs. McNamara, this is Detective Sergeant Miller with City of London police, and I am calling to regretfully inform you ..." said Detective Sergeant Miller.

Teddy heard but simultaneously didn't hear Miller's words. A blaring screech filled her head, and she sank to the ground at the base of her home office desk and wailed. Although she couldn't recount the words that were said to her by the London police officer, she knew the message was that Colin was dead.

She stayed curled up, alone, for nearly three hours, her two dogs coming to comfort her periodically, seemingly knowing that something horrible was happening. When she heard her younger son Declan's car pull into the driveway, she managed to get herself to her feet and meet him in the kitchen.

Teddy ran to Declan and threw her arms around him. "Declan," she croaked. "I have, um, I have to tell you ..."

"Mom, what is wrong?" said Declan softly.

Teddy sunk to the ground at Declan's feet, looked up at him, and said, "Your father had an accident and did not make it ... I am so sorry."

"What? Did not make what?" he asked in brewing disbelief.

"Your, um, your father, Declan. He passed away. There was an accident at a tube station in London. I don't have the details of what happened. I am so sorry, Declan. I am so so sorry to tell you this."

Declan ran up the stairs to his room, screaming, "No way, no way!"

Teddy ran after him, knowing she needed to follow.

"Honey, I am in disbelief, too. But I need you to ..." she could not finish.

The mother-son pair slumped down next to Declan's bed in a heap of tears. Sadness, madness, and disbelief seemingly consuming every ounce of them.

As always in motherhood, there was another unenviable job she was required to do. Teddy knew she had to pull herself together and tell her older son Ronan, who was away at college, as well as Colin's parents. Despite her devastation, she moved into some sort of out-of-body state that allowed her to take care of these two horrific, albeit necessary, tasks.

"Declan, I need to call your brother. Do you want to be with me for that? It is your choice," Teddy said tenderly, not knowing where this sense of calm and strength was coming from.

"Um, Mom, if it is alright with you, I do not think I can

be here when you tell Ronan. I just can't. I am sorry, but I still do not believe this. I just don't, and I just won't." Declan trailed off, tears still running down his fair face.

"Declan, you can go. I understand. I really, truly do," she said and meant it.

Teddy sat back and thought before she hit Ronan's number on her phone. He was in his dorm, she could see from her tracking app, but that didn't mean he was with people. She didn't want him to be alone to hear the news. Teddy decided to call the dorm's rector and see if he could be with Ronan for this call. Mercifully, Father Mark picked up the phone and agreed to go to Ronan's room on the second floor. Father Mark was, of course, gracious and supportive when Teddy told him the horrible news.

Teddy awaited Father Mark's text intended to signal that he was with Ronan. Her phone pinged. She summoned every ounce of motherly strength she possessed.

"Hello, Mom, what's wrong? Father Mark just asked to come into my room," said Ronan when he answered.

"Um, Ronan. I do not know how to tell you this, but I learned this afternoon that your father was in an accident in London, and he did not, um, he did not, um... make it," sobbed Teddy.

"What happened?" screamed Ronan. The screeching started again in Teddy's ears.

"Ronan, I am sorry that I don't know the details or cannot remember them, not sure. I don't know. But something happened in a tube station," said Teddy shakily.

Teddy could hear Ronan sobbing. She could picture the devastation playing out in the austere boys' dorm room. She hoped that Father Mark was enough in-person support. Not being able to hold her precious firstborn at this devastating moment was searing pain on top of the already molten hot pain she was experiencing.

Colin's death in early September 2021 was a freak accident that only could have happened to him. He was in London on a business trip and was enjoying the pubs as he was known to do – wherever in the world he was, but especially in his beloved London. London was partially his home, having spent half his childhood growing up on a Royal Air Force Base outside of London. He swiped a pub's pint glass that must have been additive to his and Teddy's already large collection, as he was also known to do when one caught his attention. Their collection included Guinness pint glasses as well as Harp, Smithwick's, Greene King and Fuller's. This collection reminded them of the fun times in pubs on their many trips to England and Ireland. There was no way of knowing why this particular glass was swipe-worthy. But this glass, which was nestled in the breast pocket of his coat, caused what normally would have been a minor accident to be fatal.

Colin either tripped or was pushed in the Bond Street tube station in a crowd of people and fell to the ground. The CCTV footage did not definitively determine the incident as an accident or crime. The fall should have been of no real consequence. Colin, in his late forties, would have been able to handle a tumble. However, the pint glass broke, and managed to nick his jugular vein. Colin bled to death in minutes as the crowd looked on as a nurse attempted to stop the profuse flow of blood – to no avail.

It was hard for Teddy to process that the little thievery game she initiated on their second trip to Ireland – their honeymoon – caused Colin's demise. It was her desire for a particular Harp pint glass that started the unfortunate thievery habit. "It's so unique because it's embossed, Colin. I really want it!" exclaimed Teddy exuberantly. So, she asked the bartender if she could purchase it, but he declined in a very offput Irish way. He was certainly thinking, "idiot American." At the time, Teddy didn't think anything of drying out the glass and tucking it in her purse. It seemed like a victimless crime, not counting the bartender who had rebuffed her offer to buy it. But this victimless crime started what she and Colin found to be a fun-filled habit. Teddy would never have dreamed it leading to a victim-filled crime, Colin being taken away from her and their beloved sons. She would need to get rid of the collection. The family used them every single day as their drinking glasses at home. What once were reminders of good times were forever tainted. They had to go.

Chapter Seven

Teddy and Colin had built a wonderful life. They had two terrific sons and two terrific dogs. For them, that's all they ever wanted or needed. They fondly referred to themselves as the "family four-pack." Despite both Teddy and Colin coming from large families, they typically spent holidays at home, just the four-pack. The word "tightknit" probably doesn't do justice to their closeness.

They lived in Houston without any other family members for hundreds of miles. The closest being Colin's parents in San Antonio. Teddy's mother still lived in Ohio, alone after the passing of Teddy's father in 2020, and her four brothers were spread across Illinois, Massachusetts, and

Oregon. Given her brothers were much older, she didn't have a close relationship with them or their children, Ronan and Declan's cousins, because the age gap was just too great in both generations. The closeness with Colin's family was slightly better, but not much. None of them minded, really. They were content to be the four-pack.

But now, the perfect four-pack was incomplete, and there was nothing to change that unbearable fact. And for what, because Colin was having fun – as usual? Teddy loved that about him. He always found the fun wherever he was and in whatever he was doing. She never dreamed this trait would steal him away from her. And she was always the one who said she didn't want to live to be very old, much to the annoyance of her husband and children. She didn't. This was something she felt strongly about. Reaching old age felt like prioritizing quantity over quality. Her feelings about not living an exceptionally long life only intensified as her parents aged into their nineties. She didn't want to have garbage time – to borrow a sports term when teams are just going through the motions during the final minutes of a blowout – in her life. Never dreaming that it would be her husband, six years her junior, who would leave Earth first, Teddy felt anger along with grief. She didn't see this coming. She didn't have a plan like she always did. Not having a plan was tantamount to a mortal sin in her view. She didn't know the rules, which meant she was lost.

Teddy organized a beautiful Catholic funeral for Colin. Despite her grief, she wanted to ensure his tribute was reflective of him, their love and their family. The Mass and burial were typically Catholic: somber and serious. The wake was much more Colin-esque, with music Teddy managed to select through what she could only describe as guidance coming from Colin's soul. What else or who else could have prompted her to include a song like "There Is a Light That Never Goes Out" by The Smiths, which features lyrics Teddy and Colin frequently sang to each other – "And if a double-decker bus crashes into us, to die by your side, is such a heavenly way to die." Photos of her, Colin and the boys were on display. Family and friends from across the country came to show their love for Colin.

The countless times she heard, "Teddy, you and Colin were so beautiful. Please let us know if there is anything we can do for you" was making her feel claustrophobic. She, of course, hid her feelings well, always replying appropriately with a sentiment to make others feel good. "Thank you for being here. Colin loved you, and I appreciate your support." Oddly, Teddy did not interpret this outpouring as true support. She assumed the rules of politeness were motivating people's kind words and offerings of support. As a loner with fierce self-reliance deeply programmed, Teddy knew deep down she would only rely on herself going forward.

The funeral was a blur to all of them. Colin's entire family – parents, brothers, sisters-in-law, nieces and nephews – descended from their various cities across the country. Only one of Teddy's four brothers and his wife came. Unsurprising, given she barely spoke to two of them, and one was unwell. "Why would those jerks come? They never bothered to visit before," Teddy thought miserably Of course, her mother was too old at ninety-one to travel, so she was not there for Teddy either. It was the story of Teddy's life, a poorly timed life within her family. Her cousins who lived in Vancouver made the trip, for which she was eternally thankful. They were more like her siblings than her biological siblings. Although she called them cousins and they were very close, in fine Italian fashion, they were more distantly related. Describing the blood relationship was too complex, so they always just said, "We're cousins."

Teddy cannot remember anything from those early days, including the wake at The Lamb and Flag. Despite being one of Teddy and Colin's happiest places in Houston, even The Lamb and Flag couldn't make this occasion memorable or remotely happy. Despite all the kindness and love shown to her and her boys, it was a day of pain with details that mercifully would be a mist in her mind forever. Why would Teddy want to remember it? She was destroyed, as were the boys.

Colin and Ronan had grown so close. Their love of sports bonded them, but it was also the significant time Colin put into being a father to both boys. He was not an absentee dad. He spent countless hours driving Ronan to play in basketball tournaments throughout the Houston suburbs and watching Notre Dame football with him. The relationship blossomed later with Declan. The two of them bonded when Declan started to enjoy watching and playing basketball when he started high school.

Their perfect family built over the last twenty years was destroyed. They got two boys close in age, which was their hope. And they were solid kids – good students, fun, no trouble outside of the ordinary boy stuff. Teddy and Colin still had fun together despite being married for two decades. Of course, there were bumps, but all in all, Teddy considered herself one of the lucky ones. She thought she had life figured out and that she was making a good life that she would be proud to look back on, full of good memories. Breaking her five-year older or younger rule about whom she dated seemed to be her life's best rule-breaking decision. It allowed her to be with Colin and build a life she loved. But now, she was not certain what she felt about anything. Her life or her rules.

Chapter Eight

It had been three days since the funeral. Thirteen since Teddy got the news of Colin's death and had to be the messenger of the horror to her teenage sons. They were now in the hardest part of grieving. Trying to get to that horrible word ... "normal."

Teddy looked at her sons, Ronan and Declan, with tears in her eyes. They were stoic, trying to be strong for their years, nineteen and seventeen, respectively. The three of them sat in the family room where they shared so many moments together– big and small – lost in grief. The place where there was Christmas morning joy many times was now filled with a stunning, incomplete feeling. Their father, Teddy's husband

Colin, was buried three days ago. None of the now "three-pack" knew how to begin anything that looked like normal. What was normal without Colin, without Dad?

The guilt of having her sons lose their father made Teddy recall her short bit of angst about starting a family immediately following their wedding in 2001. Teddy and Colin's one-month anniversary fell on September eleventh, the day after her birthday and just a few days after returning from their Irish honeymoon that started their pint glass thievery habit. In the months following the tragedy of the 9/11 terrorist attacks, it felt like the world was spinning out of control. Anthrax in the mail and the fear of additional terrorism. Nervousness about boarding a plane or attending an event with large crowds with metal detectors and additional screening emerging all over. Even in corporate America, Houston-based Enron's corruption was exposed, taking down the corporate giant and Arthur Andersen, for its role in the farse.

The newlywed's fear of starting a family was short-lived, with Ronan being conceived in October. Teddy thought looking back that maybe it was the wrong decision. Her poor sons were facing an agony she never predicted. But how could Ronan and Declan be the wrong thing? Impossible. She shook herself back into reality.

Pulling herself abruptly back into the moment of day thirteen post-Colin's death – in their family room – just the three-pack, Teddy wiped the tears from her eyes and said, "Okay, guys, we need to start living again. We have no choice but to go on. Your father would not want any interruptions to your life. So, Ronan, that means you need to get back to South Bend, to Notre Dame, and Declan, you need to get back to classes at St. Michael's. This is an important year for you for college applications. As hard as it is going to be, we must keep going."

She would never let her sons know about her anger with their father. That was a feeling she was going to keep deep down within herself. She had to. She never wanted to be like her mother, who spoke ill of Teddy's dad daily.

Teddy's sons looked at her with complete disbelief. It had been exactly thirteen days since it happened. The astonishment on their faces communicated clearly to Teddy that they felt it was too soon to attempt normalcy.

Ronan spoke first, saying, "Mom, look, I appreciate the strong act here, but don't you think we all need more time, especially you? I know I cannot think about going back to school. I just don't care." Ronan was trying to be strong, feeling he had to assume the man of the house role. At six-foot-three and quite a handsome young man, he looked like a young adult, but he wasn't there yet. He was a college freshman who was supposed to be living out his childhood dream of being at Notre Dame. He should also be able to be his fun-loving self. Ronan was like a Pac-Man running around gobbling up all the fun pellets life had to offer. At this moment, it certainly felt like Game Over.

Declan, a young man of few words, usually unemotional, said with an atypical degree of animated conviction, "Mom, you cannot be serious?"

"Boys, what will all of us continuing to sit around here do? It will not bring your father back to us," Teddy croaked, her voice breaking. "You were your father's everything, and I am not going to let him down by not getting you back to normal. I am just not." Teddy was shaking but in control.

Teddy prided herself on being a strong person. She basically raised herself, as there was something emotionally missing from her relationship with her parents. Being by far the youngest in her family, she was a little adult her entire childhood. She was not an overly sentimental person, and she was certainly not passive. Being strong and taking charge were her ways of coping with work and personal problems. So of course, she went to her hardwired playbook in this most horrible of situations. Teddy believed she had to be strong for her sons. Although basically adults, they were still children, her babies. It's just what had to be done. Plain and simple. So, she did what any strong person would: started moving. It never once occurred to her that her sons could or should help her.

So, with that, Teddy went into action mode and booked a flight for Ronan to return to his first semester at Notre Dame. She fought back the tears, as she realized so many things Colin would never get to experience that he looked forward to with his eldest son at his alma mater: football weekends, Junior Parents' Weekend, Christmas breaks.

They had a wonderful freshman move-in weekend with Ronan back in August, just a few weeks ago, really. It all seemed so promising. Ronan was fulfilling his lifelong dream of being at Notre Dame. He seemed confident in his choice of studying finance. Teddy often joked that finance was a good fit for him because Ronan liked money and always enjoyed getting a maximum return on the least amount of effort. He was making friends quickly in his dorm. During the move-in weekend, Teddy and Colin connected with many old friends who were also experiencing the joy of bringing a child to their alma mater. Ronan had grown into quite a man. He was poised, communicative and engaging. Every adult he met found him to be an impressive young man. This was probably the reason he was frequently tipped twenty bucks when he babysat. Ronan knew how to connect with people.

"Okay, Ronan, you're heading back tomorrow. I don't want you to miss any more classes," Teddy said matter-of-factly.

Ronan nodded and left the room to begin packing. Her boys knew not to argue when their mother went into drill sergeant mode.

"Declan, what about you? School tomorrow?" she asked.

"Um, okay, I guess," Declan replied glumly. "Are you sure you don't want me to stay since Ronan is leaving tomorrow?"

"No, no, I appreciate it, D, but no. We need to get back to things," she stated firmly.

Poor Declan. He was not an emotionally astute person by nature. He was sweet and kind but reserved and preferred less communication to more. One of his go-to mantras as a child was, "Can we just stop talking about this?" This signature phrase caused much laughter among the four-pack over the years. It was typically used by him when he was getting lectured or when the topic of discussion was deemed embarrassing. His deadpan delivery of the phrase was also comical to the family. The "let's stop talking about it" guy being the one that Teddy would be leaning on just because of birth order and proximity seemed a tragic joke from the universe.

The next day, Teddy drove Ronan to the airport after getting Declan off to school. The drill of activities comforted her a bit. "I can do this," she thought to herself. "I just have to, right?"

She gave Declan the tightest of hugs before he left.

"Please be extremely careful driving, Declan, promise me," she said, trembling.

"Mom, do you not want me to leave?" asked Declan.

"No, sweets, no. I just want you to be careful, and I want you to go to your counselor or call me if you have any moments where you need someone. But, most important, drive carefully, please, please ... drive safely," she rambled.

"Okay, Mom, I promise. Ronan, good trip, bro," Declan stated in a manly tone of reassurance and then was out the door to his car.

Although the family four-pack was tight, the boys were so different and had grown apart as elementary and middle schoolers. Ronan, the social, sporty one, and Declan, the quiet, hardcore studious one. Teddy and Colin believed and hoped they would reclaim their childhood closeness in adulthood. Before the accident, lukewarm ambivalence was probably the best descriptor for their relationship. Now, they seemed to be leaning on each other a bit more. At least that is what Teddy hoped. It was always hard to read the teenage boy.

"Okay, Rooooooonan, up next. All your stuff in the car? Let's hit it," Teddy tried to say in her jovial let's get 'er done voice of the past. Her tone now, however, was noticeably flat and faded.

"Mom, please stop. You are not okay. Let me stay a few more days," Ronan pleaded. His eyes, which were a combination of green and brown, still looked beautiful despite the welling tears. Colin and Teddy called his eyes Connemara marble eyes because they resembled the marble from Ireland's west coast that they first saw in many gift shops on their engagement trip in 2000.

"Absolutely not, Ronan. We cannot wallow," she preached emphatically. "As several of my Peloton instructors say, 'We can do hard things.' We can. We are strong and we must find the strength to do this hardest thing. Go on."

When Teddy returned home from the long airport run across the expansive city of Houston, she sat quietly and sobbed for hours. The late September day was a beautiful one, but she curled up on the couch and did not move all day. She sat there alone. Colin was in the ground. She didn't even have an urn to look at, talk to or clutch in her arms. She had nothing, it seemed, at that moment. That strange wish to be whisked away to the nothingness she imagined in the beyond started up in her brain. And in her heart. "Please whisk me away God, please," she thought on repeat.

Until. Until Declan drove into the driveway, Teddy heard the driveway gate swing open with a thud. Teddy leapt off the couch and scurried into the kitchen to make herself look busy – to appear to be just fine. Just another day. It was as if a director had called for "action," and she was going to play the part of the perfect mother, well, perfectly. Inside her always swirling mind, however, Teddy was contemplating the unfairness of this being one more instance of motherhood calling on her to be superhuman. However, in fine Teddy fashion, she was not going to be the one to blink in the face of challenge. She was going to dig in.

She gazed out the window as Declan put his golf clubs in the garage and lugged his backpack in through the back door into the kitchen.

"Hi, Declan," Teddy said as cheerily as possible, fooling no one.

"Hey, Mom, how are you?" asked Declan softly.

"Um, well, I am okay," she lied.

"Being here alone wasn't hard?" Declan further inquired.

"Yes, yes, sweets, it was. But that's okay. You need to do what people your age do: go to school. You should not feel guilt or responsibility for me. Promise?" she prompted.

"Um, well, promise, I guess," replied Declan flatly.

Dealing with her sons was so hard and awkward. Declan was devastated too, and how was he supposed to deal with his grieving mother alone? Man-of-few-words Declan most certainly wanted more than anything to be left alone, but Teddy was certain Ronan told him he needed to step up and be responsible for his mother.

Seemingly unsure of what to do next, Declan marched upstairs to his room to shower. Despite being late September, it was still hot and humid in Houston, so his practice round of golf with the team left him sweaty and smelly. His strawberry-blonde hair was particularly curly due to the perspiration.

While Declan showered, Teddy grabbed one of the many casseroles, stuffed in her refrigerator, and put it in the oven. She didn't know what it was, nor did she care. She didn't know how all this food was supposed to help anything. Gestures she really did not want. Although politely appreciative of the support from friends and family, Teddy, the longstanding loner, preferred to deal with things alone. Colin was really the only person she truly relied upon. She was now back to how she grew up: alone and self-reliant.

She and Declan ate in painful silence. Although Declan's eyes were more of a gray than the crystal, bright blue of Colin's, Teddy was comforted by looking at her son, who was in many ways very much like Colin. Teddy felt that he was not scared to be himself. He didn't chase popularity and external affirmation like Ronan often did. Declan seemed content being Declan, like Colin was happy being Colin. They both possessed an inner peace Teddy admired and, in all honesty, was jealous of. Inner peace and self-happiness were not natural states of being for Teddy.

Chapter Nine

Teddy's cell phone rang, and it was Ronan. She was relieved to hear from him.

"So, you made it back without any issues?" she asked her son without even saying hello.

"All good, Mom. How are you?" Ronan asked. Teddy hit the button on her phone's glossy screen and put him on speaker.

"We're good, right, Declan?"

"Um, yeah ..." replied Declan without a trace of inflection in his deep voice.

"Well, that certainly sounds convincing, you two," said Ronan, trying to bring a little life to the conversation.

Ronan seemingly knew exactly what was happening back home. His mom and brother were sitting at the huge kitchen island in silence. The size of the island emphasized the fact that there were only two of them eating at it, making them feel even more lonely.

"Seriously, Ronan. Don't worry about us. We're fine. Just eating a little dinner. You know how we get when there is food around," countered Teddy, trying to be jovial.

"Yeah, how dare I try to interrupt your dinner," Ronan joined in halfheartedly.

"Have you eaten?"

"Not yet, but I will. Dining hall's still open," Ronan replied.

"North Dining Hall awaits. You know I know it well, Ro! Okay then, we better let you go. Ronan, thank you so much for calling. I love you," his mother said with a woeful sadness in her voice.

Teddy had eaten virtually every meal on campus at North Dining Hall as her dorm, in which she lived all four years of college, was right next door. During her time, North was viewed as the less desirable dining hall on the Notre Dame campus. Teddy had to admit that South Dining Hall was hard to beat, given it looked like the great hall featured in her beloved *Harry Potter* movies. Nonetheless, North Dining Hall held a special spot in her heart. It comforted her that her son was in a place she could easily visualize. Anything that could help during this painful time was appreciated.

"Mom, I love you too. I am not so sure this was the best idea you've ever had. I should be home," he protested.

"No, Ronan. I will not hear of it. You are just starting your life, and you must get to it. Enough said," Teddy stated with motherly authority that shut down the conversation.

"Hugs," she said.

"Hugs," said Ronan in return as they ended the call.

As Teddy cleaned up the dishes, she started to weep. Thankfully, Declan was already upstairs doing his homework. "Now what?" she thought. This was the time of day that she shared with Colin. It was "couch time" with the dogs and TV. This was Teddy's first "normal" evening since *it* happened. "What should I do on day fourteen since my husband died?" she thought. "Should I get on the couch like normal, given that it's anything but, or should I do something else?" Their terriers, Lucy and Sally, named after the *Peanuts* characters, could certainly use some couch time. They were out of sorts too. Colin doted on them, and his absence was felt by the four-legged members of the family who, instead of lounging on the floor, kept exploring the house in search of their daddy.

Teddy had no answers. So, she cleaned the kitchen as slowly as humanly possible. This task killed all of fifteen minutes. She considered starting on her thank you cards, but that sounded like a torturously depressing task. She was pleased that so many people made donations to their beloved Notre Dame, as she requested versus sending flowers or other fleeting remembrances. She could not bear the thought of her house full of flowers like her mother's was after the passing of Teddy's father just a little over a year ago. So, Teddy sat at the kitchen island, staring blankly out the window as dusk turned to night. She simply sat with tears streaming down her face, not sure if she was sad or mad. She wiped her tears away and quickly hopped out of the chair when she heard Declan's feet striking the hardwood stairs. It was pre-bed snack time for Declan already; hours had passed.

"'Sup," she tried to say cheerily to Declan.

"Nothin' ... just getting cereal."

"So, school was okay today? You okay?"

"Yeah, it was fine. I managed if that's what you are asking,"

"I am glad to hear it. I also want you to know that being sad or upset is okay and normal. Just promise you will talk to me or someone like your counselor if you are feeling overwhelmed. I am going to a counselor, and we can get one for you too. I know you said you don't want to do that, but that option is open any time you choose."

"Yeah, Mom, I get it. I just don't even know what I am feeling right now. Just trying to get through each day. And no. I don't want to talk to some stranger, okay?" Declan said quietly, almost a whisper.

"I get that, Declan. I really do," Teddy said tearfully.

She began to sob, and her son tried to comfort her. Realizing she was breaking down, she pulled away, kissed Declan's cheek, and ran upstairs to her bedroom. It was now just *her* bedroom, not *their* bedroom.

For Teddy, the loss of Colin was an overall ache. It wasn't a particular room in the house or a particular photo on the wall that would trigger a flood of emotions. It was an all-encompassing feeling that part of her being was gone. Teddy realized now that she never fully understood how much she loved Colin when he was alive. She really had let someone in. She wasn't a loner after all. With Colin, she was never alone. She was a team with Colin. She had broken her rule to be with him, and it was good – great – until it was over.

She buried herself under the covers, and that was it.

Her mind drifted to the thoughts of just being whisked away from life. These quasi-suicidal thoughts were a part of her life. Why? She didn't know. Sometimes life was just overwhelming for her with so many demands, and her brain would use this image of evaporating to nothingness to soothe itself, she guessed. These thoughts always led to sleep, which was her reprieve from the pain. Before the accident, she would scold herself for such self-pitying moments because she knew deep down her life was blessed. Now, she realized that in the past, she had no idea what true pain was. Perspective.

When she awoke the next day, she realized she had slept the entire night without interruption, which was a first since Colin was taken from her. She didn't know whether to be happy or sad. That seemed to be her constant conundrum now. Should she be happy that she had twenty-two years with Colin and two wonderful boys that will carry on his memory? Or should she be sad that their time was cut short, and their sons lost their father too soon? Was getting sound sleep for the first time in two weeks a sign that she was not grieving enough? Her mind was still swirling at the thought of virtually everything.

She slowly got out of bed. Down in the kitchen, she found that Declan was already up and eating breakfast, ready for school.

"Hi, Mom," Declan said with a mouthful of Honey Nut Cheerios and cell phone in hand, scrolling.

"Hey, sweets," she said, planting a kiss on his cheek, to which he resisted.

"Don't pull away. It will only get worse for you if you resist my affection. It is my right as your mother to bestow affection at my will," she tried to tease.

This was their typical interaction when it came to affection. Today, however, it just felt strained and hollow. After Declan shot out the door to get to school on time, Teddy lumbered to the couch. Another empty day ahead of her.

She started to tidy the house, something that usually comforted her, but didn't today. The house was the boys' teenage house, complete with a pool. They had purchased it just five years ago, so the boys would have room to have friends over and a built-in activity. Sadly, because of the affluence of the neighborhood, a house with a pool was not really the draw it was when Teddy was growing up in the '80s in a true middle-class neighborhood. The house and pool had, however, been a Godsend during the global pandemic. The countless hours the four-pack spent together in the house and in the pool during that time were now a true treasure.

Next Teddy started to write thank you cards to all the

people who showed such kindness over this horrible time. After just two, she felt spent. Writing the cards just caused her to think, and thinking wasn't a good thing at this moment. Teddy was grateful that, financially, there was no need for her to go back to work. However, this meant she had no real distractions during a time when distractions would be oh-so welcome.

Teddy's mind was typically on tasks and proving herself in every setting possible, from the playground and classroom as a child to the office and in mothers' groups as an adult. Teddy's built-in coping mechanism for everything was activity. She always felt compelled to do something and never waited for something to happen. But when she needed it most, there was nothing to do or accomplish – nothing she could do to change the facts. She was forced to just be ... to exist. Mercifully, her phone rang. "A distraction, thank you, God," Teddy thought to herself.

"This is she," Teddy said in response to the caller asking for her.

"Mrs. McNamara, this is Mrs. Lopez at St. Michael's. I am calling to find out when we should expect Declan back in school," the attendance clerk said.

"Declan went to school yesterday, and he's there today

too," replied Teddy with a confused tone.

"Well, we did not show him at school yesterday or today. We didn't call yesterday because we were unsure of your plans, given the situation," the woman said sensitively.

"So, you're positive he's not on campus right now?" said Teddy, her heart racing with abject fear.

"I am positive," the clerk replied without hesitation.

"Okay, let me get to the bottom of this situation, and I will call you back."

"Thank you, Mrs. McNamara, and I am very sorry for your loss."

"Um, yes, thank you," Teddy absently replied.

Teddy's mind was racing. What was going on? Was Declan hurt? Why wouldn't he be in school? She immediately pressed his name on her phone. It rang, but Declan did not pick up, so she texted him. After just barely completing those critical tasks, Teddy ran to the bathroom to throw up, her body not able to handle another jolt of fear.

"I understand you are not at school. CALL ME," she wrote in her text. SEND.

A minute or two later, which felt like hours, her phone rang while she was still hovering next to the toilet. Declan was on the other end.

"Where are you, Declan? Are you okay?" Teddy said urgently.

"Yes, Mom, I'm okay. I'm just at Sundown Park," Declan responded.

"I see. Please come home so we can talk about why you are not in school," she said firmly.

"Okay," was all Declan said, seemingly aware that was the only acceptable answer.

Once Teddy knew Declan was safe and another loss was not in store for her, Teddy became furious. She was, in fact, Italian furious, which is a fierce and verbally colorful state. School was the most important thing to her. She believed the boys needed to get back to it because school, unlike jobs, progressed. In her mind, the boys shouldn't miss a beat. They just couldn't, no matter what. If they did, she was failing herself in her eyes, and more so, she thought in Colin's. She could not let Colin down. She had to finish what they started with their boys.

Once she vanquished her anger with her verbal tirade, she sat on the island barstool, contemplating how to approach Declan when he got home. She was only capable of semi-calm thoughts, despite letting much of her anger release verbally before his arrival. Declan had never acted out before. He was a rule follower too. But the situation Declan was in could sway any child into atypical behavior.

Declan slowly opened the back door and went inside. He looked down at the floor, avoiding Teddy's eyes, his face and neck red from anxiety. She came to him and gave him a long, hard hug. She would have normally lost her mind, but she realized he was, of course, still hurting, and his mother's anger would not help anything.

"Declan," she said softly, "do you want to talk to a grief counselor?"

"No, Mom, I don't think I need that. I think I just needed some time alone. I will be fine. I promise. I was not ready to face people. People saying they are sorry, all that."

"I know. They think they are helping, and they are by showing they care, but it's hard to be reminded repeatedly. But do you think you will be up for school tomorrow? We have got to start doing our normal things. We just have to."

"Yeah, yeah, I'll go," he replied.

"Okay, Declan. I will give you a pass here, given the extraordinary circumstances, but don't lie. If we ever needed to tell the truth to each other, it's right now," she said lovingly. "I will always be here for you, but you have to let me in for that to happen. Does that make sense, Declan?"

"Yeah, Mom, it does. It's just that I don't want to be a bother to you. You are so sad. I just wanted to handle things in my own way, myself," he explained.

"Oh, um. I guess I haven't thought about you guys trying to be strong for me. I can see that logic. But, please, resist that temptation. We are all going to go through a lot. We're without your father, and Ronan being away is new too … We are in uncharted territory, and it's just us right now. We need to truly be an 'us' to make it, okay?" she concluded.

"Okay, Mom, I get it. I do. I will go tomorrow, and I will tell you the truth from now on. I am very sorry," he said, as he walked to the stairs to escape to his room.

Teddy went to the couch and sat and stared. It was too early to call Ronan. He was still in class. So, she dialed her friend Dana. She shared the goings-on with Declan while Dana listened, not taking a stance too soon. She listened to Teddy's feelings and took in how Teddy relayed Declan's actions and thoughts.

"Teddy, trying to get the boys back to normal is admirable. I am not surprised by your approach. It's a *you* thing to do. This seems to help you feel in control in an out-of-control situation. The boys are likely looking for the same thing. They are searching for ways to feel in control too. That's probably Declan's true motivation. As much as you hate this idea, you are going to need to get more comfortable with things being out of whack for a while. Nothing you do is going to bring normalcy two weeks after what happened. Give yourself and the boys a break. 'Iron Teddy' isn't going to truly help anyone."

"Wow, okay. I get it. I thought this was what I should be doing, but who knows, Dana? Who the heck knows?" Teddy's frustration with the roller coaster ride she was presently stuck on was seeping out. She was glad she had a friend to receive her verbal diatribe.

"Want me to stop by tonight?"

"No, I'm okay. This skipping school thing with Declan just caught me off guard. Thanks for the talk and taking in some of my venom, Dana. I am sure it is hard for you to listen to me, given what you've been through in your life. Thank you, and I'm sorry."

"Do not be sorry. I am one of the few people who can say they understand and mean it."

Dana was the only person besides her children whom Teddy was regularly talking to at the moment. After the funeral, everyone went back to their lives. Teddy would get the "thinking of you" texts from various friends, coworkers and family members, but there was no one in the thick of her grief with her. It was just her way. Teddy felt she learned through experience that others are rarely there for her. It's also likely she trained those around her not to get too close. Colin had been her person. She was all in on him, and some could say that she neglected to build a network of friends and family. Dana was Teddy's closest friend. Still, however, nothing close to a best friend. Her best friend was Colin.

Dana and Teddy worked together at LMC years ago. Then, their children's elementary school connected them once more. Their friendship, however, wasn't based on their children's friendship. It had grown so much deeper in the decade since going to lunch downtown between meetings or standing in the elementary school mom's circle chatting while the kids played on the playground after school. They assumed they would have to rely on each other to get through their children going off to college. Dana had a daughter the same age as Ronan, so they were experiencing the entire off-to-college "tragedy" together. Neither foresaw Dana needing to get her friend through an actual tragedy. Thankfully, Dana was well-equipped for the job. She was logical, reasonable and empathetic, exactly the type of person Teddy needed. Dana was Teddy's "Miranda" from *Sex and the City*. The smart, practical one. And she knew loss from her own experience of losing infant Ellen.

Dana had a daughter who was stillborn. Teddy did not know Dana when this happened but, through the office grapevine, had become aware of Dana's loss long before the pair forged a friendship. Dana was a strong, stoic type who rarely discussed her loss, but when she did share it with Teddy, it was clear that Dana's loss was felt every day.

Teddy could vividly recall sitting across from Dana, with her gorgeous crown of chestnut colored hair cascading past her shoulders, those many years ago in the food court. After many months of shared lunches and coffees, Dana blurted out of the blue, "You know, although I spent no time with Ellen other than being pregnant with her, and I have Emily now, there is no forgetting, and there is no replacing."

"Oh, Dana, of course not. Of course not. Your life will go on – is going on, but of course, your life is changed after the loss of a child, the loss of Ellen. You should never forget. I just hope the sadness eases a bit every day. Going on is not moving on; it's not forgetting," said Teddy in a tender whisper. Although hundreds of people were around them, Teddy felt as if they were the only two in the cavernous food court.

"Yes, my life is going on, but it still hurts every day. And talking about it really never helps me, so I do it infrequently. I always think people think I am weird for not talking about it more."

"There is no weird. You must do what works for you, not act how you think others want you to act," replied Teddy, reaching out for Dana's hand across the table.

Now, Teddy assumed that she would be much like Dana in her stoicism to the outside world, covering up a hurt that would never ease with silence ... a silence some may call avoidance.

She thought back to her words to Dana many years ago, "Going on is not moving on; it's not forgetting." Teddy thought maybe she should consider these words herself and discuss them with the boys at the right time.

Chapter Ten

Teddy spent the rest of the day on the couch, while Declan stayed in his room. She was not sure how early afternoon turned into evening with her not moving a muscle, but it did. All the normal things in life were happening whether she wanted them to or not. She felt like a brick: immobile and heavy. She tried reading the news on her phone's many apps, something she regularly did now that the boys were older, and she had time to read. Today, she just closed up her news apps one after the other, sickened by the news itself and the incessant bullying that seemed to never end on every topic from COVID-19 to race and gender issues.

Despite her voracity for staying up to date, being in the

know of public discourse often made Teddy want to scream. She believed the reason everyone was so busy with online viewpoint bullying is because everyone had it too good. She felt that people clearly didn't have enough real problems nowadays, so they spent their time opining on every minor transgression they experienced or didn't experience, just believing so passionately in what was "their" truth. She now knew what real problems were, and her circumstances affirmed her views. She didn't care that many would describe her take as unenlightened and unempathetic. Feeling affirmed in a view was typically accompanied by a sense of satisfaction for Teddy. Today, however, she was just deflated. Believing she was "right" gave her no boost whatsoever.

Realizing it was evening, she managed to make one of Declan's delicacies: a peanut butter and jelly sandwich. He politely humored his mother by eating and then marching straight back up the stairs. This behavior, however, was not unusual for Declan, or Ronan for that matter. Their lives were in their rooms, like most teens. Declan was studious and spent most of his time in his room studying, with perfect grades resulting. He was like Teddy when she was a student, an over-studier. Teddy normally appreciated his hard work. But now, his isolation scared her. In his early years, he focused on crafting Lego creations of every sort imaginable. As he got older, he still preferred the solitude of his room, even sans toys. With cell phones and game consoles, leaving their rooms to socialize became completely unnecessary for teens. Heaven for them, hell for parents, especially now for Teddy. What if his skipping school is just the beginning of issues with him? How was she to assess his mental state when she saw him for a total of fifteen minutes a day, and he spoke no more than fifty words in those fifteen minutes?

At a loss, Teddy called Ronan. She caught him at a good time, which was not often the case since he had started college back in August when everything looked bright and shiny.

"Hey, Ro," she said in her upbeat mom tone.

"Hello, Mom," Ronan responded in a serious tone.

"Are you okay?" Teddy asked.

"Yeah, Mom, how are things with you and that little piece of garbage, Declan?"

"Oh, your piece of garbage brother is okay," Teddy lied, playing along with Ronan's constant putdowns of his brother.

"Hmmm, I don't believe you, Mom."

"Why? Why wouldn't you believe me?"

"Well, Mom, I have you guys tracked on my phone, and he didn't go to school, Mom, so I am worried. Did you know, or am I snitching?"

Apparently, Ronan was becoming a parent in his father's absence. This was a surprising occurrence Teddy never saw coming. Ronan was a great kid, but like most kids, Ronan was focused on Ronan. His looking in on his brother's location was shocking to Teddy. She used to check the boys' locations frequently. It just didn't occur to her this week. This lapse of a simple and obvious action made Teddy realize how completely off-kilter she was.

"Oh crud, I always forget about technology. Hashtag Elderly," she said, faking brightness in her voice. "Yes, I know he skipped school yesterday and today. The school called. I just didn't realize you knew it too."

"Mom, he'll be okay. We just need a little time too, okay?"

"Yeah, I get it, I do, but I need the truth from you both. How are you doing ... really? Have you been going to class?"

"Yes, Mom, I have a lot to make up after missing nine days, and my first midterms are coming up, so I am hunkered down. It is hard to believe nearly five weeks of college are over. I cannot wait to come home for fall break, but until then, I am locked in on my classes. I swear, Mom," he said very convincingly. "I am not going to mess this up. I worked too hard to get here and probably used up all the luck I was allotted for my lifetime getting in. I have it all mapped out – how I am going to get my work made up. Fun just has to take a back seat right now. I know you cannot believe I said that, but I said it, and I mean it. Not that I really feel like going out anyway."

"Okay, I don't want to put pressure on you in a time like this, but I know your father would not want you to do anything but your very best. Your being at Notre Dame meant everything to him. So do him proud, sweetie," she said softly.

"Yeah, that's no pressure at all, Mom," he responded sarcastically.

"Oh God! I just cannot seem to get it right. FUDGE MONKEY!! I didn't mean to put pressure. I mean to free yourself to the degree you can from your father's absence and focus on you and your goals. That's not selfish. He would have wanted that. You know that's true, don't you?"

"Yes, Mom, I do. It's just really hard. Dad was the best ..." Ronan said, trailing off in tears.

Teddy and Ronan shared a cry and then said goodbye. It seemed to be what they both needed. Teddy thought how lucky she was to have such a great boy but also about how unfair it all seemed to be. It was still an unbelievable fact that

Ronan was in college. She and Colin had hoped and planned nearly every day of Ronan's nineteen years for this time of his life. And here it was, overshadowed.

Teddy was thankful for Ronan's much more talkative nature, despite it often being hard to have a two-way conversation with him because he rarely paused to take a breath once he got started. She wasn't, however, always thankful for it. She thought back to all the times he shared too much information about things like his and his friend's partying or when he talked just to hear himself talk, especially about all of his plans for studying versus actually doing the studying. His constant chatter would frustrate Teddy to no end at times. Today, she was glad for every word he gave her. She did hope that his talk of hunkering down on studies was not his typical wishful thinking versus actual doing, as it often was in high school. It was hard for Ronan to leave any Pac-Man fun pellets uneaten, but perhaps he was being honest about losing his appetite for fun during this difficult time.

Despite it only being late September, Teddy's mind drifted to the looming holiday season. "What on earth would that be like this horrible, horrible year?" she thought. "Could she and the boys take a pass and just ignore them this year?" It was too much to bear, so she tried to shift her thoughts elsewhere. But oddly, she found herself slowly ascending the stairs to find the binder of Christmas letters tucked among the photo albums on the bookcases in her room. She slid out the very same binder that held the first few letters Colin had shared with her back in the summer of 1999. Since then, more than twenty years' worth of letters outlining their lives were all at her fingertips. Memories.

"Was this a good or bad idea?" she thought. Her body seemed to move without conscious thought, and she proceeded back down the stairs and settled on the couch, Sally and Lucy jumping up to join her. She looked back at the stairs admiring the checkered tile she put on the stairs' risers. It was a little thing, but it was something she and Colin did to the house to make it unique and their own. Every single thing triggered a memory, even stairs. She just wanted to float away, but that was not an option. As usual, she had a job to do. She had to be strong. She had to see her boys through this. It was on her.

She stared at the puffy, fabric-wrapped binder that sat in her lap with her hands folded on top of it. The binder's cover was a bit of a throwback, which made sense since Colin's mom did the stitching, and his dad did the calligraphy. While holding the binder, she gazed at her diamond Claddagh engagement ring, missing her Colin terribly. "Friendship, love and loyalty," she thought. "Now it felt like sorrow, loneliness, and hopelessness." She opened the binder and flipped to the 2002 letter. She wanted to see how they, really meaning Colin, had reflected Ronan's first year. Teddy contributed a tiny bit to the letters as the years went on, but they were really Colin's reflection of the past year, outlining how he saw the year's triumphs and sometimes its struggles. Instead of her usual scan-reading, Teddy read slowly and deliberately, relishing every single word and well-crafted joke. The letter, of course, spoke of her, Colin and Ronan. Today, however, the letter spoke to her. In the past, Teddy was the letter's editor. Today, she has become its audience.

Christmas 2002

Christmas came early for the McNamaras this year, as we received the best present possible on the fifth of July. On that day, Ronan Kevin McNamara made his grand entrance into the world. Needless to say, this year has been an unforgettable adventure as we started our life with Ronan.

During the springtime, we loaded up on the baby essentials. Not just the crib but the changing table, stroller, playpen, gymini, diaper genie, bouncy-chair, bumper-jumper, boppy, car seat, swing and exersaucer. You name it, we got it. Colin took a shot at becoming a McNamara artist like his sculptor father, painting Ronan's nursery in a rainbow of colors. At Easter, Ronan bolstered his future wardrobe, as we traveled to Ohio for a baby shower at the home of Teddy's parents. Ronan realized that we were indeed ready for his arrival with the last-minute purchases of a camcorder and an SUV.

Measuring in at eight-and-a-half pounds and 21 inches, Ronan started out big and continues to skyrocket with every passing day. His unofficial statistics at five months were 20 pounds and 28 inches. If he stays on his current pace, he should be staring eye-to-eye with 7-foot-6 Rockets rookie Yao Ming sometime during kindergarten.

Following Ronan's birth, we both stayed home for a few weeks to learn all about our new son. Teddy's three-month maternity leave undoubtedly ranks as one of her favorite stretches ever, as she strengthened that special bond between mother and child. Both sets of grandparents came to Houston to meet their newest grandchild at this time. We also received visits from Colin's brother, Brendan, our Notre Dame classmates, Elaina, Ryan and O'Malley. Speaking of O'Malley, the family dog is definitely starting to show his age now that he has reached his fourteenth birthday. If having a child is a handful, then having an eccentric dog keeps all hands endlessly occupied.

Towards the end of Teddy's maternity leave, we embarked on our first family vacation, heading up the road to Dallas for Colin's college friend Fernando's wedding to Michelle. A week later, the family went mobile once more, taking a flight to Notre Dame for Ronan's baptism. Father Joyce presided over the beautiful ceremony at Notre Dame's Log Chapel, with Colin's brother Dylan and Teddy's niece Kathleen serving as Ronan's Godparents. Ronan quickly became a fan of the Fighting Irish, as his life began with Ty Willingham, the ND head football coach, guiding the school to eight straight wins.

After three months of around-the-clock Ronan, Teddy returned to work at Omni Energy. This transition was eased by granny care, as Colin's mom moved in for a month of babysitting. But Grandma's stay was just a band-aid, and Ronan soon had to face the real world. It started with a week at an assembly-line daycare, where our little boy was just a number. Then Ronan came home to an uncommitted nanny, who quickly departed for Christmas vacation. Fortunately, we finally found an acceptable daytime spot for Ronan at a nearby Montessori school. That's not to say that Teddy hasn't been tempted to hide Ronan under her desk at work.

Over the last month, we have searched for that elusive balance between work and family. Teddy continues to adapt to her new role as "Supermom, the Working Mother." Colin has trimmed back his travel with the Rockets, but media demands have grown as Yao Ming grabs both national and global headlines. Ronan has done his part to help us adjust by sleeping through the night on a consistent basis. We made our final family trip of the year over Thanksgiving weekend, driving to San Antonio. Four generations of Colin's family gathered together that weekend, as Ronan met his Great-Grandpa.

It looks like this year we've finally discovered the true meaning of Christmas letters: to gush about your children until the reader can take no more. I can tell that you're already looking forward to future installments on teething and potty training. Have a great Christmas, and all the best in the New Year.

Colin, Teddy and Ronan

The letter warmed her heart. She could hear Colin's voice in every word. It made Teddy feel better, feel something other than loss. She read it again and again until she fell asleep. With each reading, she would think of a vivid memory. The top one being the fact that Teddy's doctor told her on the third of July that she was not close to delivering, so she and Colin decided to have friends over for the July Fourth holiday. Knowing this was Colin's last hurrah, with Teddy's last hurrah having happened many months earlier, Teddy gave him permission to enjoy himself. That he did. Unfortunately, Ronan decided he was ready for arrival at two in the morning. Teddy was unsure to this day if Colin would have passed a sobriety check if pulled over on the way to the hospital.

That was their life, a series of ordinary events but oftentimes with a comical twist. To Teddy, there was no better storyteller of their special, albeit typical, life than her love, Colin.

Chapter Eleven

Declan woke up and got ready for school. He wasn't sure what he was doing. Going to school seemed futile, but staying home with his mom was not permitted. Skipping school was no longer an option either. Day sixteen after his father's death was apparently the day he had to be normal, act normal, accept this as normal. His typically organized, driven self now felt aimless. With no other realistic option available to him, he left the house for school. His mother was not downstairs as she normally was first thing in the morning. He wasn't sure if he should check on her or not. Declan, being a "let's not talk about it" kid, opted to just leave for school. "Going to school is what she wanted, so I am doing it," he said to Lucy and Sally, as they jumped up at his legs for a goodbye pat with the blissful glee of ignorance.

At school, he went to first period, AP Physics, after a long walk from the parking lot. His school was a very nice private Catholic school—all boys—in a not-so-great part of town. But the campus was pretty posh for a high school. It was a campus with several buildings and a well-manicured quad where the boys played a variety of games during free periods and lunch. Many friends at public schools who had come to the campus for SAT tests or sporting events were always impressed with his school's campus. Declan was thankful that he was not at their gigantic public high school option, which was home to nearly five thousand high schoolers. Ronan endured one year of it for his freshman year, and Declan was pleased to be the second son in this particular situation. Declan was much more comfortable in this smaller, less chaotic environment.

Declan's parents were perfectionists, especially his mother. He and Ronan changed schools in elementary school from a parish Catholic school to a small public school in their neighborhood. His parents did not think the education at the Catholic school was very good, nor did they like the pastor giving the school children fire-and-brimstone homilies straight out of the 1950s. So, they had the boys make the switch when Ronan was in second grade and Declan in kindergarten. The boys enjoyed great public school experiences through middle school. High school changed that story entirely. Once again, his parents were unafraid to make a change. They seemingly wanted the very best for their kids, and they were not afraid to admit miscalculations and take action to rectify them. It appeared to Declan that they had always been all-in on parenting, not in a helicopter way, which was the parenting rage of his youth. Somehow, his parents seemed to bring the best of their upbringings from the '70s and '80s with structure and firm expectations but also showed an active interest in his and his brother's lives.

Normally, Declan appreciated his surroundings at St. Michael's. Today, he was on autopilot as he made his way to the classroom in the largest, newest building on campus, Xavier Hall. He took his usual seat and made a tiny bit of small talk with his classmate, John, who struggled to look at Declan and did not immediately start talking about some inane gossip as he normally did. "Uh, hey Declan ... um... how are you doing, bro?" asked John. Realizing John's discomfort because John had literally never asked how Declan was doing ever before, Declan obliged, responding, "Oh, you know. Doing the best I can ... I guess." Mercifully, Dr. Fields started class, putting an end to their awkward exchange. Would awkwardness be the feeling emanating from all of his classmates, Declan absentmindedly wondered during Dr. Fields' pre-class preamble?

Declan psyched himself up mentally as Dr. Fields got started with her usual droning tone. This was Declan's first class back after the accident. It felt weird to him. Empty and pointless. Declan tried to shake off this mental vibe and pay attention. He was able to listen, but taking notes felt beyond his current capabilities.

Declan was in his junior year, an important year for college applications. Being studious and hardworking, he was not too worried about getting into somewhere he deemed acceptable, meaning a college ranked in the top twenty. Unlike his brother, Declan was fine with going to Notre Dame, but it wasn't the fulfillment of a lifelong goal like it had been for Ronan. Declan was much more practical. He wanted a good education and ultimately a good job, probably in engineering. College was a means to an end, not the end goal in and of itself, as it seemed to be for his brother and, to some degree, his parents. He wanted something prestigious as a payoff for his hard work. He was simply not singularly focused on the family tradition.

Once the class ended, he slid his notebook into his backpack, realizing he hadn't written down a single thing.

"Well, at least I was physically present, and the teacher releases her slides anyway," he thought. He ambled his way to English across the quad and was a minute late. "Great, a detention," he thought. However, his teacher didn't issue the expected reprimand, so Declan quickly took his seat and slid his notebook onto the desk. "Hmm, a bizarre 'you just lost your father' perk?" he surmised. No matter, Declan was grateful, as he had precious few detention marks against him.

He realized that everyone had a writing assignment done that he hadn't even started yet due to his absences. They were going to edit the assignment during the class session. Feeling completely out of sync with the class, Declan asked Mr. DeSilva if he could be excused from class to go work on completing the paper since he was behind. He wanted out of the class badly. Unfortunately, Mr. DeSilva sensed he wanted an escape more than a quiet place to do work, so he instructed him to work on his essay at his desk while the others edited. Reluctantly, Declan took his seat again and powered up his laptop. The blank Word document stared back at him, giving him a sense of loss and dread.

****

Ronan stayed up late the night before, trying to make up for the work he had missed while in Houston. He was exhausted when his phone's alarm started beeping at eight in the morning. Despite his mental and physical exhaustion, he got out of bed and made his way to his dorm shower. Oh, how he missed his own bathroom and king-size bed at home. Despite loving Notre Dame and being thrilled to be there, dorm living was austere compared to his life at home with his parents.

As he put on his shower shoes and got under the stream of water, Ronan thought about his charmed life with his parents. They lived in a sought-after neighborhood that looked like a movie set for a John Hughes movie like *Home Alone*. Every house was large and different, the trees were mature, and the flowerbeds made each house seem inviting. The neighborhood was not the only thing that seemed perfect. His family was perfect in his mind.

Growing up as part of the four-pack was pretty amazing now that he looked back at it. Ronan was not typically a sentimental type. Recent events seemed to have changed that. As he showered, he was happy and devastated all at the same time, thinking about the fun and love at his house on Brown Street. The neighborhood streets were named after universities and famous authors. It always irritated Ronan that Notre Dame was overlooked as a street name in his beloved "'hood." Pulling himself out of his dreamlike state, Ronan got dressed and headed to class. He was determined to catch up and make his dad proud. It's what he had to do for himself, his mom, and the memory of his dad.

His going to Notre Dame was a lifelong dream for all of them. He was accepted in December of 2020, and they were all ecstatic for months. It was hard to believe that only a month and a half ago his mom and dad were on campus dropping him off. It was picture perfect. No dark cloud was sighted on the horizon but, apparently, it was there. The entire family was feeling nothing but goodness and promise just six weeks earlier.

Now it felt tainted to Ronan, even his being at Notre Dame. Being the staunch competitor that he was, Ronan knew he had to fight the feeling that his college experience was tainted by this loss. His heart told him that his dad would be so disappointed if he let anything tarnish Notre Dame. How to combat this nagging feeling that it was all ruined was the question that had been tormenting him since he got on the plane to return to campus.

Prior to the disruption, Ronan had been enjoying college life immensely. He loved the dorm life and the many social opportunities that were now at his fingertips twenty-four hours a day. Ronan enjoyed socializing with many people, a bit of a social bee. He never had one best friend, unlike Declan, who strayed from the in-crowd but had a primary "bestie" at every school he attended, starting in preschool. Although Ronan was enjoying Notre Dame, he still hadn't really found a core group of friends. He wished he had now that the unspeakable happened. He didn't feel alone, but he didn't feel deeply connected either, making the loss of his father seem even more acute.

And Notre Dame is renowned for its proud football tradition, but even that was tarnished with his dad now gone. They watched games together since he was a toddler, and talking Fighting Irish football was their thing. Even though the team was once again in pursuit of a playoff spot, the season had suddenly stopped bringing him joy. Instead, he felt cheated that he and his dad would never share the experience of their favorite team winning a title.

After making his way through the South quad of the picturesque campus, he took his seat in Macroeconomics. Despite his physical weariness, he was tuned in and ready, all while missing his father terribly. Day sixteen was the day "going on" officially started for Ronan.

Chapter Twelve

Teddy awoke and found herself still holding the Christmas letter binder. She smiled. This was the first morning that she didn't immediately wake up with feelings of doom and dread. She looked at the time and realized she had overslept, apparently forgetting to set her alarm the night before. She frantically ran to Declan's room, expecting to see him sprawled across his bed. It, however, was empty, just a tangled mess of sheets and his comforter. "He must have gotten himself up and gone to school," she thought with surprise. However, given recent events with Declan, she immediately tracked him on her phone. His little picture showed him on the St. Mike's campus. While in the app, she took a peek at where Ronan was. There was his little picture in one of the classroom buildings on ND's campus.

"My poor little guys," she thought. "Why did this happen to them? But look, they are both getting on with it, right? Proud."

"Proud" was one of her frequent sayings to the boys. She typically didn't use a full sentence but would just smile her big smile, admired by every dentist she ever saw, and say "proud" to their many accomplishments, big and small.

Teddy was blessed with two terrific children. They were smart and both had good hearts. Those qualities sound quite basic and simple, but from observing other children as hers grew, Teddy realized those were not qualities to take for granted. There were many children who were smart, and many who were good. It was sadly rare to have both, a sentiment that teachers would actually echo in their positive feedback about the boys. She took pride in her and Colin's effort and commitment to raise boys who were frequently acknowledged as both by the adults with whom they interacted.

Teddy made herself some breakfast. This simple task revealed that she was feeling less black inside today. As she nibbled at her sourdough toast with butter, a simple pleasure she loved, she wondered why. Was it the Christmas letter? She concluded that it most certainly was the letter. She then rushed upstairs to get the binder. She found it among her sheets and decided to nestle back into the bed. She went back to the beginning and reread the letters from 1999 and 2000. The letters brought her back twenty-two years. The detail and the writing put Colin right next to her. She felt warm, as she daydreamed about those beautiful early years. Teddy was amazed at the comfort she was feeling. There were tears, of course. But more importantly, she didn't feel quite as alone.

After Teddy reread the 2002 letter that she had read no less than ten times the night before, she moved to 2003. She craved more of the feeling of comfort the letters provided.

Christmas 2003

Sooner or later, it had to happen. This looks like the year that the annual Christmas letter shifts to a play-by-play of what childish behavior took place in the McNamara household. Fortunately, most of these stunts were performed by Ronan, with Colin finishing a distant second in the tally. This past year, we constantly tried to stay one step ahead of Ronan, who seemingly accomplished a new feat with each passing day.

Ronan started the year learning to locomote, as he

rolled across the floor to each desired destination. While this method of transportation entertained his parents, it soon gave way to the more traditional crawling approach. He motored about like this for the next six months and made the jump to standing on his own just before his first birthday. Colin's brothers came to town for the birthday party, giving Ronan a chance to play with his cousin, Mary. One week after his birthday, Ronan took his first steps. And things were never the same. The challenge now is keeping the daredevil reasonably contained. When he's not climbing onto chairs and couches, he's crawling under beds and tables.

Measuring in at a bruising 35 pounds and 35 inches after 17 months, Ronan is a perfect cube. He is off the charts for his age, as his weight is that of a four-year-old and his height is that of a three-year-old. Houston Rockets scouts drop by the house to monitor his progress, as he has developed a variety of offensive moves on his Learning Hoops basketball goal.

Speaking of the Rockets, not much changed on the work front for Colin or Teddy in 2003. Both of our companies moved office locations, so we now work just blocks away from one another. Teddy had the shorter move with her company just switching spots on the Houston skyline. The Rockets settled into a new downtown arena, extending

Colin's commute from three minutes to 15 minutes. Yao-mania has calmed down in the Chinese center's second year in America, while Houston's legendary coach shrunk more than a foot over the summer, with former NBA big man Rudy T stepping aside for Jeff Van Gundy, a notoriously small yet feisty man.

Houston's year-round summers have been perfect for Ronan, as he loves the outdoors. The McNamara family has become a fixture at the neighborhood park, with Ronan making the swing-sandbox-seesaw-slide circuit with great efficiency. Other outdoor favorites for Ronan include the pool, the zoo and the backyard. Basically, if there's grass or dirt involved, count him in.

We did have a chance to have a little fun without Ronan this past year. Trips to New York, New Orleans and Austin allowed us to relive those wild and carefree days gone by. Anything to keep a flicker of that old flame alive. Ronan did come with us on our yearly trip to Notre Dame. He met with the Director of Admissions and had an informal workout with the football coaches, who are holding a spot for him in the Class of 2025.

After 15 good years, our dog O'Malley sadly said goodbye to the world. We miss having him around, but he is far from forgotten. His legacy lives on, as O'Malley has provided us with several techniques for "Ronan-proofing" the house, as our infant becomes more mobile and adventurous.

Over the last few months, Ronan has started to talk. His first word was "ball," as he pointed at it, picked it up and tossed it. Since this landmark moment, Ronan has increased his vocabulary to about 30 words and counting. He says "Mommy," "Daddy" and "Yao Ming." Other favorites he uses daily include "morning," "Amen," "night-night" and "potty." Yes, Teddy started potty training Ronan at 15 months, and he has already produced impressive results, both literally and figuratively.

As you can tell, Ronan has kept his parents on their toes for much of the past year. But it has truly been a time that we will remember fondly. And if we do forget this past year? Well, we'll be sure to remember better the next time around. Yes, we're bringing in another little McNamara in 2004! We think we can handle two, even though our double-teaming strategies will probably have to become a thing of the past. Here's wishing you a Merry Christmas and a Happy New Year!

Colin, Teddy and Ronan

Reading made her feel reunited with Colin in a way she

could never imagine. She read it again, savoring every joke and memory. She was tempted to read more letters, but she decided to restrain herself. With great effort, she forced herself to put the binder back on its shelf and make her bed. She considered making a rule about how many letters she would allow herself to read at a time or per day. Uncharacteristically, she decided against a rule and to just wing it; go by how she felt.

While making the bed, she realized that she hadn't made her bed since the tragedy. She always made her bed, firmly believing, to the dismay of the rest of the family – to whom she tried to futilely enforce this rule – that getting into a made bed felt better than getting into an unmade bed. But over the last weeks, she did not have the will nor the care. "Wow, maybe today all of us are getting back on track," she thought, given the boys were both in class and she had this pivotal bedmaking triumph.

As she made her bed, she thought about 2003. The Christmas letter often glossed over things, as it should. She recalled when poor O'Malley, the dog, not the friend, had to be put down. Colin was on a road trip, and Teddy had to handle the horrible task. Thankfully, her parents were visiting because of Colin's road trip, so she was not alone during that episode. Her parents were lending a hand because during

Colin's previous road trip that year, Teddy was violently ill with a stomach bug while alone taking care of Ronan. She truly believed she was going to die, and, therefore, she feared her son would as well. So, for the next road trip, she asked for help.

Their life was wonderful overall, but the saying "Don't believe everything you read" is a saying for a reason. There were tough times and grueling days of raising a family and being newly married. While Colin was away at NBA games and staying in the best hotels, Teddy was not thrilled with her working mother situation. They rarely disagreed, but the stress of being working parents was real, especially since Teddy's income was necessary for survival because the NBA didn't pay well for staff roles. And Colin was six years behind her careerwise, which made the financial disparity between them acute.

Their earning difference was a detail she did not give appropriate due when she was blinded by love, as is the way. She had no choice but to work when she would have given anything to quit and be a full-time mother. This feeling surprised Teddy, but it was how she truly felt. They didn't have enough money for help like a nanny or cleaning people, which would have made things a bit easier. Stressed doesn't adequately describe Teddy at this point in their lives. That newly released happy-go-lucky girl she temporarily became when she met Colin evaporated. But what Teddy wouldn't give for those types of problems now.

Riding the wave of bedmaking normalcy, Teddy was determined to take advantage of the momentum. She put on shorts and a t-shirt since it was still quite warm with Houston's unending summer weather and went for a walk in the neighborhood. Her mind wandered to Ronan and Declan. She took a deep inhale and prayed that her boys were doing okay. Lucy and Sally were thrilled. This was their first walk since Colin passed. Of course, they didn't understand what happened, but they sensed the loss and departure from normalcy. They still looked for Colin throughout the house, standing on hind legs on his side of the bed and frolicking in the side yard thinking he would most certainly come and play if they barked and ran around enough. It was a heartbreaking reminder that a key part of their beautiful mosaic was missing.

Teddy looked down at her sloppy t-shirt and shorts. She hadn't dressed properly since the funeral. Teddy sported many stylish outfits over the course of her life. Clothing was a hobby for her, a creative outlet. Being fashionable was part of her identity. She wasn't trendy, but she managed to take youthful trends and make them her own. This year, she started sporting fashion colors in her hair, not neon green or anything like that. She chose a rose gold color that was trendy and fashion-forward for a fifty-year-old woman. She wondered if her focus on clothing and beauty were partially due to her age difference with Colin. Ironic given that they would never truly grow old together. "Regardless, I am going to start wearing real clothes tomorrow and doing my hair and makeup," she said to Lucy and Sally. "I have got to do it, girls. Make me, okay?"

Chapter Thirteen

Declan arrived home around six o'clock, the typical arrival time when he had golf practice. Teddy was hoping today was a good day that would help reset Declan. When he came in the back kitchen door, his hands were full of clothes, shoes, and his backpack. Why the boy refused to use a duffel bag for his things was a mystery to Teddy. He promptly dumped everything onto the floor and went to the refrigerator without a greeting or any other word for that matter.

"Hey, Decky-man," Teddy said cheerily.

"Hey," Declan responded in his low monotone voice.

"How was today?" Teddy continued, not dissuaded by Declan's clear "don't wanna talk" vibe.

"Fine."

"Okay, tell me more, which classes did you have?"

"Physics, English, Theo," Declan said flatly.

"How bad will catching up be?"

"Not bad, Mom, I got it covered."

"Okay, I get it. You don't want to talk. But remember, we agreed that it's exactly what we need to do. So, I'll give you time to shower, but be prepared to chat when you come down for dinner. Deal?" she prompted.

"Sure, yeah," was the unconvincing response Declan gave, as he headed up the stairs.

Teddy had tears streaming down her face, burning hot. She knew how hard all of this was for her. Was it worse or better for the boys? Did it even matter? At the same time, she was exploding inside with venom thinking, "Can you please cut me a break, you selfish little jerk? Don't you know how hard this is for me too? Give me something! Your father left me too ... because he couldn't stop having fun!"

The frustration and loneliness were sinking into Teddy's bones. Because Teddy and Colin felt it necessary to start a family immediately, they always counted on living their "fun first five years" of marriage after their sons went to college when most couples did this before having children. Teddy thought of this grand plan and the feeling of being cheated once again overcame her. She could feel herself slipping into quicksand of despair. She slumped down onto her behind onto the kitchen, resting her back against the cabinet doors. She breathed deeply while praying for strength.

Moments later, with a defiant shake of her head, Teddy jumped up and decided to shake off the interaction with Declan. She was not going to let herself go down a rabbit hole with her emotions. Her grief counselor told her a good tactic was to use other activities to interrupt downward spiraling feelings. She instead decided to reach out to Ronan. She thought of other people she could call, her sister-in-law, her mother-in-law, her cousin. But as usual, Teddy kept her support system small and tight. Mercifully, Ronan picked up after a few rings.

"Hey Sweet Petite, how are you?" she asked brightly, using one of her many made-up names for her sons. She switched the call to video. She needed to see Ronan.

"Doin' fine, Mom, just studying. I'm pretty behind and midterms are coming," he said, as if his mother needed reminding.

"Do you think you can get some relief given your

circumstance? Doesn't seem like a lot to ask."

"I don't know," Ronan responded.

"Well, I don't know why we didn't think of this before, but I think you should talk to your advisor," Teddy continued.

"Yeah, maybe, but I just feel like putting things off now will just snowball later, you know what I mean?"

"I get what you are saying, but it is worth talking to your advisor, regardless? What you've been through is not something that only takes a week to heal. Promise me you'll talk to her. What's her name, Ms. Pugh?" Teddy said with no uncertainty in her motherly tone.

"Right, will do. Yes, that's her." Ronan said in hopes of ending this line of questioning.

"So, how are Jason and Joe?" Teddy said switching gears asking about his dorm roommate and neighbor.

"Good, but hey Mom, I really need to go and study. Can we talk some other time?" Ronan said abruptly.

"Oh, sorry. Of course, sorry," Teddy responded.

She sat there waiting for the oven to finally reach four hundred degrees, wishing she could jump in and burn herself up and turn to dust. She understood Ronan being busy. But understanding didn't mean that him not having time for her didn't hurt. "Who was going to have time for her now?" Teddy thought bleakly, knowing she could not, she should not, burden her sons. She actively thought how she was not going to be like her mother, who dumped emotional garbage on her as a way of life. The semi-good feelings she had managed to conjure today seemed to have left as quickly as they came.

Teddy mindlessly threw some French fries into the oven and started cooking two lonely hamburgers in a skillet. Two. She wanted to cry again but restrained herself. Just a couple of months ago, they were the four-pack. She was ready to be a three-pack with the fourth a phone call away. She had been preparing for years for Ronan's matriculation to college. But, of course, nothing could have prepared her for cooking for two in September of 2021. That was supposed to happen in September of 2023!

She called Declan down for dinner. They sat quietly eating at the island in the kitchen. Teddy had the countertops replaced along with many other things in their home. The house looked nothing like it did when they purchased it. Teddy had a gift for spiffing up houses—not renovation, just superficial adjustments that were unique and intriguing. Making their houses into their homes was something Teddy immensely enjoyed. The boys and Colin loved the Brown Street house. It wasn't fancy by their elite neighborhood standards, but it was homey and filled with their memories. This was their fourth house in the area, and it was definitely the house the boys viewed as their childhood home.

As they finished dinner, Teddy noticed the strained silence between her and Declan. She desperately wanted to bridge the gap, to find a way to connect with her son.

Declan fidgeted around on the counter stool, seemingly finding it uncomfortable that his mother was not engaging him in conversation, especially since she said they were going to talk at dinner.

"Mom, are you alright?"

"Well, no, Declan. I am not," she responded tersely, providing no further details. Her curt reply placed Declan in the uncommon position of having to extract information from his mother.

"What exactly is wrong?"

"I sort of had a decent day today, and then you not wanting to talk and your brother not wanting to talk either just bummed me out, to say the least," she responded candidly.

"Oh. Sorry, Mom. I kinda figured you were upset because that's the only time you do not talk. I'm really sorry about not talking when I got home ... But what do you mean today was kinda okay?" Declan asked with atypical probing skills.

"Well, I just felt better. I made my bed. I went for a walk. I just sort of felt a bit less empty inside, I guess."

"That's good, right? What do you think caused you to feel a bit better?"

"Strangely, I think it may be the Christmas letters, Declan. I read a few of them over the last day, and they just gave me comfort. I don't know. It just happened."

"Huh, that's cool, Mom. I'm really glad to hear that. Maybe I need to give that a try because although I was at school physically, I wasn't there in my head, if you know what I mean."

"Tell me more," Teddy said, employing her usual Oprah-style conversation skills.

The mother and son talked for twenty more minutes. Declan shared his feelings and challenges. They were connecting for the first time since *it* happened. Teddy was having a feeling of thrill and relief at the same time. The highlight of the conversation was Declan agreeing to see a grief counselor. Both he and his brother originally declined this support in the very early days after the news. Teddy let it go for a while but planned to attempt to get them to talk to someone a little later after things were not quite as raw. This was her moment with Declan, and she was pleased that she successfully seized it.

"Do you really want to read a letter, Decky Duck?"

"Yeah, I do, Mom," he replied, flatly ignoring her use of this ridiculous pet name she concocted when he was young.

"Yay, yay, yay, go to the couch, and I'll get the Christmas letter binder, and we can read 2004 together. It's your big arrival in the world, Decky!" And just like that, Teddy felt that the day might just rebound, as she ran up the stairs to get the book. On her way up, she passed the two-story wall on the stairs' landing that had roughly twenty canvas-printed photos from their many family vacations. Teddy saw this wall every day, multiple times a day for years. With repetition, it became invisible to her, as things do when you take them for granted. Like the Christmas letters, this wall that was often overlooked was giving her simultaneous comfort and sorrow. Bittersweet.

Christmas 2004

And Declan makes four! In 2004, the McNamara baby count caught up with the parents. Our new addition has caused all sorts of defensive adjustments for us. Just after getting comfortable with a double-team to keep Ronan contained, we now employ man-to-man defense at all times. Colin is usually assigned the two-year-old tornado, while Teddy handles the less mobile, more dependent infant. Here's a recap of what's happened this year in the McNamara house.

The year started with a few notable changes. Ronan moved to St. Bernadette School, where he learns foreign languages dressed in his dapper uniform of plaid overalls. Yes, it's quite hilarious listening to him count, "Uno, dos, tres ..." Teddy also made a major switch during her pregnancy, returning to LMC, the global consulting firm, as their director of marketing. The new job has given her much-needed flexibility, as she works from home a couple of days a week. Colin continues to work with the Rockets, who returned to the playoffs for the first time in five years. Fortunately, their postseason run was short-lived, as we didn't need any conflicts with the baby's arrival. Logistically, we were all set for number two – moving Ronan into a big bed and turning our guest room into a nursery. Little did we know that you're never truly ready.

Our five-year plan played out to perfection. Declan joined our family on June 11 – exactly five years to the day that we first met each other. We were eagerly expecting him a few weeks earlier, but he came just three days before his due date. He's now six months old with the sweetest disposition, always smiling and clutching his mommy. He's still balder than Ronan was at birth, but he has the same linebacker build as his big brother. Both sets of grandparents came to Houston in July to meet Declan and celebrate Ronan's second birthday. Colin's brothers also dropped in over the summer to welcome the new arrival.

Ronan – who has nicknamed himself "Rony" – continues to entertain us with each passing day. He has grown from a baby to a boy over the past year, stringing together sentences and reciting his ABCs. Play-Doh, books, flashcards and puzzles stand out as his favorite activities. Ronan also loves music, as his tastes range from Sing-Along Bible Songs to Queen's Greatest Hits. He gives a powerful rendition of "We Will Rock You!" His most-prized toys are Playmobil and Thomas the Tank Engine, which are two of Colin's favorites as well. More than toys, Ronan likes getting his hands on CDs, telephones, remote controls and a variety of other items deemed "off-limits." Possessing the self-confidence of an All-Star, Ronan often refers to himself in the third person and loves watching home videos of himself. On the very exciting potty-training front, Ronan mastered the drill, recently becoming the first McNamara grandchild to pee standing up. Of course, he is the oldest McNamara grandson ... but that's just a technicality.

Having a pair of boys has definitely turned us into homebodies. It's just much easier being at home base, with all of the equipment, toys, childproofing, etc. Trips to the neighborhood park have become the most frequent excursions. The four of us did make it to some Astros games and a Wiggles concert, signifying that we officially crossed over the line into parenthood. Our big family trip was to Notre Dame for Declan's baptism and the win over Michigan. A few months later, the boys dressed up as Fighting Irish football players for Halloween and were repeatedly mistaken for members of this year's mediocre squad. We did take a kid-free trip to Atlanta for the wedding of Colin's college roommate Steve and realized that might be the way to go for the next few years. Airplanes and babies just don't mix. Nothing's quite as scary as a toddler upchucking on his daddy at 30,000 feet.

So there you have it. It may not have been as action-packed as previous years, but never underestimate the adventure of taking care of a pair of McNamara boys. Needless to say, we wouldn't change a thing. Here's wishing you all the best during this Christmas season!

Colin, Teddy, Ronan and Declan

"You were such a 'bubzer' of a baby, Declan," Teddy said, using a favorite made-up word.

"Dad sure had a way with stories, didn't he?" Declan said, ignoring the "bubzer" comment.

"Oh yes, he did. I think you know people frequently complimented him on his letters for their humor and even told him they couldn't wait to get the letter each year," Teddy said.

"Yeah, I can see that. He sort of makes the ordinary seem interesting."

"Indeed, he did do that well. Did reading that make you feel any better?" Teddy asked.

"Well, I guess a little better and a little worse. I mean, it is a nice way to remember Dad, but I immediately started thinking about this year's letter, and that made me sick just thinking about it."

"Bittersweet, I get it. I think bittersweet feelings are what we are going to have to endure frequently for a while, Declan," Teddy said while giving him a tight hug.

"Maybe you can get together with A-A-Ron this weekend," said Teddy, calling Declan's best friend by the nickname that became popular after the substitute teacher sketch in the *Key & Peele* TV show. She desperately wanted to lighten the mood before Declan escaped the emotional scene.

"Yeah, I should. I have not seen him since the, um, you know, funeral," said Declan uncomfortably.

"Yes, it will be good for you to get together. Play b-ball, whatever. Just do normal stuff. It was very nice of Aaron and his parents to come."

While Teddy sunk into the couch in the family room after Declan retreated to the kitchen, she heard him call Ronan.

"Odd," she thought, "he never calls Ronan without me."

She comically strained to hear but really couldn't because of Declan's low, quiet voice. To fill the void, she let her mind wander to the first year with Declan. Teddy still couldn't believe as a full Italian that she had a bald baby with gray blue eyes! Declan had grown up to be a slender adult despite his start as a chunky baby. Colin also left out that Declan got teeth at four months old which cut short his time being breastfed.

Teddy chuckled to herself as she thought of the time that sweet baby literally bit her nipple, making it bleed. Those days were hard, despite Colin reflecting them as all fun and games in the letters. Being a working mom was a raw deal in

Teddy's mind. The "you can have it all" thing she was sold as an '80s female was a laughable mirage. But she absolutely loved being a mother and wouldn't change that part of their story for anything. She sometimes felt that she must have made it all look normal, all of the juggling.

Ronan told her when he was about fifteen that she made the working mom thing look easy. He was intending to pay her a compliment. She knew this, but she also immediately knew she had done her sons a disservice if they perceived it this way. She promptly told Ronan that appearances are deceiving and that playing both a full-time mom and a full-time professional was beyond difficult. Teddy made it clear during their conversation that Ronan should never expect or assume that his spouse should do the same.

***

Declan decided he should call his brother about this Christmas letter thing. But he was also desperate for a snack, so he retreated to the kitchen, hoping his mom could not hear the call. As he rummaged through the pantry to find something crunchy and salty, he tapped his brother's icon on his phone.

"What?" answered Ronan in his warm, brotherly way.

"Mom has been reading the Christmas letters. She and

I just read the 2004 letter where I make my first appearance," said Declan softly without so much as a greeting to his brother.

"So?"

"Do you think that's a good idea?" Declan replied.

"Well, I don't know. I guess it's like looking at pictures. How did she seem?"

"She said they make her feel good, like Dad is there." Declan answered.

"Well, then maybe it's not weird or anything to worry about," said Ronan.

"Okay, well, it made me feel weird about the upcoming holidays," Declan shared.

"Yeah, I hear ya. It's all weird, Deck. You doing okay?" asked Ronan.

"Yeah, I have been attending classes, but that's about it. I am there."

"That's a good first step," Ronan said supportively. "I am flippin' dying with catching up and midterms coming up. I cannot wait to be back home in a couple of weeks for a rest and to see how Mom is. Glad ND gives a weeklong fall break. Most schools don't, so consider that, slimy, when you are applying to colleges."

"Okay, I will keep it in mind, and I will do what I can to keep things on track here, Ronan."

"I know you won't believe me, Deck, but I am locked in on school. I am not going to play around like I usually do. I am going to do what needs to be done to get good grades from the start. I am not going to get in a hole that I have to dig out of. You know, my signature move. And most importantly, I am doing this for Dad. It's the least I can do, right? Make him proud? I realized I don't want Notre Dame tainted by Dad's death. He would hate that!" Ronan stated emphatically, despite Declan never asking or questioning his work ethic.

"Yeah, we'll see," chided Declan. "It is a noble motive. But you are having some fun, right?"

"Of course. I am not a saint, as you know. In fact, the other night the juniors in my dorm section made all the freshman go out to Flaherty's. It's the bar with the big golden dome behind the circular bar. I got really wasted, and the juniors dared me to sneak behind the bar and climb on the golden dome. And I did it. It was crazy! I may become a legend."

"Oh boy, well, I am glad you are not living your life as a studying monk, but I hope Mom doesn't find out about this."

"How would she find out? It's all good. I gotta blow off some steam, and I guess a bit of rage, ya know," Ronan justified.

"Yeah, I guess. Just don't rage too hard. Dad didn't try to taint Notre Dame for you on purpose. It's just life," Declan commented.

"I know, but sometimes I am still pissed. Aren't you?"

"Sure, this is all messed up. I just don't want to cause Mom any more heartache so watch yourself."

"Ooh, trying to boss me around, Declan?"

"No, just sayin'. I guess I won't make a big deal about Mom reading the letters then, if you don't think it's bad," replied Declan, bringing the conversation back to his reason for calling.

"Yeah, I mean, what real harm can it cause?" Ronan asked rhetorically.

Despite the story about the golden dome climbing escapade, Declan was surprised at how much Ronan was dialed into school. Some may have diagnosed him with being in denial, but Declan didn't think he was. He knew his brother ached inside, probably more than himself, but like his mother, Ronan was a doer. Declan surmised that Ronan was going to apply himself in a way he never had before to cope with his pain.

As he continued to shovel his beloved Cheese Chex Mix into his mouth, Declan wondered about the best strategy for him to deal with his feelings. The letter was nice to read, but that did not seem like enough. Maybe the grief counselor would help. He doubted it. But he had promised to see someone, so he would give it a try.

Chapter Fourteen

Teddy caught the word "Christmas" from the one-sided conversation she could barely hear with Declan in the kitchen. Teddy thought with complete revulsion that made her gasp out loud, "The actual holidays! What on earth would that be like now?"

Teddy had not given anything besides the current day much thought since Colin's death. Living in the moment was horrible enough. Thinking about the future was beyond her current capabilities. She thrashed around in bed but could not relax into sleep, as she obsessed thinking about Declan bringing up the holidays after reading the Christmas letter. She thought it had been a good idea to read those letters. Maybe ... probably not.

She texted Dana to see if she was awake. It was a gift. She was, so Teddy hit her name on her phone. Dana had been moved to Teddy's 'favorites list' on her phone. Teddy could not bear the thought of removing Colin from the list just yet, but adding Dana was a step in the process Teddy had agonizingly decided to take a few days ago.

"What's going on?" asked Dana, trying to hide the concern in her voice.

"Are you sure it's an okay time to talk?"

"Teddy, seriously, what's going on?"

"Well, I've read some of Colin's Christmas letters over the last few days, and they made me feel pretty good. It was like being with him, ya know? Then tonight, Declan and I read the 2004 letter together, the year he was born, which was really nice until he said it made him dread this year's holidays. Then, he actually called Ronan right afterward. I could not hear much of their conversation, but I did hear the word 'Christmas,' so I am pretty sure Declan called him about reading the letter with me."

"Okay, gosh, yep ... logical. How did this make you feel?"

"Well, first it made me feel like I did the wrong thing by reading the letter with him. Encouraging him to read it, actually," Teddy's voice cracking and tears starting to form, the sting. "We had a really good conversation tonight for the first time since it happened. I shared with him that I was reading the letters, and that I thought they were helping me, so I brought up the idea of him reading one. And we did. Then his comment about dreading the holidays made me absolutely sick about the coming months. I have not thought about anything but the day I am in since it happened. His comment made me think about what used to be the best time of year. How can it be that anymore? How do I even do a holiday season? If I didn't have kids, I wouldn't care, but the boys..." Teddy trailed off in tears.

"Breathe, Teddy, breathe."

They sat silently on the open phone line except for Teddy's sobbing for several minutes. Dana was the kind of person who knew how to hold silence, well in this case sobbing, and not talk until it was the right time. Teddy was grateful beyond measure for the astute emotional intelligence of her dear friend. Years of being a recruiting professional honed Dana's listening skills to perfection.

Once Teddy's tears wound down, Dana said, "Teddy, you didn't do the wrong thing by sharing the letter with Declan. And please stop beating yourself up about and second guessing every interaction with your sons. Keeping Colin alive in your hearts and minds cannot be wrong no matter how you do it. As for the holidays, just try to put that out of your mind right now. October just started. Just do early October. There is no benefit to thinking about what's ahead right now. I know that's hard for you, my planner friend, but your planner nature needs to take a back seat right now. Okay?"

"Okay, I guess. It was just a jarring thought. I know it doesn't need to be solved now. Thanks for walking me back from the edge, Dana. But, without something to focus on, I know I am going to have a hard time not fixating on the holidays. You know my lovely obsessive personality. Maybe I should have gone back to work. I just hate my profession so much. I looked at this, this, this … situation as a way to finally walk away from thirty years of misery. But now, I have a massive void with nothing to fill it but memories."

"Yes, it is true that you have too much unfilled space in your days to be healthy. But I am going to push back and say that a bright spot in all of this horror is that Colin was able to give you the dream of not working in your profession. You always wanted that, especially when the boys were young. But not working in corporate marketing and not working at all are two different things. You've been given a gift of financial independence, albeit in the worst way, but what if you thought about work you would like to do? And in your situation, you do not need to factor in financial need like you've always had to. The golden handcuffs are off, Teddy. You can – and Colin would want you to – pick yourself up and do something that gave you joy or purpose, or whatever the hell you want!"

Teddy's mind flooded with visions of herself playing at her chalkboard in her basement, teaching her neighborhood friends math. It was the vivid image that always popped into her mind when asked what her passion was.

"My God! I really should stop paying the grief counselor and start paying you. You have blown my mind. You are right. I am so paralyzed thinking I should do nothing but take care of the boys, but they are seventeen and nineteen years old. It's still an important job but not a full-time job. And I am free now. I cannot remember the last time I was free to choose. Alright, it's late. I will stop my stream of consciousness babbling. I cannot thank you enough for this earthshaking talk. You da best! I hope you know that."

"Any time, Teddy. Really. You know that don't you?" said Dana as she hung up.

Teddy sank back down into her pillows. Turned them all over to give everything, including herself, a reset on the night. Teddy settled into the covers and thought, "Teaching. Maybe I should once and for all become a teacher."

Teddy tried to pursue teaching during a short stint between marketing jobs. It had always been the money that kept her in the corporate game, giving in to the highest bidders. Now, however tragic the circumstances, that need was gone due to the substantial life insurance settlement she was about to receive. This revelation made Teddy feel better – albeit with a twinge of guilt – and the conversation with Dana had fully awakened her. She needed some relaxation. With this thought, Teddy got the binder and read another letter. She needed comfort, the letters being her only true source.

Colin was always so festive. Teddy cherished his love of the holidays. There were even years when Teddy wasn't overly supportive of the annual Christmas letter – too tired, too frazzled, too annoyed for holiday cheer – but Colin always came through. He wouldn't let anything stop him and his Christmas spirit. Teddy decided that she needed to step up and not dread the upcoming holidays; she needed to be positive for herself as much as the boys.

Christmas 2005

For the first time in forever, no earthshaking changes rocked the McNamara household this year. But it's not like life has been quiet, with two little boys endlessly imposing their will. Recently, the challenges of parenthood have started to feel a bit more manageable, though. Either that or our ability to block out the madness has gotten better and better.

What's life like these days? Well, there's the park, the zoo, the beach and the children's museum. Basically, Ronan calls the shots when it comes to our social calendar. Lately, he's even begun picking which restaurants we frequent. No Chuck E. Cheese's, fortunately. Instead, he has taken a liking to sports bars. Heaven knows where he gets that from.

Declan celebrated his first birthday this year, and Ronan tallied number three. These marked our first ventures into themed parties, as Thomas the Tank Engine filled Declan's event, and Ronan enjoyed what was certain to be the first Charlie Brown party for a kid in decades. Declan's done an admirable job keeping up with his older brother, often engaging in wrestling matches over a favorite toy or simply for bragging rights.

The biggest family events of the year involved Declan, as he learned to crawl, walk, talk and breakdance. Unfortunately, as the second child, Declan's milestones haven't come with the same hoopla as Ronan's. While Ronan received Neil Armstrong attention with one small step, Declan has been Buzz Aldrin, needing giant leaps just to elicit a response. Declan makes sure that he doesn't go unnoticed, however, displaying his Irish temper and Italian attitude whenever things don't go his way. A redder head cannot be found when he is angry.

Declan's transition to toddler has made travel tolerable once again, as our foursome logged successful journeys to both sets of grandparents as well as Colorado. The addition of a double stroller became a lifesaver for the airports, where Ronan always entertains bystanders by taking off his shoes at the security checkpoint. One of our family trips came as part of the Hurricane Rita evacuation, as we joined two-and-a-half million Houstonians fleeing for safety. Fortunately, the false alarm left our home and city safely intact.

We also had the pleasure of leaving the boys in Grandma's hands for a kids-free football weekend in South Bend. A night at the Linebacker Lounge gave us welcome relief from parental responsibilities, but some stress came the next day via an instant classic between Notre Dame and USC with its tragic "Bush Push" ending.

Having one too many T-Macs in his life, Colin chose his wife Teddy over Tracy McGrady and left the Rockets in the summer. A decade in the NBA was long enough, and a PR firm called Ryland Associates offered an opportunity to reclaim nights and weekends as family time. A November return to Toyota Center with Ronan marked Colin's most enjoyable basketball experience in eons.

Teddy, who received a promotion to senior marketing director, put in her bid for "Wife of the Year" by securing tickets to the World Series. At the Fall Classic, Colin witnessed his White Sox claim their first championship in 88 years against the hometown Astros.

Ronan continues his love for music, taking piano lessons and composing his own melodies. He has asked Santa for a guitar so that he can play his favorite song, Van Morrison's Brown Eyed Girl. Ronan is extremely excited for the holidays, telling us recently that "Christmas is the day that Jesus was boring!" Here's wishing you a not-so-boring Christmas.

Colin, Teddy, Ronan and Declan

Boy, did this letter bring back memories for Teddy. She always felt so rushed back in those days with full-time work and two small boys. She was certain she didn't really savor the fleeting time in her life with small children. In fact, she was horribly jealous of stay-at-home moms who, from her vantage point, seemed to have nothing but time on their hands. She knew that was not entirely true, but it was true that she harbored deep jealousy, warranted or not.

How could she savor anything when she was on a treadmill that just kept getting faster? Wake up at five-thirty to exercise and get ready for work before the kids got up. Get the kids ready and take them to daycare. Work all day. Rush to get them before closing time. Feed them. Spend "quality time" with them. Bathe them and put them to bed so it could all be repeated four more times before the merciful weekend came.

Teddy recalled and was now not proud of her malicious thoughts every time she would catch her stay-at-home mom neighbor seemingly carefree, waltzing down the driveway to get her newspaper to enjoy with her coffee, while Teddy backed out of her own driveway with two small boys strapped into their car seats on her way to daycare, then work. This is the plight of moms, no one way to play the role, so we are left assuming others' ways were somehow easier or superior.

This letter, which only reflected the high points, let her savor that special time in her and her young boys' lives. Memories are so funny. The bad is really overtaken by the good in the vast vault of the mind. Teddy realized that after the given year, she had never read the Christmas letters from the past, until now. Reading them was a vivid walk through her adult life with Colin when she began to become the person she wanted to be.

These letters were her life's memory collection, and it pleased her that it was rich and her life with Colin was good … it was meaningful. Easy and meaningful rarely come in the same package. Taking the risk and doing the work to become a family woman was the right move those many years ago when she met Colin. Because Colin always saw the positive in life, Teddy was going to try to embrace that beautiful quality now more than ever. "Taking on Colin's positivity could be my personal tribute to my sweet husband," she whispered to no one but herself.

"Ugh! I want to read the rest of them right now, girls," Teddy said emphatically to Sally and Lucy, who looked puzzled by the outburst.

However, she forced herself to put the binder aside, still close to her in bed, but closed. She didn't want to use up all the comfort stored in these pages too quickly. As Teddy drifted off to sleep, she envisioned her family as they were in the mid-2000s. Of course, toy wooden trains were part of the picture that put her into a calm night's sleep.

Chapter Fifteen

Declan was in Mr. DeSilva's class, participating in the discussion about George Orwell's *1984*. He was feeling pretty good, normal. Despite hating the book and its bleak outlook on humanity, he was engaged in the class conversation.

"Thoughts about the rat scene?" prompted Mr. DeSilva.

"That was so gross. I am scarred for life," shouted Devin Saunders at the top of his lungs.

"Ooh, I loved it, Mr. DeSilva. So cool," contributed Jake Smiley.

"Well, I can see we've reached our limit for thoughtful

discussion today, gentlemen. We can leave it at that," said a resigned Mr. DeSilva.

While walking out of class, Mr. DeSilva called for Declan to come to his desk, which was in the middle of the circular arrangement of chairs designed for group discussion.

"Any chance you have a free period now, Declan?" inquired Mr. DeSilva.

"Yes, just one," replied Declan uncomfortably.

"Let's chat, Declan. Have a seat next to me."

They moved two student desks, so they were sort of facing each other but with the double desk space as a bit of a barrier Declan appreciated.

"Declan, you probably don't know that my wife passed away two years ago from breast cancer."

Declan shook his head in reply.

"Well, I tell you this because I obviously know about the passing of your father. Please know how sorry I am for your loss."

"Um ... thank you. Sorry to hear about your wife too."

"Thank you. Death is one of the hardest parts of life. I can tell you time helps. But I can also tell you that the loss is always a part of you."

"Well, yeah. I guess. Yeah," stammered Declan with great agitation.

"Declan, I am not trying to upset you. I guess what I am trying to do is connect with you beyond being your AP lit teacher. I want to be a resource for you during these early days as you cope. I know you skipped school a couple of days at the very beginning. You seem to be doing remarkably well, but grief is sly. It can get to you when you do not even see it coming. What I am trying to say, and saying it badly, is that you can reach out to me any time you want. You already have my cell number because I gave it out at the beginning of the school year, right?"

Declan took his phone out of his backpack and found the number under DeSilva in his contacts.

"Yes, I have it."

"So, what are you doing to manage these days?" asked Mr. DeSilva.

"Well, I am going to a grief counselor. It's okay. I am just not sure I am even grieving yet. I may still be in shock. And I want to be strong for my mom. My brother is off at college, so it is just the two of us."

"Yes, yes, is Ronan doing okay at ND? We were all so happy he got in. I hope this isn't ruining his entire experience."

"Kinda weird, it may be helping him focus on school instead of partying," Declan replied. "He wants to do well for our dad. Says he is studying harder than ever before."

"Well, that is quite admirable. He is an impressive young man, as are you. I want to help you, so know that my door, phone, e-mail—all the means of communication—are open to you."

"Thanks, Mr. DeSilva. I appreciate it." And surprisingly, Declan, the "don't want to talk about it" boy, meant it.

Chapter Sixteen

Teddy spent a good part of the day contemplating teaching and other jobs she might enjoy. Her love for hair, makeup, and clothing got her thinking about various potential professions. Hair stylist? Makeup artist? Shop girl? Teddy had her nails and toes polished for as long as she could remember, since being a young girl of four or five. Likewise, she would tell her mother to "kiss me hard" so that her mother's lipstick would transfer to her own little lips. It was oddly fun thinking about something she wanted to do and not thinking about it with a million caveats, such as what people expected of her, what it would pay, and what the hours were – the whole litany of extraneous factors she had to balance previously.

Teddy could not recall a time when she had the freedom to do exactly what she wanted and to consider only her desires, likes, and dreams. Growing up was spent pleasing her parents. Early adulthood was consumed with showing the world she was a successful female, a modern woman, in massive contrast to her mother. The mother-of-children-at-home stage was all about her children. Her choices were for them. Caring so deeply about others made her a new person, a better person, but it caused her to continue to push down her own dreams of professional fulfillment.

As she thought, she realized she was not contemplating a new career to please anyone or to make herself appear good enough for someone to like or love her. Sadly, this may be one of the few times this fifty-something-year-old woman felt this way. In many ways, pursuing a new career was a breakthrough of substantial proportions in her life.

Her phone buzzed, having forgotten to turn on the sound this morning. It was her mother-in-law, Sue. Teddy scolded herself for not keeping in better touch with Sue since it happened. Colin was Sue's only biological son. Although she was the consummate stepmother to the other children, there was no doubt the loss of Colin deeply affected her too. No parent should have to endure the loss of a child, thought Teddy as she answered. She knew she needed to do better with

Sue.

"Hi, Sue," Teddy said, striking what she thought was an appropriately positive yet sorrowful tone. The last thing she wanted was her mother-in-law interpreting her voice as either too chipper or too gloomy.

"Hi, Teddy, how are you?"

"Thank you for calling, Sue. Sorry I have not been better about calling. I am sure you understand ..." Teddy trailed off.

"Yes, I do, but we would love to hear from you and the boys more. We worry," Sue said.

"I know you do, and we do not mean to make you worry. I am just so focused on them, and I guess me. I suppose that is selfish," admitted Teddy.

"Well, no, we do not think you are being selfish. It's just hard," sniffled Sue.

"You and Richard have been nothing but good to me; I promise I will do a better job of staying in contact. I am sorry," said Teddy, reverting to one of her many rules – elderly parents are always right – even when they are wrong.

Getting what she wanted, Sue asked Teddy how she was doing. Teddy shared about reading the Christmas letters.

This delighted Sue because she was the original Christmas letter author in 1972, their matriarch one could say.

Teddy also mistakenly mentioned thinking about a new career.

"You are looking for things to do already?" inquired Sue with a shrill tone in her voice.

"Well, just thinking about things," stammered Teddy, as if guilty of something.

"I just think you need to take your time and be there for the boys. You don't need money. Colin left you in a good place, didn't he?"

"Yes, Sue, I am fortunate. And my priority is the boys. Of course they are. Always have been and always will be," Teddy responded as if defending her very essence to her mother-in-law.

"How is Ronan doing at Notre Dame?"

"He seems okay and very focused on schoolwork. I will know more accurately when I see him in a couple of weeks for fall break."

"And Declan?"

"You know Declan, hard to read him even in the best of times. He is seeing a grief counselor, so I think that is good."

"Yes, that one is tricky. Stay on top of him. And I wanted to ask if you wanted to come here for Thanksgiving. We are starting to plan."

This invite made Teddy cringe, as she had intentionally lived in somewhat isolation in these weeks following the tragedy, not really wanting to talk to anyone. The McNamara Thanksgiving would be diving into the deep end of the small talk pool. This holiday gathering typically included around twenty guests, with just a few of them being family. Teddy froze in fear thinking about how she would have to engage in conversation with people she had only met once or twice.

"Oh gosh, Sue. I cannot begin to think that far ahead. I will let you know soon, though. I have given it no thought."

"Okay, hun. Love you."

"Love you, Sue. Bye."

Thankfully, Declan strolled in just as Teddy hung up with her mother-in-law. Otherwise, she would be fuming about the call. First a guilt trip, then commentary on what she should be doing during this unthinkable time and an invitation to Thanksgiving on top of all that! Bah!

Teddy grabbed him and gave him a big hug, using Sue as the excuse. "Your grandmother told me to hug you."

"Okay, okay," replied Declan. "Which one?"

"San Antonio grandma, of course. How was school?"

Teddy did not know what came over Declan, but whatever it was seemed to make him share his conversation with Mr. DeSilva with her. She found it to be nice, but she also felt a bit skeptical about the interaction as Declan relayed it to her.

"So, he knows you are seeing a grief counselor, right?"

"Yes, Mom. I told him."

"What kind of person is he?"

"I don't know what to say. What does that mean? He's an English teacher, Mom, a nerd. What do you want me to say?"

"Well, I don't know. Is he nice, sincere? You know ..." Teddy followed up.

"Really, I don't. He is not some weirdo creep, if that's what you are asking."

"Yeah, I guess I don't know what I am asking either. I guess it's nice and caring. I guess I am just being overly protective. Can you blame me?" Teddy ended with a bit of a skeptical laugh. "So do you feel like your actual grief counselor is helping you?"

"I don't think there is any magic. Trying to forget is a stupid thing to do. I guess she is helping me learn to live with the fact pattern," Declan answered quite eloquently.

"That is a powerful statement, Decks. Learning to live with the fact pattern. You have always been able to cut through the garbage and get to the heart of things. I admire that about you, kiddo. So, you want to continue? I realize you have only gone twice, and I would like you to continue, but I want you to be open with me."

"I know I typically don't like to dwell on problems," Declan said with a laugh as they both knew his disdain for talking about difficult topics. "But I think talking to her is an okay thing for me right now. I'll tell you if that changes."

After Declan disappeared to the depths of his room, Teddy retreated to her phone to kill some time, scrolling away on Instagram for the first time in weeks. The first time since *it* happened, Teddy was sure. Nothing caught her eye, just ad after ad, it seemed, until she came to the ND YikYak feed. YikYak is a site where college kids post funny comments and sometimes pictures specifically about their school. It is kind of like reading a bunch of inside jokes. Prior to her life turning upside down, Teddy really enjoyed the frivolity and an inside look into today's college students. Today she felt like she was ready to reconnect with some college fun and humor. One post stated, "Who is the legend that climbed on the golden dome at Flaherty's last night? We need a name. Identify yourself." The question refers to a photo of a boy atop the replica golden dome behind the bar. Teddy laughed at the college hijinks. Ha! Such fun. Then she zoomed in on the photo on her phone screen, realizing it was Ronan.

No longer finding the photo funny, Teddy looked at Sally and Lucy in despair. "What the eff?!? Now Ronan is going off the rails. What am I supposed to do?" she asked of her four-legged friends. Teddy forced herself to breathe deeply and calm herself before engaging with Ronan on this topic. She said a quiet prayer for strength. After a minute or so, she pressed his name on her phone screen, praying he would pick up the phone.

"Hello," answered a groggy-sounding Ronan.

"Hi, Ro, is this a good time to talk?"

"Uh ... sure, Mom, what's up?

"Well, um, Ronan, I was looking at YikYak on Instagram. What do you think I saw there?" Teddy asked, keeping her tone even and soft, forcing her fiery Italian temper to stay at bay.

"Oh boy, I assume you saw the photo of me at Flaherty's on the dome. Right?"

"Yes, Ronannnnn. What on earth is going on?"

"Mom, it's no big deal. The juniors in my section made all the freshman guys go out. That's all."

"That's all. You climbed on a what, a seventeen-foot golden dome replica in a bar! Did you get into trouble?"

"Well, I got kicked out, of course, but nothing serious happened."

"But, Ronan, you obviously were well past just having a few drinks, right?"

"Well, yeah. I admit I was pretty wrecked."

"So, you were wrecked on a Wednesday night as an underage freshman and were thrown out. And I am not supposed to worry about this behavior given the circumstances. And, honestly, given any circumstances, Ronan. I don't want to lecture, but I need to know what is going on with you. Are you coping or not?"

"It's complicated, Mom. I am working hard at school. But I am also in college, so I want to live it up. And, yes, sometimes I am angry. Mad about Dad leaving us and, selfishly, tainting this time for me at Notre Dame. I don't want to feel that way. But, okay, I am admitting it. I am embarrassed to admit it but, yes, sometimes I am mad. Then sometimes all I think about is making him proud. It's just a lot."

"Oh, Ronan, I do understand the anger. Believe me, I do. And I understand the partying. It's just hard for me to differentiate normal college drinking and crazy behavior from grief drinking and crazy behavior. Do you know what I mean?"

"Yes, I get it," Ronan acknowledged. "I promise, it's just college stuff. I am not drinking to hide my feelings. And I am not putting fun first. I am putting school first. I swear."

"Would you humor me and see a grief counselor?"

"No, Mom, I don't have time for that, and it's just not for me. Please trust me. Pleassssse."

"Ronan, I hope you know how hard it is for me not to fly up there to see your face to believe you. But I must have faith that your father and I raised you to be strong and make good choices, so I am going to believe you."

"Thank you, Mom. That means a lot."

Chapter Seventeen

Despite the days feeling like they dragged on without making any discernable progress on the calendar, it was time for Ronan to come home for fall break, mid-October, a little more than a month since *it* happened. Teddy would feel much better being able to gauge Ronan's wellbeing in person. The dome climbing episode at the bar gave her angst. And she kept being reminded of it as other social media sites kept sharing it with jokes about Notre Dame football climbing up the rankings.

She hoped coming home was going to be a good thing for Ronan, but with the current situation, she was unsure if it would not have been better for him to have gone home with a friend. Not coming back to the disrupted scene of his family in the house they so happily shared may have been a better choice for him, in retrospect.

The flight arrangements for his trip home had long since been made by Colin when he plotted out the entire semester's travel in mid-July. He was so proud of Ronan. They were more like buddies than father and son when Ronan got older, always bonding over sports. Teddy loved their relationship because it was so different from the relationship she had with her parents. Her parents were unmistakably parents. There was no confusion about that. Old Italians do not blur the line between parent and friend as had become the custom with Colin and Teddy's generation.

Declan seemed to settle into his classes after his truancy "hiccup," as Teddy preferred to think of it. So, as she drove the long trek to the airport to pick up Ronan on that clear October Friday night, she felt okay. "Okay" was a triumph in her mind. Declan sat quietly in the passenger seat as usual. If Teddy didn't talk, neither did Declan.

The chaotic airport arrivals pickup zone was its usual frantic scene. She managed to navigate to a spot where she wasn't forced away by the police and waited for Ronan to appear. Without too much waiting time, he lumbered out the revolving doors and made his way to the car. A strong, manly hug for Teddy and a "Get out of the front seat, you slimy jerk" order to Declan, and they were on their way back home. The conversation in the car was stilted. Ronan answered Teddy's questions, but it was certainly not a natural conversation.

"How do you feel about your tests?" Teddy inquired.

"Fine, I think it all went fine," Ronan replied with no embellishment.

"How are your pals, Jason, Joe …," Teddy persisted.

"They are all good," Ronan answered.

"Did they all go home too?" Teddy followed up.

"Yeah."

It was a riveting ride home. Teddy decided to just leave it. No reason to press right now. It was hard for her to let it go, but she managed. When they came in the door, the dogs were thrilled to see Ronan. This seemed to loosen him up a bit. "Thank God," thought Teddy as she pulled out some snacks she had made since the pickup at nine-thirty at night was well past dinner time. The three of them sat at the kitchen table awkwardly eating in near silence.

"That was a very unsatisfying beginning to Ronan's time at home," Teddy said out loud in her baby-talk voice to Sally and Lucy, who were staring up at her as she cleaned the kitchen before bed. Maybe she had not prepared herself enough. Maybe she naively thought it was going to be a good week versus a hard week, a building block week. With the realization that this time may not serve as some sort of magical reset button, she desperately needed comfort, so she immediately went to her reliable source, the Christmas Letter binder. She tucked herself into her bed and opened it to 2006.

Christmas 2006

Bigger meant better in 2006. A bigger house, bigger vacation, and, most importantly, bigger kids. Not to knock the early years of parenting, but having both boys reach the two-year mark makes a big difference. Here's a look back at this year and our family's biggest moments.

We began the year by deciding that it would be a good idea to move our boys into the same bedroom and make Declan's nursery a playroom. This flawed thinking led to months of bedtime delays, waking up through the night and overall restlessness. If that wasn't enough of a sign that the old house was no longer a great fit, our plumbing and foundation teamed up to deliver a vicious one-two punch that left us with just one bathroom for a two-month stretch.

All of this chaos helped us make the not-so-big two-mile move into a much bigger and newer home. Now not only do the kids have their own rooms again, but the place also features a garage apartment that Ronan has dubbed "Grandma's House." An expansive backyard and multiple play areas keep the boys occupied for hours, helping to ensure that they're worn out by day's end.

This summer marked five years of marriage for us, so we celebrated with a week in London. Colin's mom watched the kids while we turned back the clock to those carefree days of little responsibility. The pubs, clubs, concerts and shops were all fantastic, but the highlight for Teddy may have been sleeping in until lunchtime on a daily basis. Of course, after a week, we were ready to come home and be with our kids. And a week after that, we were ready to go back.

The biggest change has really been how much the boys have grown up this past year. A year ago, they basically lived under the same roof and did their own thing when it came to playtime. Now they fill their days playing together, chasing each other, wrestling one another and conspiring against us. Teddy's flexible work arrangement means that she gets the majority of the abuse, as the boys team up against her.

This year, we also took on the task of getting Ronan into our church's school. As ridiculous as it sounds, the lengthy process to get him a pre-K spot felt as rigorous as our college applications to get into Notre Dame. Along with starting his new school, Ronan has kept us busy playing soccer, swimming and diving, bike riding and tackling Colin while wearing his football helmet and shoulder pads. Superheroes and Star Wars figures have also become favorites of Ronan. And, to show that they truly grow up fast, he recently told Colin upon leaving the Thanksgiving Day Parade and seeing the Rockets Power Dancers dance their way along the route, "I loved the pretty girls with not all their parts covered!"

Declan's getting bigger by the day as well. While we rented a train for Ronan's birthday bash, Declan is now obsessed with everything Thomas the Tank Engine. He is either playing with trains, talking about trains or watching shows about trains. An intervention may be necessary in the not-so-distant future. The family even had to take a trek to Austin so that the boys could ride on the "real" Thomas that tours around the country. One more thing about Declan: he is a jigsaw puzzle master, completing them in no time, especially when they include pictures of — you guessed it — trains.

That pretty much covers all of the big stuff for us. We wish you and your family all the best this Christmas season!

Colin, Teddy, Ronan and Declan

"The girls with not all their parts covered," thought

Teddy. This made her laugh out loud just as it had fifteen years ago when she first read the draft Colin shared with her. As she continued forcing herself to pace the reading of these gems, Teddy sunk down under the covers and called for Ronan and Declan. That trip to London had been something special. The night of a royal concert featuring a lineup of '80s stars at the Tower of London followed by partying at a nightclub until four in the morning was certainly a highlight then and now. Teddy laughed at the memory of finding the bar receipt for two hundred British pounds years later in her desk. And what about the two young posh couples they befriended at the club that night dancing the night away? Where were they now? Did they ever think about that crazy American couple who were surely ten years older and invaded their Saturday night out? Teddy hoped they were all together and doing well. Not like her, alone … abandoned.

The boys appeared in her doorway, and Teddy said, "Time for my tuck-in!" They looked at each other sheepishly but complied with giving her a goodnight kiss on the cheek. The boys tucking her in became a tradition when they were teenagers because they stayed up later than she did! Teddy required a lot of sleep and getting into bed at nine o'clock was her go-to move. She chuckled to herself thinking about when Declan used to say "rooooom serrrrvice" in a mock Irish accent and smooth out her covers. He started this bedtime tuck-in habit after being at a fancy castle hotel in Ireland one summer as a tween. Teddy loved getting "rooooom serrrrvice" from her little strawberry blonde cutie.

Ronan saw the binder on the table next to Teddy's bed and asked, "What's that out for?"

"I enjoy reading them. They seem to be helping me cope," Teddy said. "I just read the 2006 letter when you were four and Declan was two. You have a quote about loving the girls with not all their parts covered, referring to Rockets cheerleaders at the Thanksgiving Day parade. Do you remember that?"

"No," replied Ronan blankly.

Letting his flat reply go, Teddy asked, "Declan, in 2006 your love of Thomas the Tank Engine was ignited. I realize you know about your train obsession, but now we can pinpoint the specific year it started. Kinda cool, huh? I find these letters amazing at helping me remember details. They are gratifying."

"If it is making you feel good, Mom, you should do it. I liked reading the one the other night with you," said Declan.

Ronan made no comment, and they both left the room after some fairly mechanical "I love you's." They were teen boys after all. A tragedy doesn't change that fact.

Teddy tried not to worry about Ronan, but she restlessly went to sleep wondering about his vibe. However, her dreams were not of worry for her children. The dreams took her to her childhood basement where she spent hours at her chalkboard playing teacher, alone or with friends. It mattered not to Teddy as a little girl. She was happiest at that blackboard.

When she awoke recalling the teacher dreams that seemed as if they repeated all night, she did not know what to think. Was this the answer to the question Dana had posed? Was teaching what she was called to do now that every circumstance had changed? But then guilt flooded into her mind, tsunami-like. Teddy could hear Sue's skepticism ringing in her ears. Maybe it was selfish to think about herself and making a new start.

Teddy did not know the rules of losing a husband. There was no playbook that could tell her the perfect steps and the perfect timing. And feeling guilty, being judged, not executing perfectly were among the most feared things for her. "Maybe this whole job thing Dana brought up is not the right track," Teddy thought as she flopped back down onto her pillow.

The week with Ronan home should have been a wonderful time. That's how Teddy always envisioned it before the accident. Colin would have been so thrilled to see his son, watch sports, and relax with him nearby. Teddy would have been happily cooking his favorite meals and taking him to his favorite restaurants. Teddy was, after all, Italian, so relating over food was in her DNA. Ronan loved food, so it was a match. He stayed in his room most of the time and was not his usual talkative self when he intermittently emerged. The only bright spot was when he got his quarter grades. All A's and one B+. Those marks were remarkable under any circumstance, but given Ronan's situation, they were truly amazing.

"Ronan! I am so happy for you and so proud," Teddy exclaimed, hugging her son as he showed her the report on his phone.

"Thanks, Mom," he replied. "I really couldn't have asked for anything better. These are the best grades among my guys. I really had to work hard to make up for the time I missed, but it looks like I did it."

"You really did," said Teddy joyfully.

"I hope you know now that I am not drinking too much and overdoing it with the fun. I am studying and applying myself," Ronan continued.

"Ronan, it's not that I was doubting you. I just want to ensure you are not adopting unhealthy behaviors given the circumstances. That happens to a lot of people who experience loss like you have," Teddy replied trying to keep the tears contained within her stinging eyes.

She was so proud of the strength her oldest son had shown in the face of true disruption and difficulties. Before this year, her children had not faced much adversity in their lives, she was happy to say. You really never know how a child, or an adult for that matter, will respond. In this case, Teddy was thrilled that her son seemed to be decently coping and was certainly staying focused on his coursework. At this point in the grieving process, she didn't think she could have asked for anything more. She hoped, however, that she was not just being naïve.

The three-pack went to their favorite Mexican restaurant for the Wednesday night fajita special. This was a fairly regular occurrence for their family because Colin loved nothing more than deals. It was the first time they had been to the cozy dining spot without their father. They enjoyed a quiet meal of mixed beef and chicken fajitas.

In the past, a fajita meal with the family was a frantic scene, with the four of them struggling to serve themselves efficiently with the flimsy tongs, as the meat was served family style on a sizzling hot metal contraption. Tonight, with just the two boys, sans Colin, the competitiveness was diminished. Teddy thought to herself how she would give anything to have the chaos of the four of them trying to eat this meal again.

Interestingly, Declan seemed to be the most talkative of the three.

"So, who are you most excited to see back at school?" Declan asked his brother.

Declan never threw out questions to start conversations. Teddy sat back to see how Ronan replied.

"I don't know, I guess Joe," said Ronan in a terse reply.

"Who is he?" followed up Declan. Teddy was flabbergasted at Declan's continued questions.

"Next-door neighbor," Ronan said curtly.

"Is he your best friend?" continued Declan.

"Hard to say. There's a good amount of people I get along with," Ronan responded.

"So which class do you like the most?" Declan asked, switching topics.

"Probably Econ, why?" said Ronan, seemingly getting irritated with the questions.

"Just curious," said Declan.

"Yes, Ronan, although you've been home, we've not gotten to really talk much. We are interested in your life," added Teddy.

"Well, my life is just fine, as you can see, so can we stop with the questions?" Ronan said, shutting down the conversation, which was clearly his endgame.

"We just miss you, Ronan. We want to hear about your life. Don't get mad at us, well at me," said Teddy with tears in her eyes.

"Look, I got good grades," Ronan stated. "I thought that would show you that I am fine. I mean, as fine as fine can be right now. I just don't want all the questions. Take my actions and the results I showed you. I feel like you are doubting me."

"Oh no, I am not doubting you." Teddy responded. "I see how you could feel that way. I will lay off."

The three finished their meal and quietly left. During the car ride home, Ronan took Teddy by surprise and asked if he could drive to College Station, an hour and a half away, to visit friends who were attending Texas A&M. Teddy was crushed but kept her sadness inside. She allowed Ronan to go up on Thursday and come home on Friday. She wasn't going to spare more than twenty-four of her precious hours of

Ronan's fall break, despite it probably being the best thing for Ronan. He needed to do normal things. She knew that. But she wanted to be selfish. Was that really so bad? So uncalled for?

At home, another startling thing happened involving Declan, which mercifully interrupted the pity party Teddy was having in her head and heart. He asked her if she wanted to read another Christmas Letter.

"Sure, let's ask Ronan too," she said.

"Hey Ronan, come down," she yelled up the stairs. Ronan came to the top and declined Teddy's offer to read a letter. She didn't press him and let it go. It took all of Teddy's patience and restraint not to cause a confrontation.

"All right, Declan. It's just going to be you and me, bud," Teddy said brightly to cover her sadness that Ronan declined the offer.

"I read 2005 and 2006 on my own, Declan, so do you want to read starting at 2005 or jump to 2007? It's up to you," Teddy asked as they settled on the couch.

"Let's skip to 2007; I will read 2005 and 2006 on my own if that's okay with you, Mom."

"Okay, 2007 it is!" said Teddy.

Christmas 2007

It's Christmastime, and what does that mean in the McNamara household this year? Just an endless parental chorus of "Santa's watching" as Ronan and Declan pester one another nonstop. Our days have become increasingly filled with wrestling matches and keep away. Yes, they've reached that special stage in their relationship. Archrival? Best friend? It's anyone's guess. Here's the blow-by-blow account of the family's 12-round bout in 2007.

If he's not taking on his little brother, Ronan can usually be found in the backyard playing sports with Colin or Teddy. Football, baseball, basketball and soccer all found a place in the heart of our little four-sport athlete this past year. He insists on changing jerseys to match the sport he is playing in the backyard and becomes quite the intimidator when donning his football helmet, shoulder pads and mouthpiece. He has also turned into a little sports almanac, like his father, retaining vital information about the NBA playoffs, World Series and the BCS college football rankings. Other sports highlights for Ronan this past year included making his first basket, meeting Astros All-Star Craig Biggio, going to his first ND game, running the bases at Minute Maid Park, losing his training wheels and scoring his first goal in soccer. Of course, he'll be quick to tell you about *all seven of his goals, so we're working with him to keep that ego in check.*

Declan continues to grow up as well, but he remains as feisty as ever. His strong will keeps his parents on their toes, as he has the uncanny ability to turn the simplest request into mission impossible. Among Declan's big achievements this past year were learning to write his name and to stop sucking his thumb. Declan's love for trains appears to be never-ending, as he can amuse himself for hours with these toys. He also enjoys riding around on his train, drawing trains, reading train books and watching shows about trains. If only he showed a fraction of this interest in getting dressed, eating his dinner or going to bed.

As for us parents, we both landed new jobs this year. First, Colin got hired by Neelan Fuller, the biggest law firm in Texas, to do PR. Coincidentally, Colin's new building connected to Teddy's, leading to frequent lunch dates in the nearby mall's food court. Yes, it felt like high school all over again. Sadly, after just a few months of holding hands in the halls, Rogers, another consulting firm, wooed Teddy away to the other side of downtown. She now leads their energy marketing and continues her flexible schedule, giving her the added bonus of being a referee to a three-year-old and five-year-old every afternoon. We did manage to escape from the clutches of the children for a few getaways, taking in a weekend in Malibu and then hanging out with 65,000 of our closest friends at the Austin City Limits music festival.

While the kids can be impossible at times, they both continue to be sweet and loving boys for at least a good 15 minutes a day. I guess, as parents, you take what you can get. Here's wishing you and your family all the best this Christmas season!

Colin, Teddy, Ronan and Declan

"What do you mean I was feisty?" asked Declan.

"Ha! When you were little, you had quite a temper," answered Teddy. "I know you've heard this story before, but I think it illustrates your feistiness best. I had to call your father to meet me at a toy store because you literally had a rage fit about leaving the store because there was a train table with trains you wanted to stay and play with. You were out of control. I couldn't get you in your car seat. It was a complete meltdown. Your whole head turned red, and you were screaming, your body stiff with toddler rage. You were insane, my friend, and that episode did not advance the image of redheads and their commensurate tempers."

"Why didn't that story make it into the letter?" Declan asked with no sense of remorse for his past devilish behavior.

"Well, I think your father liked to put everyone's best self forward in these letters. Although it would have been comical if he had worked that crazy tale into the 2007 letter. I think that was the year that happened. If you choose to write Christmas letters when you're an adult, you can decide how to present the antics of your kids! And Declan, you really were the sweetest little kid more often than not. You were the scrunchiest nibbly pibbly!"

It felt good to laugh and to use all of her made-up terms of endearment for her son.

"That was nice, Declan. Thanks for doing that with me," said Teddy as Declan made his way to the stairs.

"Sure, Mom. I kind of see why you like reading them. And you know, you better never use those silly names in front of my friends! You have slipped up once or twice, and that did not make for a great day at school," Declan scoffed as he ascended the stairs to his room.

"Hey! Notre Dame has a 'Ginger Run' every year in March. All the redheads on campus do a little run. Looks fun on Instagram. Another positive for ND, Decks. But no pressure," yelled Teddy with a laugh, as Declan vanished to his room without acknowledging this fun-filled tidbit about Notre Dame.

Declan, like Ronan, was a combination of Teddy's and Colin's features. But being close enough to Declan on the couch to see his gray-blue eyes that clearly came from Colin simultaneously warmed and tore her heart.

***

"When I write my own Christmas letters," thought Declan. "Hmmm, never really thought about doing my own letter, now or ever, really."

This exchange with his mother seemingly put the vague idea of taking up the task of writing the 2021 letter into Declan's head.

Instead of going to his room, Declan went into Ronan's. He was greeted with typical brotherly love.

"Get out," Ronan said blandly.

Declan ignored him and continued with his reason for invading his brother's space.

"You know Mom has been reading these Christmas letters, right? Well, they are making me think about this year. What are we going to do?" inquired Declan.

"Nothin'," said Ronan stubbornly, not wanting to discuss this topic.

"Well, I was thinking that maybe you and I could write

the letter as a tribute to Dad. You know, keep the tradition alive ..."

"That's a no, I've got too much on my mind, and I just find reading those letters gruesome."

"Okay, well, what do you think if I try to write it?"

"Go for it, little man," Ronan replied, somewhat annoyed. "Go. For. It."

Chapter Eighteen

The week with Ronan at home wore on, with him continuing to be reserved. Teddy wondered if it was Colin's death or just the typical adjustment of a child who thinks he is now an adult coming home to visit for the first time. She had been warned of this first visit home phenomenon by other mothers. Teddy concluded it was likely a bit of both. The only material information he shared about his social life was about a bet he made with a dorm friend about the Major League Baseball playoffs. The loser had to do something called Edward Fortyhands.

"What the heck is that?" Teddy exclaimed. Teddy enjoyed her boys being older so she could swear. She was fond of more hardcore swear words when really upset, but she still tried to keep a lid on it when she was with her sons, despite them being teens.

"Well, the loser has to have forty-ounce beers duct-taped to both of his hands, so he loses use of the hand until the forty is gone," explained Ronan.

"I don't get the name," said Declan, ignoring the far more absurd part of the story.

"Oh, *I* get that part," said Teddy. "There is an '80s movie called *Edward Scissorhands* where Johnny Depp, the *Pirates of the Caribbean* guy, plays a weirdo who has scissors for hands. But seriously, Ronan, you think this is a good thing to be involved in? I don't worry about social drinking, but this kind of stuff scares me."

"Mom, it's fine," Ronan replied dismissively and walked away.

Declan and Teddy just stared at each other shaking their heads. They were all struggling, and Ronan was not making it easier this week. Teddy was happy that Declan seemed to be stable. He was going to school and doing his normal activities. She was checking. She was sure.

Declan's vibe seemed better too. He wasn't a laugh a minute, but he never was. However, he was not as dark as he seemed just a few weeks ago. He seemed to be managing.

"At least one of them seems to be doing okay. One at a time?" she guessed to herself. The song lyrics to Annie Lennox's "Walking on Broken Glass" popped into her brain. Teddy could hear her smooth voice singing, "Now everyone of us is made to suffer. Every one of us is made to weep." Although the song is about a breakup, Teddy felt that these particular lyrics may indeed be true and certainly applied to her current existence. Her sons' lives too. Maybe everyone's. She didn't know. Maybe even the breakup sentiment was applicable to her too. The result of the incident was that Colin left her, broke up with her. And the irony that the song's chorus was the repetition of the words "walking on broken glass" did not elude her. She realized she must be deeply missing Colin because he was the one who always created soundtracks to their lives with pop songs, not Teddy.

Another strange irony flooded Teddy's spiraling mind. She always thought Colin should be a writer. She often mused about novels set in a professional sports environment that he could write because of his inside knowledge of the unusual and often unbelievable NBA world. She thought there was ample hilarious material for a fun story. She also tried to persuade him to write a book based on his Christmas letters. Colin rejected that idea outright, saying he thought about it, but the only way he could see telling a story based on the letters was to have one of us die in the story. He said he would never write that on a page. Ever. Looking back, Teddy saw her audacity of laughing at his superstition. It was a clear tempting of fate that she could see clearly now.

It was likely unrealistic for her to think that it would be easier for Ronan since he was away. He had double the adjustment, being away for the first time and adjusting to the loss of his father whom he loved dearly. "Give it time," Teddy thought for what seemed like the millionth time in the month since Colin died. How could it have only been just one single month?

That evening after dinner, Declan asked to read another letter with Teddy. She asked if they should invite Ronan to join, and Declan said no. Teddy decided to leave it at that and not interrogate Declan about his older brother's mental state.

They settled into their respective spots on the couch and opened the binder. "Okay, 2008, here we come," Teddy said brightly in her new fake, positive voice, which she had been honing to perfection since the accident.

"Wait," said Teddy, "Did you ever read 2005 and 2006?"

"No, but maybe I will take the binder after we read this one and I'll do some catchup reading."

"Sure, of course you can take it," said Teddy. Her heart was warmed by Declan's continued interest in the letters.

"You know what is interesting, Mom? I talked to Mr. DeSilva for a bit today and I mentioned that we were reading these letters to help us feel better. You will never guess what he told me! He said he and his wife—the one who died a couple of years ago—did Christmas letters too. I never knew anyone else besides us and Grandma and Grandpa who did them. So weird, right?"

Ignoring the information about Mr. DeSilva and his letters, Teddy asked, "When did you talk to him?

"This morning during community time," Declan said. "Just for a few minutes."

"What else did you talk about?

"He asked about golf. We talked about that."

"So, how did our letters come up?"

"Well, I guess he asked if anything was giving me joy right now. After giving a couple of seconds thought, the letters just popped into my head, so I told him. I could tell he thinks it is very cool and good for me."

"Hmm, okay," Teddy responded. "I am surprised you are okay with this guy chatting with you. "

"Yeah Mom, I am. It's no big thing. Can we read now?"

Christmas 2008

Christmastime is here, and we hope you enjoy your annual McNamara gift of kindling for the Yule log. Both flammable and informative, here's a recap of all that happened in 2008.

With the boys now six and four, the party never seems to stop for Ronan and Declan. Bunk beds have brought them closer than ever, as Declan abandoned his own bedroom to become Ronan's roommate. Parties have become all the rage for this dynamic duo, hosting a Super Bowl bash, a Halloween sleepover and birthday extravaganzas at the Astros' ballpark for Ronan and Galveston's train museum for Declan.

Declan is now transitioning from trains to Transformers being his favorite toys, as Teddy comes to grips with her "baby" getting bigger. This Halloween, Declan demonstrated this new allegiance with a costume choice of Optimus Prime, replacing last year's selection of Thomas the Tank Engine. While he still has a soft spot for trains, Declan has also branched out to embrace new animated friends in

Scooby-Doo and Alvin & the Chipmunks.

Ronan's love for sports continues, as he got his first taste of Little League with a season of T-Ball. After a handful of at-bats, he was already plotting his career as a major leaguer, casually mentioning, "When I sign my first contract, I'm going to make sure it has a 'no-trade' clause." Of course, with the changing of the seasons, the wide-eyed kindergartener launched aspirations of becoming a two-sport athlete. This enthusiasm was further sparked after he won a "Take a Texan to School Day" contest, receiving a classroom visit from Houston Texans wide receiver Andre Davis. When Ronan's not playing sports or talking about sports, he's drawing sports pictures, as he has taken quite an interest in art as well. He seems to be taking his religion classes seriously too, evidenced by him declaring, "That guy trespassed against us" about a person who cut us off on the freeway.

Weddings in Teddy's family made for a pair of fun vacations. Teddy and Ronan ventured up to Toronto in the winter for her cousin Giancarlo's wedding, filling their free time with snowball fights and snow angels. Later in the year, the four of us headed to San Francisco for the wedding of Teddy's niece and Declan's Godmother, Isabelle. This fun-filled trip also included an Alcatraz boat trip, cable car rides and a Giants game on the Fourth of July.

To avoid hours of lines and countless inconveniences, we decided to try something different for our yearly kid-free getaway, a Caribbean cruise ... on which we encountered hours of lines and countless inconveniences. Colin will forever treasure those memories at the ship's sports bar, where South American soccer was the only viewing option. Since that trip didn't really hit the spot, we later partook in a much more satisfying vacation with our first post-Katrina return to New Orleans. 3-for-1 drink specials, how we missed you so.

Speaking of hurricanes, we were fortunate enough to escape to Notre Dame the day before Hurricane Ike shut down Houston's airports. A three-day trip extended to ten days away, as our house lost power for two weeks. The trip featured the unveiling of the Lou Holtz sculpture created by Colin's father. Ronan, who ranks the Fighting Irish in the "Bottom 25," recently saw old highlights of Holtz and spoke to the TV screen, "Can you please be Notre Dame's coach again?"

Our boys have recently given us the greatest gift imaginable: the sleep-in. No, not them – us. Upon waking up on weekends, Ronan has been making breakfast for himself and Declan. And it doesn't stop there. The two will then entertain each other for hours before deciding to check on us. Seeing 10:30 am flash on the alarm clock is truly a dream. Here's wishing all of your dreams come true this Christmas season!

Colin, Teddy, Ronan and Declan

"Transformers," said Declan making his goofy Declan face of bulging eyes and a stretched-out mouth. "I don't remember Ronan ever taking care of me in the mornings though. Are you sure that really happened, or did Dad just make that up so we would look good?"

"That's 100% true, Declan. I know Ronan is a little hard to take sometimes as a brother, but he loved you then, and I know he loves you now," replied Teddy.

"I'll take your word for it, Mom," said Declan as he took the binder and went to his room.

"Do you remember being away from home when our house had no power?" asked Teddy.

"No, umm, not really," said Declan.

"It's okay, you were young. It was truly horrible. We were stuck at Notre Dame for several extra days, then we flew back to Texas only to head to Grandma and Grandpa's house in San Antonio, four hours away, for about a week. It was a crazy time trying to take care of you guys away from home and attempting to keep up with work. Even the unveiling of your grandfather's Lou Holtz sculpture was a horror. It poured down rain during the unveiling ceremony, and the tailgate fields were seas of mud. You and Ronan loved clomping through the mud, though."

"I am going to take the binder up with me, Mom, okay?"

"Sure, Declan. Of course."

The sculpture unveiling reference made Teddy think about Colin's family. Colin's father was a professional sculptor. He was a fine arts major at Notre Dame in the '60s but soon realized he needed a real job to support his growing family, so he joined the Air Force. After a long military career, he was blessed with a second career of sculpting. The sculpture unveiling weekends at Notre Dame were always during a football weekend because the sculptures were of the coaches who won football national championships for the school.

They should have been fun family reunions. They, however, always seemed to be fraught with chaos. It seems to come with the territory when you are trying to coordinate across more than twenty-five people spanning three generations. Teddy had hoped that she had found the family she was missing when she met Colin, but it was just another filled with unusual personalities and unnecessary conflict.

***

Declan opened the binder to the very beginning, which did not immediately reveal his father's letters but rather letters written by his McNamara grandparents. The letter-writing tradition started in 1972. Declan had no idea it started so long ago. Years that started with a nineteen seemed a long mystical distance away from his time exclusively in the twenty-first century. He decided not to skip ahead to his dad's letters but to genuinely immerse himself in the Christmas Letter heritage and read his grandparents' works. He settled back into the pillows on his bed and started reading the typewriter-written letters from the '70s. To Declan, a child born in this Millennium, typewriter font seemed foreign and strange. "Are these hieroglyphics?" he mused.

Reading the retelling of the story of his grandparents' courtship – the divorced Air Force man and the former nun who had previously dated fifteen years before reuniting – and the early years of his father's uniquely blended family was interesting. Declan had heard these stories before but seeing them in print made them seem more real. Or maybe he just cared more now that his dad was gone. Anything that helped him feel close to his dad was interesting to him. Declan realized that what you treasure is all about perspective. The memories he uncovered through the letters were becoming increasingly valuable.

The 1973 letter introduced his dad, Colin, to the McNamara family picture and the family's move to London due to an Air Force assignment. Although his dad was just an infant, Declan suspected his father's love of London started then. His dad loved to visit London, read about London, curate his massive music collection heavy with British artists, and most of all, mine online and print media for new pop British music knowledge. Even his mother couldn't fully understand how her husband found the obscure facts that he did and, more importantly, how he kept such information in his head, some of it being more than thirty-five years old.

"Twenty years of letters documenting his grandparents', father's, and uncles' lives," thought Declan. "Then, my dad's twenty plus years of letters on top of that. I really need to carry on the tradition, especially for Dad. How can I just let it end?"

Chapter Nineteen

The last day of Ronan's fall break came, and Teddy drove him to the airport. Ronan and Declan said goodbye in a curt manner symbolic of the entire week before Declan drove off to school in his gleaming black Jeep. Declan loved his manly wheels.

Teddy and Ronan had a nice chat on the forty-minute car ride to the airport along the ugly billboard-laden Houston freeway. That was just it. It was nice. It was polite, but it just didn't feel good. Ronan was doing well when it came to school. His quarter grades showed that loud and clear. He said his social life and friend group were good.

"Was that to be expected? Was something wrong?

Should she do something?" Teddy thought to herself as she made the drive back home. When she pulled into the driveway, she realized she had no concrete recollection of driving home. She apparently had been on autopilot with her thoughts and worries consuming the front of her mind.

Teddy entered the house. It was dead quiet, a sound she used to cherish, but now it annoyed every fiber of her being. She went to a go-to coping mechanism, cleaning. She started straightening up the family room, folding blankets left strewn across the couch from last night's "snuggle buggle" time with the dogs, "snuggle buggle" being another of Teddy's frequently used made up phrases.

She was so thankful for the dogs. Sally was the sweet and fuzzy Cairn Terrier who looked like a little bear, and Lucy was the energetic Westie. Like many Westies, she was indeed just like Lucy from *Peanuts*: feisty and bossy! Not only had the critters made it easier to handle Ronan and Declan having the nerve to become young adults, but they were also her constant and loving companions during this grotesquely lonely time. As all dogs do, they unconditionally loved her. For that love she was thankful.

Teddy flopped on her newly straightened-up couch and asked Sally and Lucy out loud in her doggie baby-talk voice, "Is it odd that this teacher, this Mr. DeSilva is taking an interest in Declan? Or is he just being a good person, a good teacher?"

"Sally, you say he's just a good guy," as she continued talking to herself. "Good. I sure hope so. With so many creeps in the world, you just never know."

"Wait, what? Lucy, you think it smells fishy? That's just your sister, Sally. She's been sunbathing again, and that always gets her a bit stankified."

With her pretend dog conversation behind her, Teddy moved upstairs. She took on Ronan's room first despite its lack of urgency since he would not be back to occupy it until Thanksgiving. She tore off the blue sheets of his bed sending ND Bear, a huge teddy bear with an ND football jersey that Colin's parents gave Ronan when he was born, flying to the floor.

"Sorry, ND Bear," muttered Teddy half-heartedly. The holidays she thought to herself with a shiver. The word "how" kept repeating in her mind, an incessant loop, taunting her. "How am I going to do this, any of this, much less the holidays?" she finally said out loud, as if hoping ND Bear would have some answers.

Teddy found the Christmas Letter binder in Declan's bed open to a 1985 letter written by her in-laws. "Hmm, he's reading the legacy letters too. Interesting." Teddy's mind floated to this Mr. DeSilva again. Christmas letter writing Mr. DeSilva. Was something amiss? Teddy decided to act. It was kind of a rule she had. She had to find out a little bit about any adult her children spent time with outside of class, whether it be a coach, counselor, priest or teacher. Even though Declan was seventeen, she decided he was still not too old for her to screen this guy who seemed to be inserting himself into his life beyond being his lit teacher.

Teddy slid behind her laptop. She realized she had not been behind her laptop since the accident. She did not miss the screen at all. Her work had become nothing but hours of responding to e-mails and inane meetings. Quitting seemed more like breaking up with her laptop than leaving an actual place of employment. But teaching, she imagined, had little time behind a laptop, or at least it was balanced between actively doing something with other humans and using our new appendage in the modern age, the laptop.

She pulled herself from the reverie of imagining what it would be like to be a teacher, perhaps a literature teacher like this Mr. DeSilva character. Sue's voice then invaded her head. The conversation played back in her mind: "You should focus on the boys right now. Colin left you in a good place. You don't need money."

"Ugh, am I a horrible person for thinking about me for one damn second? I guess I am," gasped Teddy out loud. "Fine. I will do as a good mother should, focus on her children. Mr. DeSilva, here I come."

Teddy poised herself at her laptop and typed.

To: Sdesilva@smcps.org

Subject: Declan McNamara

Dear Mr. DeSilva,

I understand from my son Declan that you have been taking an interest in him beyond the classroom given the recent tragedy that has struck our family. That is very kind of you.

However, as you can imagine, I am very protective of my children at this point in time. I would like to come to the school and discuss the situation with you. Please let me know some date and time options that work for your schedule.

Regards,

Teddy McNamara

Send.

Teddy felt good about asserting herself. She and Colin used to joke that the Depeche Mode "Everything Counts" song lyric stating "everything counts in large amounts" should have been "everyone sucks in large amounts." Sadly, Teddy kind of believed that sentiment. And in this case, she needed to be sure Mr. DeSilva meant no harm, did not suck in some horrible way. She rarely met with the boys' teachers because they were both good students and, in Declan's case, exceptionally so. He was likely in the hunt for valedictorian, which is no small feat at a college prep school that is strongly academically focused.

Teddy picked up the binder and sunk into the pillows on Declan's bed. She flipped through the pages to get to 2009's letter. As she did, she remembered a little nugget that did not make the letter. In 2004, she took a business trip to her company's headquarters in Times Square. She was about eight months pregnant with Declan, and this was to be her last work trip before her due date.

Times Square was never her favorite place, and this episode solidified her displeasure with the New York City landmark. Teddy waded through the fanatical crowd of Insane Clown Posse fans overtaking the streets because of an MTV show called *Total Request Live* that was shot in a studio with windows facing the streets, causing fans of its featured acts to swarm outside. Unfortunately, this mass of scary painted faces obstructed her access to her normal, boring, non-groupie-inducing office building. She literally held on to her large belly to protect Declan from the crazy fans with black and white painted clown faces. This story made her laugh in 2021, but not so much in 2004. She often wondered how she made it through many points in her life as a working mother. The clown crowd was certainly one experience she was not sure how she survived.

Thankfully, she and Colin had a strong relationship. But make no mistake, there were times when she was completely spent and frustrated with her situation. That trip was one of those times. She changed jobs to get more money and a flexible work arrangement, which were seemingly good things. But changing jobs at six months pregnant and traveling through eight months was difficult. But Teddy always did what she had to do. There is goodness in that quality, but there was untold frustration too.

Christmas 2009

The McNamara household enjoyed many memorable moments over the last 12 months. For starters, Ronan and Declan each lost their first tooth. Ironically, no crying took place at either milestone ... until the next mornings when the child who didn't lose a tooth felt woefully slighted by the Tooth Fairy. For times like these, we have had to ban "NO FAIR" from our vocabulary. "I WANT" might be next on that list, as we try our hardest to prevent the bratification of our two boys.

In Little League, Ronan transitioned from coach pitch to the 40-mile-per-hour heat of machine pitch. The competitiveness has risen among the youngsters and even reached the stands. Colin is embarrassed to admit that he had a moment as the stereotypical "Little League Dad" when he got into a debate with an umpire who had lost track of the pitch count. Possibly more pathetic, however, was Colin's continual tracking of our seven-year-old's batting average, as Ronan went 26-for-31 through the machine pitch season.

For Spring Break, the boys stayed with Grandma while we let loose in London and other historic towns around England. Highlights included a Gordon Ramsay pub, the London Eye and the musical Oliver! starring Rowan Atkinson. The majestic towers of Oxford made Teddy feel like she stepped into the world of Harry Potter, as she had recently discovered her inner geek by plowing through those seven fantasy novels. In Stratford-upon-Avon, Colin dragged Teddy to an unplugged concert by Nik Kershaw, a British pop star from the '80s. It's clear that Colin is getting old when his two favorite concerts from 2009 – this one and another by Men at Work's Colin Hay – were both acoustic sets from guys who haven't made the charts in 25 years.

Summer started with Ronan and Declan celebrating

their birthdays at an Astros game with several friends. We then had two stays at the Hyatt Lost Pines Resort near Austin. Here, our boys enjoyed the outdoors with horse rides, flag football, s'mores, bikes, a putting green and, everyone's favorite, inner tubes on the lazy river. The rest of their summer was spent around the house drawing Star Wars pictures, building Lego creations and shooting Nerf blasters.

This fall, Declan started at St. Joan of Arc, reuniting with Ronan after three years at separate schools. Ronan loves art to the point that he has begun teaching "art class" to his first-grade classmates. Declan likes school too, but the Pre-K grind might be wearing on him, as he recently complained, "God needs to make weekends longer!" As for Colin's favorite line from our five-year-old quote machine, it's the rhetorical question: "If you're not bad or good, are you a jerk?"

Soccer and baseball consumed the fall. Declan's shining moment from his first year in sports was scoring a goal in his season finale, while not-so-humble Ronan is quick to boast about his undefeated soccer season. In October, the boys got their first dose of Chicago, seeing the Cubs at Wrigley Field and the entire city from 103 stories high at the new glass-bottomed Skydeck. On this trip, we also witnessed a rare Notre Dame win in South Bend. Fall finished up with

Ronan and Declan impressing their grandparents in their school's musical program at Thanksgiving.

This year's arrival of a Wii has led to countless hours of playing Lego Star Wars and John Madden Football. Consequently, Ronan has absorbed the entire Madden playbook and provides entertainment on NFL Sundays by yelling at the coaches to call the "Tight End Drag" or put in the dime package. With this kind of guy talk, Teddy has started to feel outnumbered as the lone female in the house. We thought that bringing a sweet girl puppy might even things out a little. Unfortunately, our new little Westie, Molly, is just as feisty as either of the boys.

So that wraps up things for us this past year. Have a great Christmas season, and, in Ronan's words, we wish you, "Peace on Nerf, Goodwill to Men!"

Colin, Teddy, Ronan and Declan

What Teddy wouldn't give to let loose in London again with her husband. They always had such fun together. That was really a credit to Colin. He always found interesting and unique things to do and just made the best of things no matter where he was in the world. She loved herself most when she let herself be the fun Teddy that Colin brought out in her. She wondered if she would ever be that Teddy again.

Even their frequent house parties – with no guests invited – were special. Colin would put on music from his vast library of pop music, and they would drink beer, talk, and sometimes dance as if they were out at a club or bar. They only needed each other to have a good time.

Reading this letter didn't seem to help her like the others had. This letter hit a nerve. Between this letter and the trying visit with Ronan as well as the concern that was brewing with this Mr. DeSilva, Teddy was exhausted. She went to her bed and slept the rest of the day. She found sleep was her only escape from her new life as a widow. The thoughts of vaporizing off the planet soothed her to sleep where she didn't have to think. Didn't have to worry about her boys. Nothingness felt like peace.

Teddy had so looked forward to the empty nest time. She thought at that time her sacrificing would be over. Now it seemed she wouldn't get the euphoria of being an empty nester, just the loneliness and the continued sacrifice of being a mother, putting all of her energy into ensuring her sons were going to make it.

Her brain seemed to have shut down with Colin's departure. There was always something going on in her head – something to do, something to improve, something to investigate, something to just ponder. Her idea factory brain was more legitimate than the commercial-free satellite radio idea that Colin frequently mocked her about. In her work, she came up with many clever marketing techniques, like giving away high-end pens to encourage small business owners to allow her company to assess their electricity usage and provide a price bid. All it required was signing a piece of paper that would normally end up in the trash without such an incentive. The boys were frequent beneficiaries of her constantly churning mind's ideas. She dreamed up service projects, essay topics, and even summer book club groups. Some of her ideas were more appreciated than others by her sons. The summer book club and service projects were not very well received in the moment.

But without Colin, her brain and body just wanted sleep.

Chapter Twenty

During a free period at school, Declan opened a fresh document on his laptop. He stared at it and finally typed, "Christmas 2021." His free period was forty minutes. In that time, he started the letter six times. Each time, he reread his opening lines and repeatedly hit the backspace key to erase his feeble attempt.

"How on earth did my dad do this for more than twenty years?" thought Declan in frustration. He really had no idea how to start. He was a decent writer for his schoolwork and even for the community magazine articles he wrote as a student reporter, but this was a completely different challenge. And the situation was so hard, with his dad's passing, which was the whole reason he was even attempting this. Declan's mind spiraled in circular thoughts. "Maybe this was a bad idea, like Ronan thought," Declan said out loud to himself. His friend Juan looked at him puzzled as if to ask, "Are you talking to me?" Without responding to Juan's look, Declan packed up his stuff. He was happy that it was time to head to class. That seemed much more manageable than attempting to write this letter.

"What's a bad idea, Declan?" asked Juan, who followed Declan out of the student center.

"Do you really want to know?"

"Uh … yeah, idiot. I wouldn't have asked if I didn't wonder."

"Okay, well, my dad used to write these Christmas letters every year telling people about our lives over the past year. They were our Christmas cards, basically, instead of just sending photos of ourselves like everyone else does," said Declan.

"Oh yeah, man. I think I have seen one or two of those things. So, what's the bad idea?"

"Well, my mom has been reading them to kinda help her during this, um, you know, time. I got the idea of maybe writing this year's letter since my dad, uh, cannot do it obviously."

"Wow, that's cool, Deck."

"Amazingly hard. I don't know if I have it in me on many levels. You know? The writing, the memories it brings up. All of it. And my dad's letters were funny. It's hard to be funny in writing, bro ..."

"Yeah, especially since you are not the least bit funny Declan. Joking, bro! Seriously though, if I can help let me know. I can read drafts for you, whatever. You know you can count on me, okay, Declan?"

"Yeah, okay. I guess," said Declan feebly. His friend's offer of support was nice. He was just feeling overwhelmed.

When Declan returned home after school and a short golf practice, he found that his mother was in bed sound asleep at five o'clock. This worried him because he understood she was trying so hard to be strong for him and his brother. He knew she was exhausted as a result of her "keep calm and carry on" operating model. She probably has no energy left at all. He let her be and went to his room, where he found the Christmas Letter binder open to a different page than he left it. He realized his mother had clearly been in his room because it was tidied up. He felt guilty. I should be keeping my own room clean, especially now. He made a mental note to do better. He read the 2009 letter and wondered if it was still helping her to read them. Declan understood that his father was no longer with them through a freak accident, yes, but he also understood it was due to a bit of fun-seeking for which his father was known. He was old enough to surmise that his mother likely viewed this as a bit of a betrayal, despite never once hinting at such feelings. Declan just wondered. It was likely an unanswerable question because he was certainly never going to ask the question of his mom, and he was sure his mother would take her feelings to the grave on this topic. She was just like that.

Declan reflected on his attempt to start the letter earlier in the day. "Maybe this is just too hard for me to do," he thought. "Maybe it wasn't even a good idea in the first place."

He sat on his bed staring at the binder, touching the plastic-sleeved pages, wondering how his dad produced these each year without fail. Declan was never involved. His dad kind of went into mad scientist mode and a letter resulted. The black box approach left Declan with no recipe to follow.

Declan decided to read the 2009 letter, which his mom had obviously read earlier in the day given that was the page left open on his bed. He laughed to himself at the stories and his quote. "Did I really ask, 'if you're not bad or good, are you a jerk?'" he said out loud. Actually, it's a pretty astute question for a pre-K kid, he decided with pride in his younger self. He also reflected on Lost Pines. He and his brother loved their races around the lazy river to the degree that you could actually race in one. But being boys, and with a jock brother like Ronan, competition seemed to be available in anything at any time.

Declan then went back to where he left off in his grandparents' letters. The letters were a look back at details he would never hear about otherwise. Apparently in 1982 his dad was into the movie E.T., which Declan vaguely knew about, and Ziggy, whom he had not a clue.

He continued to read, now noticing a marked style difference between his father's and his grandparents' letters. His grandparents were a standard chronicle, while his dad's works seemed to take it up a notch with a little more humor and a definite focus on the kids versus the adults. Declan realized that he now had a writing style to think about if he pursued the endeavor he was fiercely contemplating. He strongly preferred his father's work, but that made the task at hand even more difficult to think about. Declan never prided himself on his humor. Thoughts of chucking this idea crept into his mind once again.

"Dad made his letters fun, and I would want mine to be the same," Declan thought to himself. "That's going to be impossible since the most unfun thing ever just happened to us."

He turned his attention to his schoolwork, which was a much more comfortable task than attempting to put something on the page for the Christmas letter. At five-thirty in the evening, he decided that he should wake his mom. He had no idea how long she had been asleep, but sleeping all day long probably wasn't a great idea for her. Declan found himself acting like a parent as he went into her room and looked at her sleeping calmly. Weird.

His mother easily woke when he softly touched her shoulder. "Oh goodness, Declan, hey ..." she said flustered. "Five-thirty! I cannot believe I slept the afternoon away."

"Hey, you must have needed it," Declan said calmly. "Wanna take the dogs for a walk?"

"Sure, that's a good idea, sweets. Let's do it," she replied.

His father was their regular dog walker. His mom could be considered intermittent at best since he died. The dogs' excitement was beyond their norm over the prospect of a walk, which was always a bit extreme anyways. All his dad had to do was open the closet that housed their leashes and Lucy and Sally assumed a walk was on the horizon. They would jump and dance in their dog way until their leashes were on and headed out the door. The "girls," as his parents often called the dogs, brought them so much joy. Today, the spunky terriers were out of their minds with excitement. Once they finally got their leashes on despite all their jumping, they started down the street.

"Declan, I clearly need to do a better job with the girls. I need to walk them more. Look at how crazy they are right now. Please help me do that by bugging me about it. They deserve more than just couch time. I gotta step up my game, in a lot of ways."

"Sure, Mom," was all he said. He was not going to weigh in on her stepping up, even though he did not think she needed to put that kind of pressure on herself. He felt more comfortable just avoiding the statement.

"I had my weekly meeting with Mr. Z today. I guess I am starting to see the benefit from what he is trying to do. I just hate the monthly written updates I have to do," said Declan, referencing the teacher that ran the Learning Resource Center at his school.

The previous spring, Declan had been diagnosed with

a learning difference that affected his reading speed.

"That's good. I know Mr. Z is an acquired taste. But he helped Ronan quite a bit and I think he will do the same for you. When your father and I first encountered him at a school presentation, we thought he was a bit out there. But, with actual experience with him, I get his value. So, I am glad you are warming up to working with him," said Teddy, appreciative for a substantive update the walk seemingly coaxed out of Declan.

They lived two streets over from the first tiny 1940s bungalow Teddy and Colin purchased, one of the few original houses yet to be knocked down and the lot rebuilt with a McMansion. It was the house Ronan and Declan came home to as infants out of the hospital. Declan suggested a route that didn't pass their old house. He figured it was best to avoid more memories. They all enjoyed the neighborhood. What's not to love about a neighborhood that looks like the one in *Home Alone*? The dogs particularly loved it. They were thrilled to be out with their mama and their brother. Declan and his mother walked in silence, enjoying some fresh air. When they returned, the dogs were happy and tired. Declan suggested reading a letter. Teddy was a bit reluctant.

"I don't know," Teddy said. "Maybe I should take a break with that."

"Really?" replied Declan. "I've really been enjoying them. I've even gone back and read Grandma's and Grandpa's letters."

"That's good," Teddy said. "I have to admit, I have never read theirs, other than the first one."

"They are not as good as Dad's, but they are kinda cool," replied Declan. "Come on, let's read 2010. I read 2009 earlier today because the binder was open on my bed to that letter. Ronan and I are goofy in these letters, aren't we?"

"Okay, let's read one. And, yes, you two are goofy, to say the least."

Teddy attempted a hug and a stomach tickle to which Declan backed away. She seemed to have pushed her luck and needed to realize that seventeen-year-olds don't want hugs and stomach tickles.

Christmas 2010

Well, the McNamara family is all set for Christmas. Teddy outdid herself with a candy cane decorative theme throughout the house. Colin loaded the tree with the family's favorite ornaments, and, most importantly, Ronan and Declan completed their wish lists for Santa. Now comes the best part of the season – the boys' extra-good behavior down the stretch to ensure that Christmas Day is Pay Day (along with being Jesus' B-Day, of course). It's so nice to not hear Declan scream, "Ronan, you are a middle finger!" – which everyone knows means "all the bad words in the world combined." During this peaceful time, here's a look back at some highlights from 2010.

Early in the year, the family escaped to a white wonderland – the Canadian Rockies. Ronan and Declan rarely see one snowflake in Houston, so this problem was rectified with a week in Banff and Lake Louise. The boys got to experience the simple joys of snow – building a snowman, having snowball fights and riding a toboggan – along with more extravagant adventures – dog sleds, horse-drawn sleighs and gondola rides. Ronan will surely have fond memories of his first-time skiing, while Declan may never shake the image of a herd of elk charging after him.

With spring comes baseball, as Declan joined Ronan on the Little League diamond. Always a comedian, Declan's antics didn't often find an audience during the ballgame. He did show promise as a hitter, but his fielding range seemed limited to balls that would roll in his direction and stop at his feet. Ronan continued to love the sport in his machine-pitch league, hitting his first home runs and catching a few pop-ups behind the plate.

In the summer, the boys visited both sets of

grandparents, getting a chance to fish with Colin's parents in San Antonio and garden with Teddy's parents in Ohio. Colin and Teddy also embarked on a little getaway, hitting New Orleans with Notre Dame friends. The summer closed with the annual trip to Lost Pines resort near Austin, where the boys (Colin included) can never get enough of lounging in inner tubes along the Lazy River.

The new school year brought with it a new school. Ronan and Declan now go to Kendall Elementary, which is a five-minute walk down the street. Both boys have made a great adjustment to their new surroundings. Declan, now in kindergarten, has learned to read like a champ, tackling classics like Fun with Dick and Jane. While Declan likes school, his heart still belongs to his Lego creations and Molly, the new family dog. Although he did recently tell the Westie, "You can't go to school 'cause you don't know nothing."

Now a second-grader, Ronan conquered the 300-page Harry Potter and the Sorcerer's Stone. However, Ronan insists, "I like the movie because it goes faster, and it doesn't actually involve your brain." Ronan also joined the Chess Club and compiled a near-perfect record in matches with the family. Teddy's shining moment this year was the school project in which Ronan declared her as "His Hero," while other children made choices like Peyton Manning and

Jackie Chan. Talk about building up a lifetime of brownie points in one fell swoop!

As these final few "silent nights" are enjoyed before the big day, here's wishing you a Christmas filled with peace and happiness!

Colin, Teddy, Ronan and Declan

"That middle finger thing is hilarious," said Declan, laughing. "I need to bring that back."

"Yes, yes, maybe you do," said Teddy, feeling a lot more lighthearted than earlier in the day.

"So, Dad wrote these, right, Mom?" inquired Declan. "Yes, he was the primary author. I edited, and I also gave ideas, but they are truly his baby, so to speak," replied Teddy.

"Were they hard for him to write?" continued Declan.

"Well, he started jotting notes down throughout the year, and that made it a bit easier to remember material that would be good for the letter. But your dad is just a funny guy and a great writer," said Teddy, not realizing she referred to her late husband in the present tense.

Declan noticed the verb choice but didn't say anything. They were having a nice conversation. No need to knock things down. Because of his letters being here in the present,

Declan determined that his father could accurately be referred to as presently a great writer. His logic-driven brain felt good about this conclusion.

"I'm really impressed with how he writes them. They aren't as boring as Grandma's and Grandpa's," Declan commented.

"Well, your dad wrote and edited as a major part of his global communications job at the law firm and in media relations with the Rockets. He was basically a professional writer. And he has a lot more humor than your grandparents. And it's just a different time now than when they were writing theirs. Much of your dad's humor would have been viewed as irreverent back then. So, don't judge. Context is important to keep in mind. Everyone has their own style. What matters is the care that goes into them," said Teddy, always one to take the opportunity for a teaching moment with her children.

"Good point, Mom. I am gonna go study. Call me down for dinner. Thanks," Declan said as he bounded up the stairs. What his mother said about the care that went into the letters being the most important thing, not the style or how well-written, gave Declan a boost as he settled into his math homework.

Chapter Twenty-One

Looking back at 2010 gave Teddy a sense of satisfaction. They decided to change the boys from the Catholic elementary school that Ronan attended for three years and Declan one. Reflecting upon it, this was an important change. The public elementary and middle schools turned out to be the perfect academic and social preparation for her two boys. The Catholic school was just too small and stifling, with the added jab of being socially treacherous for the boys as well as she and Colin. It was hard for Teddy to believe that this little parish school had such student and parent cliques. But worst of all was the fire and brimstone pastor. His arrival was the final straw.

The public elementary and middle schools Ronan and Declan attended were heavily focused on academics as "magnet" schools, serving both boys well. Teddy recalled the stress of making the choice to change schools. The stress level was similar to the decision to hold both of her summer birthday boys back a year grade-wise when they were in Pre-K. She and Colin analyzed and stressed terribly, but the years proved the school change and the holdback decisions to be sound ones. The holdback decision gave Colin and Teddy an extra year with their boys before they set off to college. Although Colin would not get that with Declan, the fact that he had an extra year with Ronan at home felt triumphant given the circumstances.

The trip to Banff and Lake Louise was the first in a series of magical vacations they took with the boys. Everyone thought they were crazy to do such grand trips with small children. That was another decision Teddy did not regret. There is precious little time with them as children, so seeing the world with them before they don't want to be around parents felt like the right strategy to both Teddy and Colin.

The memories created on their trips were tremendous. Not the big sightseeing events, but the little things like the vivid memory of Declan running in terror from a quasi-stampeding elk. The family with these two small children was standing about ten yards away from the herd of elk, enamored by the way they were just hanging out and eating grass near the resort's restaurant. Because of their location, Teddy and Colin assumed it must be safe. When one of the elk's antlers fell off – who knew that was even a thing – the entire herd rushed toward the family. Fortunately, they ended their pursuit quickly. Declan later read that fifty yards was a safe distance to keep between elk and people. Teddy did not feel like the mother of the year after that episode, but to this day, she could not help but smile at the simultaneous fear and hilarity she felt seeing the back of Declan's red-haired head running away in fear.

In need of a snack, Teddy headed into the kitchen, reached into the refrigerator, and saw a container of guacamole. Seeing the container brought her back to the time Colin, the bargain hunter, bought a container of guacamole for her that was about to expire, so it was fifty percent off. He told Teddy about his great bargain and added that buying guacamole for her was a loving gesture, given his hatred of the stuff. He wouldn't even let it touch his plate in restaurants. It was always an elaborate conversation with the waitstaff over the necessary omittance of the guacamole for his order. He went on to say that this meant that his love for her was not expiring, only the guacamole. This monologue was then embellished by him singing, "Don't throw it all away, our guac, our guac. Don't throw it all away, our guac," to the tune of the Bee Gee's song "(Our Love) Don't Throw It All Away."

The memories were seemingly endless and everywhere. Now guacamole was triggering memories!

Teddy's phone rang, and it was Ronan saying he was finally back on the Notre Dame campus after a very long, delay-filled trip.

"Glad you made it. It's never an easy place to get to, especially from Texas," she said.

"Yeah, it was pretty brutal. I am not sure these flight connections to South Bend are worth it. I would have been much better off taking the bus or train," Ronan replied.

"Well, your father made this arrangement for you to fly in and out of South Bend because he thought it would be easier for you on the first trip. He had your best interest at heart," Teddy responded. "Declan and I just read the 2010 Christmas letter."

"You guys still into that?" Ronan asked blandly, as if something had changed since he left that morning.

"Yes, Ronan. It's nice. There was a funny line about

Declan calling you a middle finger, which you guys thought meant every bad word in the world combined," Teddy said, laughing.

"Yeah, I'll admit, that's pretty good," said Ronan. "Remember when he said I called him the B-word to get me in trouble while we were riding scooters? The little idiot wrote it on a piece of paper instead of saying it to you when he tattled, and he spelled it 'B-I-C-H.' After that, we started saying 'chib' when we meant the other word."

"Funny stuff! See!?! These letters are strangely helpful. Aren't these little tidbits good to remember?" said Teddy emphatically.

"Yeah, okay, gotta go. Just wanted to let you know I was here," said Ronan as he hung up, not waiting for a reply.

Teddy thought she felt a little thawing in Ronan. She hoped so. While getting out the ingredients for their dinner, Teddy decided to see if Mr. DeSilva replied. She deleted some junk e-mails that came in before Mr. DeSilva's e-mail, stating that he would be happy to meet any afternoon at three o'clock, which was right after school ended. Teddy figured it would be best to meet once Declan was gone from the campus anyway. Teddy, who was not a procrastinator, replied that she would be there tomorrow at three.

"Boom. I am going to figure you out, Mr. DeSilva," said Teddy to Lucy and Sally, who were waiting for their second scoops of food.

Teddy wanted more, so she read 2011's letter, delaying herself from what she felt was a horribly depressing task: cooking dinner for two. Then, of course, Teddy felt terrible thinking that cooking only for herself and Declan was depressing. She was lucky to have Declan home with her. She should be more appreciative, she scolded herself. The vicious thought cycle that trapped her.

Christmas 2011

As the restless anticipation of Santa's arrival builds in the McNamara home, it's always nice to take a moment to think about the gifts we've received in the 12 months leading up to this Christmas countdown.

This year, Ronan graduated from the children's menu – both at restaurants and in life. With steaks and omelets now topping his list of favorite foods, the third grader got his first taste of football – full contact in helmets and pads with the Texas Football League. Playing left tackle, Ronan found himself torn between protecting the quarterback's blind side and watching the TFL's number one draft pick – Jacoby Lawrence – streak down the field for touchdown after touchdown. Ronan's intensity for the game was not limited to his time on the gridiron, as playing Madden NFL 12 and managing his fantasy football team stood out as his favorite at-home activities.

Declan's longtime Lego love has transitioned into an overall interest in creation and design. The first grader will absorb an episode of his favorite show, How It's Made, and then be off to construct a character, vehicle or tower. After every one of his projects, Declan amazes us with his attention to detail and impressive finished product ... as well as his uncanny knack for leaving the floor covered with scraps of paper, tape and fabric.

After ditching Ronan and Declan on our past transatlantic getaways this year, we caved and brought them along. And they didn't ruin it! In the UK, we retraced the footsteps of both Henry VIII and Harry Potter – from the Tower of London to Platform 9¾. We also hit the rails, visiting Oxford University (where several Harry Potter movies were filmed) and Scotland's capital city of Edinburgh (where JK Rowling wrote the Harry Potter series). In hindsight, the Harry Potter thing probably got a bit out of control ... as evidenced by Rupert Grint's restraining order against Teddy.

In London, the boys loved Andrew Lloyd Webber's The

Wizard of Oz and Hamleys — the famous seven-story toy store. Teddy was a big fan of London shopping as well, as she was treated to a diamond ring from Liberty to celebrate 10 years of marriage. Colin also celebrated the milestone by taking the family on a weeklong tour of the city's finest pubs. Such responsible parenting!

We did enjoy our anniversary, minus the kids, with a weekend in New Orleans, which was a little less classy. Highlights included a naked bicycle race (not us) and 72-ounce beers (definitely Colin). Teddy must be on the edge of her seat for what awaits at the 25-year mark: 2 -for-1 bowling on $3 pitcher night?

One final item: Please note our new address, as we have just settled into our new home. This marks our third house within a two-mile radius. I'm sure you are anxiously awaiting our future change-of-address announcement to the house next door. In the meantime, here's wishing you a wonderful Christmas season!

Colin, Teddy, Ronan and Declan

Teddy sat frozen, thinking back to that trip. The boys were so young, especially Declan at just six years old. The poor little guy was so small that he was frequently smothered on the London Tube because the trains were so packed with adult bodies. Now that the adventures of the family four-pack were cut short far too early, Teddy was so happy that they had these times together. With that positive thought that kept her anger at Colin at bay for the moment, she pulled herself off the couch and into the kitchen to make some type of sustenance for herself and her youngest.

Chapter Twenty-Two

Up in his room, Declan didn't begin studying right away. He decided to take a page out of his dad's "handbook" for letter writing by jotting down notes. Given that he didn't know this task would present itself to him this year, Declan didn't have the luxury of taking notes along the way, but he would do his best to reflect on the year and think of highlights and items for comic relief.

- Ronan graduated from high school

- They went to Sedona for a vacation

- Worked at BioGen

- Ronan went to ND

- Dad

That was it. Five items landed on Declan's list of topics, with the fifth simply listed as "Dad."

"Man, this sucks," he thought as he put the list away and went to something a lot less aggravating: AP Algebra II. Declan's coursework was rigorous. His goal was to at least get into Notre Dame and maybe something even more prestigious. His other goal was to beat Ronan's impressive SAT score. Nothing like brotherly rivalry to bring out the best in academic performances. To be fair, Declan was naturally studious and a more serious student and person than Ronan.

As his mind worked on the numbers, it strayed to thinking through how he would deal with his father's passing in the letter if he did indeed write the damn thing. Once again, he began to doubt himself and his conviction.

Mercifully, his mom called him down for dinner and interrupted his mind's fight between numbers that always resulted in a solution versus the unsolvable madness that was this letter and the root cause for his attempting it: his father's passing. Unlike numbers and problems in his Algebra work, nothing made sense about his family's situation.

Declan and his mother made small talk as they ate their "naked pasta," as his mother called pasta with just butter, olive oil and salt. It was one of their favorite dishes, and they quietly enjoyed it that evening, as always.

Declan kept toying with the idea of telling his mom about trying to write the letter, but he kept stopping himself. There was something inside of him that just knew the comfort she was getting from reading the letters would not translate into the idea of writing a letter this year without her husband.

The silly dish of "naked pasta" that his mother had made for him without his asking crystallized his feelings. His mother and father always anticipated his and his brother's feelings and needs. Being the children of the household, neither he nor his brother did that very well. The simple act of his mother making something he loved to eat motivated Declan to write the letter as a gift to her, as opposed to a project with her, where she would inevitably bear the bulk of the work and anxiety. If it became a joint project, she would feel the pressure he was feeling. He wanted to spare her that, and if it turned out well, the letter would be a sign from him that they were going to survive this. Yes, plain pasta gave him the courage to take on the daunting Christmas letter task. If they liked the finished product, they could mail it to friends and family. Otherwise, it could be something the family shared only as a three-pack.

Declan knew he was blessed to have his parents. He heard stories from other kids about the crazy things that went on in their houses, and he was always thankful for the stable environment he had always enjoyed. He was one of the lucky ones, even though having two parents was cut short.

At dinner a year or so ago, the topic of abortion came up. Ronan brought up if Teddy's mother chose to have an abortion rather than have Teddy after a nine-year gap in her childbearing career. The boys contemplated what would have come of them if they had a different mother. Would they even exist? Declan arrived at the conclusion that he would still be him, but "just not as on top of stuff." Teddy laughed until she had tears in her eyes. The entire family appreciated his unique way of showing his appreciation for his mother's organization and support. Something inside of him wanted to be there for his mom now – during her greatest time of need.

"This letter could be just what she needs, and I am going to make it happen, no matter how tough it is," he thought with resolve.

After dinner, Declan asked his mother if she wanted to read another letter. She confessed that she needed a little jolt that afternoon and already read 2011. Declan didn't mind skipping years. He knew he would ultimately read them all, albeit out of order. They settled in on the couch, as was becoming a nice little habit for both of them and grabbed the binder. Lucy and Sally also enjoyed this extra couch time with

Declan, as this Christmas letter-reading habit continued on.

Christmas 2012

Christmastime is here again, which means it's time for another play-by-play account of all that stirred in the McNamara house over the past year.

Declan embraced martial arts this year and joined the local dojo. He is clearly into it, as he puts up with Colin's constant singing of "Glory of Love" from Karate Kid, Part II. The eight-year-old has advanced to yellow belt-blue stripe, his fourth belt in nine months, and now trains in an accelerated program called the Black Belt Club. His interest in martial arts even has a distant connection to Declan's other passion, Lego, as he has become a big fan of its ninja toys called Ninjago. Declan's Lego love made its way to school, where he impresses classmates with his mechanical creations at their weekly robotics club.

Ronan continues to find nonstop joy in the wide world of sports: playing, rooting, fantasy GM-ing, hobnobbing and, most recently, sportscasting. He donned the anchorman blazer and went viral with his YouTube video, "Notre Dame's #1 Fan," describing Irish football's magical run to atop the polls. In competition, the 10-year-old helped his baseball team win the Longfellow Little League championship and then led his hoops squad in scoring – accounting for more than ¾ of its points. As parents, we somewhat convinced ourselves that Ronan wasn't a ball hog and was simply operating within the flow of the offense. Colin also used his old connections to give Ronan a chance to meet two of his sports heroes, Dirk Nowitzki of the Dallas Mavericks and Arian Foster of the Houston Texans.

Teddy made one of the biggest changes in the family this year, exiting the corporate world on a full-time basis. She formed Teddy McNamara Marketing, giving her the opportunity to share her talents with clients while allowing her the freedom to enjoy the family much more. She also fulfilled her lifelong dream of teaching, contributing frequently as a substitute at our sons' school. Teddy often brings home notes of admiration from her students and even received the following word problem from one of the kids: Ms. McNamara has 2,000 pairs of shoes. She keeps them in 20 boxes. How many shoes are in each box? The bigger question is this: How did this student know the number of shoes in Teddy's closet?

Colin was promoted to media relations director at Neelan Fuller in the spring, and the law firm recently announced its combination with London-based Horton Bridgewell. Colin told Ronan that the transaction would make the firm the third biggest in the world, to which Ronan quickly responded, "Are you talking about the number of employees or profit? Because I'm more concerned about profit," When Colin wasn't fielding tough questions from reporters or family, he did enjoy a guys weekend with his brother Brendan and Notre Dame classmates in Oklahoma, watching the Fighting Irish upset the Sooners enroute to a perfect regular season.

So, while we're really trying hard not to be the obnoxious Notre Dame fans that people despise, it's a challenge when you have two ND grads who were married on campus and even had their boys baptized there. We're strongly considering a trip to Miami for the title game next month, although we still need to find game tickets. That feat might require a Christmas miracle from Santa Claus or his shady cousin, Scalper Claus. Here's hoping that your dreams also come true this holiday season.

Colin, Teddy, Ronan and Declan

"Remember me subbing at your school?" inquired Teddy.

"Yes, I know you really liked doing that, Mom."

"Yep, it was a lot of fun. Remember, all the kids loved me! You were all so sweet and cute then. Good memories,

Declan. Really good memories," she said, giving her son a big squeeze, which he tried his very best not to retreat from.

"Okay, Mom, I am heading upstairs. Do you mind if I take the binder?" Declan asked.

"No, of course not, Declan. Here you go," Teddy responded, handing him the book.

Chapter Twenty-Three

She sat back, thinking about how the real story of her departure from corporate life at that time was not completely voluntary. The new leadership at the firm decided they disliked her flexible work arrangement, so she was given ninety days to move on within the company. She chose not to look for something else and leave the firm quietly, but still, she grappled with the notion of being basically fired. She thought back to how much she loved subbing, which she was trying out as a way to decide whether to pursue teaching at that time.

However, the financial stress of her not maximizing her earning potential reared its head when a former boss begged her to come back to work for him. The big paycheck would help with the increasingly expensive children, and college expenses were less than ten years away. Annual tuition increases indicated that Notre Dame would be eighty thousand dollars per year if that long-term family goal came to be. So, she pushed her dreams to the side and did what was necessary for her family.

Much more importantly, she wondered if reading these was healthy for Declan. Ronan obviously did not think they were a good idea. Declan seemed to be into them. Ugh. One upsetting thought led to another.

Now that she had a meeting with Mr. DeSilva scheduled, what was she going to say? Accuse him of being a child predator? What had he really done? Shown an interest in her son during a hard time. My God. What was she doing? She needed rules! She needed guidance, but alas, there was none.

With those upsetting thoughts, she called Dana. There was a little of the usual small talk, check-in type stuff. Then Teddy launched into the reason for her call. Teddy was glad to hear that Dana was coping well with her daughter being away at school and that Emily was doing well at Stanford. But she was eager to get Dana's take on the letters and DeSilva.

"Do you think it's unhealthy to let Declan read the

Christmas letters?" asked Teddy. "Tell me the truth."

"Oh, so you are still reading them. Great. To answer your question though, no. Why on earth would it be unhealthy?"

"Well, I don't know. The holidays are obviously going to be hard this year, and I don't know if continuing to immerse Declan in all these memories is good for him. The letters are helping me, but I just don't know if it's a healthy teen activity – even though I started it with him," Teddy said, feeling guilty.

"Well, how has he been lately? I know he skipped school in the beginning and was not sharing with you," responded Dana.

"He's shockingly been more communicative than he normally was, prior to the accident even," said Teddy, realizing what she had just said. Declan was opening up, not shutting down. "That has to be a good thing, no?"

"Yes, then I think you have your answer, Teddy."

"Bahhhhh! I guess I am overthinking things. I am just so fearful of not getting this right. But who the heck knows what right is in this situation?"

"Precisely," said Dana. "You are not forcing him to read them. Rather, it sounds like he is seeking the connection, and you are seeing positive behavior and reaction from him, not negative. So run with it."

"I hate to keep you, but there is one more thing."

"I'm listening," replied Dana.

"Declan's English teacher has been talking to him about his feelings and stuff," explained Teddy.

"When?" asked Dana.

"Well, I guess in free periods or their community time type thing."

"Oh, got it. I thought you might be saying that he was talking to him about his father in class or something insane like that. Glad that it's not that."

"No, no. It seems like proper timing and place, but, regardless, should I be concerned?"

"Gosh, I don't know why you would be, unless he is talking about weird stuff. Is he?" asked Dana.

"No, no, no. It seems all normal. Like they talked about golf and, somehow, our Christmas letters came up too. I guess he is just trying to be a friend to him. He apparently lost his wife a couple years ago, so I suspect he thinks he can be more empathetic than most people."

"Hmmm, well, let it play out then."

"So, would you say my meeting with this DeSilva character tomorrow would be overkill?"

Dana let out a little chuckle.

"Not laughing at you, Teddy. No, it's not overkill. It is your right. And I can understand how on eggshells you are about, well, everything. So, more for you than Declan, go chat with the guy. Do you know what he's like?

"Deck just said he was a nerd."

"Well, great, go have a chat with a little English teaching nerd. Just try not to interrogate him too badly, Teddy! He is Declan's teacher, and you do not want to scar him."

"Okay, yeah. I will go easy on the dork! Thanks for the consult. Always appreciate a sanity check. Maybe tea on Saturday?" said Teddy.

"Yes, let's go to the tearoom. I'll make reservations," said Dana.

Teddy sat back, thinking about how to approach Mr. DeSilva. She laughed about Dana fearing for the poor guy. She really could not prepare for this chat. It was not like some sort of work meeting where she knew precisely how to organize herself. Again, there are no rules for talking to the teacher trying to befriend your teenage son after the death of his father. Imagine!

Completely exasperated, Teddy pulled the 2012 letter back towards her. The memories came rushing. Ronan's video that they posted on YouTube was absolutely adorable. He was a little fourth grader decked out in a sports coat and tie, giving an analysis of ND's football season and the march to the national championship game. The visual of Ronan and Colin recording this precious footage in their kitchen was priceless, mainly because Ronan's voice was still so high, yet his delivery was so serious. There was no script and only a few takes.

Ronan and Colin's love of sports was at the core of their relationship. This production was forever proof of their love because what's on the Internet lives forever. Teddy believed Colin somehow passed his detailed and analytical love of sports genetically to Ronan. She hadn't watched the video called "Notre Dame's #1 Fan" in many years, so she pulled it up on her phone and simultaneously cried tears of joy and sorrow. She had not thought of this piece in her precious memory collection for quite some time.

Chapter Twenty-Four

Declan had a new resolve, and that meant reading the rest of the letters to give him full knowledge of the letters' foundation before making his own attempt. He wanted to create the letter and have it ready for Thanksgiving. He felt sharing it on that day would be a good way to kick off the holiday season. A way to pay homage to his dad but to demonstrate to his mom that they could do it. They could persevere.

He knew Thanksgiving was his mother's favorite because it started the festive month ahead. She seemed to like the buildup more than the actual events of Christmas and New Year's. He hoped that his letter could provide some positivity to what would most certainly be a bleak holiday season.

Declan realized that he not only needed to read the letters for comfort and enjoyment, like his mother was doing, but that he needed to read the letters like he would for a literature class. Dissect and analyze them for things like style, tone and storytelling construction. Although his junior year was filled with many tough Advanced Placement classes important for his future college options, Declan was committed to making the letter a top priority. This gift to his mother and tribute to his father just mattered more to him. Something being more important than school was a message he rarely heard in his house, but he just knew this was an exceptional time. Declan knew he was right.

He sat back and read the letters that his mother had read without him. Those were of the early years of which he had no true recollection except for the planted memories from his parents' storytelling and their meticulously kept photo albums, which were another product of his father. His mom always joked that Colin was the only male scrapbooker on earth, to which he would say, "They are not scrapbooks. They are photo albums." In later years, Colin embraced the word scrapbooking to describe his hobby, even joking about it with friends and dubbing himself "The Crinkle-Cut Gangsta" in reference to the craftmaking scissors.

Declan's parents truly loved each other. They used to "play argue" about who was going to do a certain chore, each genuinely proclaiming they wanted to do whatever that given unglamorous task may be. Declan realized now that they were a cohesive team that he didn't entirely see at the moment, when he would think to himself, "Are you people crazy? Arguing over who is going to pick up the dog poop? It seems backward ... with you two actually fighting over who gets the chance to do it?" They treated each other well and were always giving to each other in big and small ways. Declan wondered how you find a match like that.

Looking around his room, Declan could not deny the many Lego references in the early letters. His room still had many of his more advanced sets on display. Hogwarts Castle and R2-D2 were two of his triumphs for which he still felt a sense of pride. He read his way to 2013, where he and his mother left off. Declan felt a bit guilty about reading without her, but he knew he had to do it to achieve his goal.

Christmas 2013

2013 kicked off with a boom as the McNamara family dashed off to Florida for an early January getaway. Universal Orlando's Spider-Man, Harry Potter and Despicable Me 3D rides provided a fun opening act before the main event in Miami – the BCS National Championship Game between #1 Notre Dame and #2 Alabama. Since Teddy witnessed the last Irish championship firsthand in 1989, Colin and Ronan headed to this title match after a day of family tailgating. Of course, the bout turned out to be a first-round knockout, with the Irish on the losing end. The blowout was unfortunate, but the overall experience was truly once in a lifetime.

Football season quickly shifted to basketball, which remains Ronan's passion. This year, our 11-year-old played on three teams and participated in camps with Notre Dame, the Houston Rockets and "The Beard," James Harden. Ronan's love of hoops extends beyond playing the game, as athlete-branded shoes and, if you can believe it, socks now top his wish list. The Rockets gave him a great gift by acquiring Dwight "Superman" Howard on his birthday. Colin and Ronan shared their second championship experience of the year at the NBA Finals, witnessing the Spurs take down LeBron and the Heat in Game 5 before San Antonio, too, saw its title hopes fade away in Miami.

While one of our boys hits the hardwood, our youngest son literally splinters it! Breaking boards with spin kicks and hand chops illustrates Declan's martial arts achievement, as our nine-year-old has progressed to the intermediate level of red belt-brown stripe. When Declan's not causing destruction at the dojo, he's building at home, constructing masterpieces in Lego, origami, wood and, even digitally, on his favorite videogame, Minecraft. Declan also received his First Eucharist this spring, and the picky eater gave God the seal of approval on the Communion host with the comment, "I don't know what's in that, but it's sure tasty!" We celebrated Declan's special occasion with his grandparents and Aiden, Declan's Godfather and Colin's brother, at his favorite Japanese steakhouse.

The year's big family vacation brought us to Ireland and England. On the Emerald Isle, the boys got to play soccer with their distant Irish cousins and visit the exact Cliffs of Moher ledge where we got engaged way back in 2000. Other Ireland highlights included archery at Dromoland Castle, horseback riding through the Gap of Dunloe, exploring the prehistoric fort Dun Aengus on the Aran Islands and kissing the legendary stone at Blarney Castle. Colin felt like the luckiest leprechaun when we stumbled upon "free admission day" to Ireland's castles, prompting a whirlwind of fortress tours broken up with the requisite pub stops.

In England, London forever provides new adventures, as we experienced its newest skyscraper called the Shard, the punk scene at Camden Market, a theatre production of

Charlie & the Chocolate Factory and Teddy's favorite, a tour of Warner Bros. Leavesden Studios where the Harry Potter movies were made. For a little kid-free fun, we caught Harry Potter star Daniel Radcliffe in the West End play The Cripple of Inishmaan and British pop star Robbie Williams in concert at Wembley Stadium. The boys found sheer delight in the little things on the trip, like the street juggler known as "The Man with Big Balls" and an equally sophisticated game they created themselves called "Count the number of private parts in the exhibits at the British Museum!"

Another notable highlight from this year was our 2,000-mile cross-country drive to Notre Dame, where Teddy and the boys participated in the school's alumni family volunteer camp. The kids really enjoyed their week of helping out at the thrift shop, soup kitchen and retirement home, while Teddy introduced them to dorm life and dining hall food under the Golden Dome. We hope to make this a family tradition for years to come.

Speaking of traditions, that just about wraps up our annual Christmas letter. Kiddo updates: Check. Vacation updates: Check. Work updates: Don't bore the reader. We wish you and your loved ones the very best throughout this special season!

Colin, Teddy, Ronan and Declan

Boy, that was a packed year, thought Declan. This letter had sort of the obvious checklist for the writer. He chuckled to himself, wondering if his dad could see him right now in his attempt to fill his writing shoes. He sure hoped his dad was watching and could give him the strength and talent to pull it off.

Declan continued reading letters until he fell asleep just before 2020's letter, his dad's last.

Chapter Twenty-Five

Teddy wandered upstairs around ten that night. She kept dozing off on the couch, so she decided she should just go to bed. Another day behind her. She looked in on Declan, and there he was with the binder on his lap, sound asleep. She picked up the book, noticing that it was open to 2020's letter. The end, she thought sadly, with no more of Colin's letters to come.

She rolled Declan over and covered him up. She threw herself into her bed and cried, clutching the binder.

On her way to St. Michael's the next day, Teddy could not stop thinking about teaching. She assumed driving to a school was why these thoughts crept into her brain. She scolded herself, however, as she was supposed to be thinking of Declan and the potential creeper. And how she was going to politely interrogate him. Mom duty first, Teddy's needs second. Isn't that the mother's oath?

The families at the high school were extremely supportive. Of course, the Mothers' Club jumped into action, setting up delivered meals. In this instance, Teddy was thankful for being part of a tightknit high school community. Oftentimes, Teddy had to battle with her love-hate relationship with the mothers she frequently encountered, especially the hyper-involved ones. The level of competition and judgment between the different types of mothers annoyed Teddy to her core. Wasn't it all hard enough without the high school-like games, she would frequently think to herself. There is no right way, and it's all hard. Any path should be acceptable.

But it may have been Teddy herself who was her worst enemy because she crafted the hardest situation for herself. She was a full-time working mom but attempted to operate like a stay-at-home mom, which included home cooking, chauffeur duty and involvement at school. Her flexible work arrangement, which allowed her to work a compressed schedule and leave the office for afterschool pickups at three o'clock, was a blessing and a curse. Jamming a full-time job into fewer hours so she could leave early and rush to a second job of motherhood. Yay. Later, when she was able to work from home full-time, long before everyone did because of COVID-19, she found the same blessing and curse combination. Yay, no commute, not so yay that she felt compelled to do household chores like laundry during the workday.

Teddy loved the campus. The giant, sprawling oak trees created a canopy over the quad that was idyllic. She walked the sidewalk to Xavier Hall to meet DeSilva. She still did not know what she intended to say to this man, never having a conversation remotely close to this situation. She felt a bit embarrassed about questioning his intention, but she was committed to exercising her right to find out about him. She was in "mama bear" mode.

She found his office on the second floor of the administrative building and knocked on his half-open door.

"Come in," Mr. DeSilva's baritone voice called.

Teddy took a breath and pushed the door fully open. "Hello, Mr. DeSilva?"

"Yes, are you Mrs. McNamara?

"Oh yes, so sorry not introducing myself," said a flustered Teddy.

Mr. DeSilva did not look like the teacher nerd she envisioned. Mr. DeSilva was about fifty-five years old and handsome as could be. Dark hair, a hint of silver at the temples, tanned skin, and warm chocolate-brown eyes.

Gaining her composure, Teddy said, "Thank you for taking the time to talk to me today. I appreciate it."

"Happy to, Mrs. McNamara."

"Well, I am not sure how to start. I guess first, it seems that Declan is doing fine in his studies in your class. Am I right about that?" Teddy asked.

"Indeed, Declan is a tremendous student. He works hard, but he also really uses his brain. Some of the perspectives he brings to class are quite unique and well-formed for a student his age. More like a college student than high school."

This brought a delighted smile to Teddy's face.

"That is terrific to hear. I am glad he has kept up that quality. Since kindergarten, his teachers have always commented that, while he's on the quieter side, he asks some interesting questions and brings unique perspectives. Glad it didn't die as he grew up with society and peer pressure beating that quality out of him."

"Ha! No, your Declan is keeping his edge."

"So, um, the other thing I wanted to chat about is your talking to Declan about the loss of his father, um, my husband," Teddy commented.

"Yes, I don't know if he told you that my lovely wife passed away two years ago from breast cancer," shared Mr. DeSilva. "That experience made me think that I could be a resource for Declan. Maybe pay it forward because I was lucky to have people around me to help me through it."

Teddy's frosty, broken heart melted a bit, hearing Mr. DeSilva share his loss of someone he clearly loved deeply and express his kind intentions toward her son.

"I am very sorry to hear that, Mr. DeSilva. Declan may have told me. Yes, I think he did. I am not my usual sharp self these days. I am sure you remember the haze," responded Teddy.

"Yes, I do remember the haze. And I am very sorry for your tragic loss too."

His smooth voice and deep eyes calmed Teddy. She no longer feared he was some sort of crazy person, but she was still going to ask more questions. There was something about him. Teddy wanted to learn more about this Mr. DeSilva.

"Thank you. I just want to be sure anyone talking to Declan about this topic is good for him. I am sure you can imagine that my protective mama bear instincts are on high alert."

"I understand. I am very sorry that I overstepped. I can see that now. It was not my intention. Maybe I should have contacted you first. It really all came about organically one day. I just felt compelled to reach out to him and engage on this topic. I did not have a plan or a specific goal."

"Well, I guess I am comfortable with it now that I know you a bit. It just felt a bit odd when he told me his English teacher was sort of grief counseling him," Teddy explained.

"Oh goodness, no. I do not pretend to be a grief counselor. I am still on the road to recovery myself. I just want to be a resource for him. Ahem, and I am a literature teacher, by the way."

"Goodness, I am so sorry that I misspoke about your subject, Mr. DeSilva! I did not mean to insult you. Declan uses the terms interchangeably, so I have followed suit. I understand there is a difference! And, sorry for the interrogation. I see you mean well. We all need as much meaning well as we can get."

"I did not interpret it as an interrogation. And you can

call me Sam. You do not need to call me Mr. DeSilva," he said.

A slight tingle went through Teddy when Mr. DeSilva mentioned his first name.

"Oh no, I have a rule that teachers should be addressed formally, even by parents. Just a little thing I have," Teddy said brightly with a bit of a giggle.

"Very well, Mrs. McNamara, I will follow your lead when I address you," Mr. DeSilva said politely with a bit of a sparkle in his eyes.

"So, do you mind if I ask you about teaching? I am considering getting into that field. Your perspective would be helpful to me. I always saw myself teaching elementary school when I was young, but now, if I get into it, I think junior high or high school may be a better fit for me."

"Of course, I absolutely love teaching, and we certainly need more good teachers today!"

Teddy and Mr. DeSilva talked for nearly forty-five minutes. Neither realized the time was passing, and the clock was about to hit four o'clock. It just came easy and natural for both of them.

"It's almost four. I better let you get back to it, and I want to be home before Declan comes home from golf practice. I don't like him to be in the house alone. So depressing ... Oh gosh, sorry. I didn't mean ..." said Teddy, realizing she may have hit a tender spot for Mr. DeSilva.

"Yes, you are correct. Home alone can be depressing, so yes, go and beat Declan home," Mr. DeSilva replied tenderly.

Their eyes locked for a mere second then Teddy whisked herself out the office door. She stood outside the door in the hallway to gather herself. What transpired in Mr. DeSilva's office was perplexing to her. There were moments of what she thought may have been flirting. Or maybe she was so old she did not even know what flirting was anymore. The guy was just being nice. She scolded herself for these bizarre thoughts and walked briskly to the car so that she could arrive home before Declan.

Chapter Twenty-Six

The days slowly advanced until Saturday finally came, the day of Teddy's lunch with Dana. It was the first social thing on her calendar since *it*. It felt good to do something from her pre-accident life. Teddy preferred to think of it as pre-accident versus pre-death, pre-widow or all of the other ways in which to phrase "before my husband died."

She and her friend frequently met for lunch to just talk. Their relationship moved well beyond bonding about their children, which many adult female relationships really are at their heart. In fact, they often didn't discuss their children at all. Their relationship was one of kindred spirits. They were both practical and real – in a world of impractical and unreal in their affluent neighborhood, where every other car seemed to now be a Tesla. Of their group of Kendall Elementary moms who regularly chatted after school on the playground, Teddy and Dana were the only two who didn't have spectacular divorces with infidelity stories that seemed straight out of trashy novels. Never did it cross Teddy's mind that she would be spouseless for a far more horrific reason.

Right before she was about to head out the door, Dana texted, asking that she bring the Christmas letters. Teddy found it an odd request given Dana had been a recipient of the letter for more than fifteen years now, but she complied.

At their cozy antique table, surrounded by unique tea-themed wall art, they ordered their favorite: a honeysuckle fig oolong tea. The delicious brew was comforting. Teddy couldn't remember the last time she tasted it. As she sipped quietly, Dana shared how hard it had been with Emily at college.

"You think you are ready, but then you are home alone thinking, my reward for having raised a competent child is to be left high and dry. All you get is a phone call here and there," laughed Dana, covering her sadness with jokes.

"And when they do call, it's short and sweet. Transactional almost. I hear ya," Teddy empathized. "How is

Diego handling it?"

"Well, you know," Dana replied. "He is quiet about it. But he does make comments about how he doesn't hear from her. But he also doesn't call her. It's a game of 'pride chicken' for him, I think. I know he misses her, but he's not going to be the one frequently reaching out."

"Yeah, I can see that with Diego. Men, they are just a strange bunch, right?"

Teddy knew it had been hard for Dana to send Emily off to college. Dana and Emily were extremely close, and Dana was rightfully so very protective of her. Having a stillborn child prior to Emily seems like a quite reasonable impetus for being protective of your only child. Teddy's tragedy didn't leave much open airtime for Dana to discuss her struggles. Teddy was mindful today to focus on someone other than herself. Dana shared that she realized that she just needed to let herself feel all the feelings, mourning that the mom-with-kids-at-home part of her life was over.

Teddy always felt thankful to have two children, but Dana sharing her feelings about her only child made her realize how much more difficult her circumstances would have been if Ronan had been an only child. It was hard to see him off, the buildup being worse than the assigned "say goodbye for now" time when she and Colin left him in his dorm. Dropping Ronan off at Notre Dame was the last significant milestone they shared. "I guess it was fitting," thought Teddy to herself while continuing to sip her tea.

Thankfully, Dana really enjoyed her job in Human Resources. She went back to work full-time when Emily was about ten or eleven. It's a very good thing that she is so entrenched in her career, now that her only child is out of the house. Teddy realized that she was not entrenched in anything but grief.

Dana turned the conversation to Teddy. They discussed the holidays, which loomed ever closer.

"I'm starting to get used to daily life," Teddy said. "But holidays of peace, love and joy just feel like a hurdle much too high for me and the boys. A complete farce, in fact."

"Yes, I understand how that could appear completely beyond your capabilities. What are you thinking of doing?" asked Dana.

"Ronan is coming home for both holidays, despite Thanksgiving being such a short break. I just need him home. And being alone up there would be horrible for him. I guess I will just do our normal 'at home' holidays. We rarely went anywhere when Colin was alive, so I don't feel compelled to go to his parents or to anyone in my family now. Sue, Colin's mom, invited me. But … no, thank you."

"Makes sense. You know you and the boys are welcome to our house if a change of scenery might help."

"Hmm, yeah, maybe. I guess I need to really start thinking about this. It is now November," said Teddy, in disbelief that she had made it nearly two months without Colin.

"So, what about these letters?" inquired Dana, changing tact.

"What do you mean?"

"It sounds like they are a positive thing, curious how you are feeling about them and whether you will do one this year."

"Yes, I think they have been positive for me and for Declan. But absolutely not; I will not be writing one without Colin. First, I am not capable and, second, well, I just couldn't," said Teddy tearfully.

"Understood," said Dana, reaching across the tiny table to comfort Teddy but being careful not to knock down the tray of afternoon tea goodies, including finger sandwiches, scones, macarons, and tiny pastries.

"Could I see them? I'm just so curious about them as a collection, I guess," asked Dana.

"Sure," Teddy responded, handing over the covered in its gawdy Christmas fabric cover and calligraphy letters declaring it 'The McNamara Family Christmas Letters.' Dana held it up to Teddy and said laughingly, "I take it you did not select this cover!" She then carefully leafed through each page enclosed in its plastic page protector.

"This really is amazing, having Colin's entire childhood and then your lives together chronicled like this," said Dana in awe.

"I agree. Although I've read them for the last twenty-two years, I never focused on the collection of them until Colin was gone, obviously. I agree that there is something unique about the story they tell. Even if sometimes the story is stilted towards the positive," Teddy chuckled.

"What do you mean?"

"Well, as you can imagine, these gloss over the hard times. Like one of the reasons for our first move was because a pedophile moved in next door! There are several references to my job and various flexible arrangements that I maneuvered for myself. My constant job changes were a play to 'stay alive' with a career while doing my best impersonation of a full-time mom. Colin made it all sound so easy, while it was the exact opposite. I realize that wouldn't make good Christmas letter reading, but it is one thing that jumps out at me as I look back, among other things, of course. There are some cute stories. It's hard for me to believe that I am now finally not working, and it's just me and Declan at home. I would have killed to not work much earlier. Anyway—stuff like that, I'm rambling."

"I can see what you mean about the bright and shiny take on everything, but I will tell you, as an avid reader of these, the letters were a Christmas highlight in our house," said Dana. "Mind if we read one together now?"

"Um, really? I, I guess," said Teddy, completely unprepared.

"Which one?" asked Dana.

"Well, I stopped at 2013 last night. I am trying to space them out because I am dreading how I will surely feel when there are no more letters to read."

"2014 it is," said Dana as she opened the binder to the proper page and began reading aloud.

Christmas 2014

As holiday greetings go digital, it's becoming a bigger

challenge to find the perfect letterhead for our annual Christmas letter. This stationery struggle has even driven Colin to hoarder status, as he now stockpiles these precious paper rations for future years. We may not prepare for Houston's formidable hurricane season, but we've got Christmas correspondence covered through 2017!

Our 2014 was highlighted by a summer vacation to Hawaii. On Kauai, a sunset catamaran cruise along the Na Pali Coast stood out as a favorite moment for Teddy – and not just because she thought Colin looked Selleck-esque in his Magnum PI Hawaiian shirt. Riding the North Shore waves, Ronan and Declan were quick learners in their first surfing experience. Declan proudly proclaimed to us many times, "I never fell off my board!"

We were on cloud nine when our plane tour flew us over locations from Raiders of the Lost Ark, Jurassic Park and Fantasy Island (Yes, we were in "dee plane! dee plane!"). On the Big Island, we loved Punalu'u Beach with its giant sea turtles and stunning black sand. Hovering above volcanoes oozing lava in an open-air helicopter and snorkeling among the tropical fish also amazed us.

A getaway to the Big Apple at spring break was full of entertainment. We absolutely rank Rocky the Musical as an all-time theater favorite. Sadly, the show's Broadway run lasted only slightly longer than Apollo Creed did against Ivan Drago. Other Manhattan memories included "The Art of the Brick" Lego sculpture exhibit, ice skating at 30 Rock, a Knicks game at Madison Square Garden and the St. Patrick's Day parade – a Guinness-fueled, all-day event that would wear out even the most spirited leprechaun.

As far as kiddo updates, Declan continues to matriculate through the elementary school ranks, with the fourth grader building complex Lego devices and making intricate Minecraft designs in his free time. Declan is advancing toward a black belt in martial arts, breaking boards with his hands and feet, sparring with classmates and mastering his weapons arsenal of a staff, sword and nunchucks.

Ronan transitioned to Walter Cronkite Middle School, an acclaimed school and famous news anchor's alma mater. We were convinced of its academic prestige when our son came off the school bus asking Teddy, "What's a lap dance?" He has also started playing AAU basketball on a team affiliated with the Houston Rockets, whose star player, James Harden, came to cheer on the youngsters from the bench.

On the grown-up front, Teddy's consulting business allows her to share her marketing talents while keeping the family running smoothly. For Colin, the global expansion of his law firm has resulted in business trips to his favorite place in the world, London.

We hope you enjoyed our holiday update, now in its 20th year. We look forward to sharing future editions for years to come ... or at least until electronic communication eliminates the US Postal Service altogether. For this Christmas season, we wish you the very best!

Colin, Teddy, Ronan and Declan

Teddy had tears in her eyes when Dana finished and looked up from the page. No more words were spoken. They just paid the bill and walked to the parking lot.

"Thanks for sharing the letter with me, Teddy," said Dana, giving her friend a tight hug.

"They really are special, aren't they?"

"Yes, they are, Teddy. A real gift. Even though Colin glossed over your working mom situation, he meant well. You know that?" Teddy gave Dana a knowing smile.

"Yes, I guess it's just part of me admitting that I am mad at him sometimes. His stupid accident was more than a bit his fault. I guess raging at the letters in my mind is more allowable than raging about him for leaving me," Teddy sniffled.

The pair of friends stood quietly for a few minutes while Teddy gained her composure.

"Hey, sorry this lunch ended up being all about me again. I really wanted to focus on you. I am glad you shared how you are feeling about your life being in transition. I think you are on the right path. Just feel the feelings," said Teddy resignedly. "There's no other way. Thanks for the sage advice, friend."

The friends hugged goodbye, and then Dana abruptly said, "Wait, did you interrogate Mr. DeSilva? I nearly forgot about that poor nerd."

"Ha ha, you know, Dana, I don't eat raw red meat for breakfast. I am nice and polite! Yes, we met. It was good. He does not seem to be a sociopath. So, mother duty number five hundred and fifteen – ensure son is not engaging with sociopathic teacher – is complete."

"Good, I kind of figured the English nerd would be fine. And Teddy, more people around you guys is not a bad thing right now."

"Yes, you are right," Teddy agreed. "I need to loosen up a bit, I suppose. It's just hard for me. I still feel that I need to be in lockdown, a bit of a pandemic-era approach to things, until I know we are all safe. And, by the way, friend, Mr. DeSilva is not a nerd. That's all I am going to say. Leave them wanting more is the saying, right?" laughed Teddy as she hopped in her white VW Beetle.

Dana's confused look made Teddy laugh out loud as she drove off. It had been a while since she had a bit of a laugh.

Back home, Declan scooped up the Christmas letter binder that his mom had put on the counter when she returned from her lunch. It was a Saturday afternoon, and he had some time to put towards drafting the letter. However, he had one more letter to read before he felt like he could try again, and the binder was mysteriously gone earlier in the day.

"Did you take the binder somewhere, Mom?" he asked.

"Yeah, I went to lunch with Mrs. Ramirez, and she asked me to bring it. We read the 2014 letter, the year we went to Hawaii. Great trip, right?"

"Yes, it was good, except for that little incident," Declan reminded Teddy.

"Yes, let's be like how the Christmas letters leave out the bad stuff. Let's just not revisit that episode, Declan," Teddy said, laughing.

Yes, there was a Teddy meltdown caused by Declan not

eating the mac and cheese that was given to him at a restaurant due to it having cheese sprinkled on top. They had specifically requested "just plain Kraft mac and cheese" to avoid such a meltdown. Teddy blew a gasket, walked out of the restaurant, and demanded to fly home immediately without the kids and Colin. She looked back at that particular meltdown and had no real explanation for why something like that set her off so severely. Teddy, unfortunately, had a long fuse and often said nothing about what was bothering her and then exploded at a seemingly insignificant thing. That insignificant thing was Declan being stubborn, as usual, about food.

Teddy recalled how stressed out she was back in those days. Even on a vacation to Hawaii, she had a hard time letting go of her anxiety, often caused by trying to be superhuman and caring for every detail of everyone around her. Sunscreen, hats, flip flops, activities, water bottles and preferred food for everyone. It all seems trivial now, but on that trip, it was the old saying of "death by a thousand paper cuts."

However, she was embarrassed about that meltdown. Teddy often overlooked and minimized the stress of parenting. She liked things to be organized, well-executed, and basically ... perfect. She was oftentimes tough on herself and her family to achieve it. The pent-up rage of a perfectionist parent was also another likely rationale for her behavior on that trip.

"But we persevered, and we all rebounded right Declan," continued Teddy. "We've got to keep trying to move on. We're a family. It's what you do!"

She gave him a hug, which he unexpectedly leaned into before he started on his way to his room. As he walked away, Teddy joked, "You know, Decks, you are just lucky your dad didn't put in the story about you telling us what girl's private parts looked like after apparently seeing some while changing swimsuits at summer camp! Remember, 'Mom! It's a line,' you declared while gesturing a horizontal line in your private area! Remember?"

Teddy laughed, and Declan rolled his eyes.

"Yes, I remember, Mom. Thanks for refreshing my memory, though. Just great," said Declan with teenage revulsion.

Chapter Twenty-Seven

The last letter Declan's father authored was filled with the highlights of 2020, a very strange and stressful year. But his dad was fully capable of making a global pandemic funny. Ronan didn't hurt the mood of the letter, given he was admitted in December to Notre Dame. Even 2020 was a good year for the McNamara family, while being amongst the worst in memory for the world at large. Having survived 2020, they had no reason to suspect 2021 would be the year that would markedly change their lives forever. But it was.

Declan closed the binder and decided it was time for him to make something happen with this letter. He decided that he needed to start the letter with humor. His dad did this for 2020, which was truly a horrible year, so he figured it was what his dad would have wanted.

After staring at the blank Word document he created weeks before, Declan had a thought. He could bring up the idea of cover songs, suggesting that he, Declan, was doing a cover of his dad's original works. "Yes, this felt right," thought Declan. He knew his dad would appreciate a music reference.

"Help me, Dad," Declan said, looking up at his ceiling in an effort to conjure his father's guidance.

He toyed with some opening lines, until he felt like he struck a tone that was in step with his dad's voice. These few sentences took nearly forty-five minutes to write. Writing is a tough gig. Declan was glad he planned to be an engineer.

After that effort, he needed a break, so he called his brother. He wanted to get Ronan's view on the highlights of the year besides the obvious: Dad's death and his move to South Bend.

"What do you want, Declan," said Ronan as a greeting.

"Wanted to talk to you about the Christmas letter I am writing. I want to see what you think are the year's highlights besides, you know," stammered Declan.

"So, you are really gonna do this thing then?"

"Yes, Ronan. I am. I think it's a good idea that Mom will

really like," he pushed back with conviction.

"Okay, okay. Well, when I think of the year, I think of, well, me, bro! My graduation, my move to Notre Dame and of course, the accident. How on earth are you going to handle that topic?"

"Don't worry, I will handle it. What about the weeklong freeze in February that left us without power for days, the joy of vaccinations, our trips to ND at Easter and to Sedona in June?" replied Declan.

"Yeah, those are things to mention. You can mention our summer jobs with G's company again this year if you want and remember you were confirmed ... with the best sponsor possible," added Ronan, referring to himself.

"Oh yeah, those are good. Thanks, Ronan," said Declan. "Anything funny you can think of?"

"Hmm, well, maybe the fact that Dad got us Suns/Lakers playoff tickets and spent an entire evening driving us back and forth from Sedona to Phoenix, a two-hour drive each way, so we could go to the game, not him and Mom. Seems crazy and funny to me now that I look back on it," said Ronan. "But very Mom and Dad."

"My outdoor graduation was in the middle of a thunderstorm, which was a good time for all, as I recall,"

Ronan continued. "Oh, and I went to Chicago for the Shamrock Series football game and had quite a wild weekend. I could see a dad joke with some sort of reference to that '80s movie. The one about the kid skipping school. Cannot think of the name."

"*Ferris Bueller's Day Off?*" supplied Declan.

"Yes, that's the one. Dad would like that reference, I think."

"Man, we're forgetting that we all had COVID except for Mom," Declan added with disbelief.

"Yeah, another gift I gave to the household," said Ronan sarcastically because he was the likely culprit who came down with the virus first.

Even though he got sick, Ronan was pleased that his parents did not limit his social activity since he was a healthy teenager with one year left with his high school friends. Declan and Ronan had a reasonably normal senior and sophomore year of high school despite the pandemic because their school went back to in-person classes in the fall of 2020. It could have been vastly different had they still been at the public high school, which operated with online classes the entire '20-21 school year.

"Poor Mom, she never got it and had to wait on three

of us for a span of four weeks because Dad and I didn't get it until the end of the two-week quarantine mark with you!" added Declan.

"What a year ..." Ronan trailed off.

"So, how are you, Declan?" asked Ronan.

"Fine and good," said Declan, as that was the brother's shared auto-response to every parental inquiry from: how are you, to how was your day, to how was your night out.

"I'm okay, too," said Ronan. "I am focused on my grades. I swear I am."

"Hey, man, I hope you are. I am not doubting or judging. Do you remember Mr. DeSilva? AP Lit?" asked Declan.

"Yep, I remember him. Not a bad guy. We had to talk too much, though, in that class. I hate that. Just give me the numbers. That's why I am going to be a finance bro!" exclaimed Ronan.

"Yep, you are definitely a bro. Anyway, you know, he's been talking with me every once in a while about what happened to Dad. He's pretty cool. His wife died, so he gets it," shared Declan cautiously, never knowing if his brother would ridicule him.

"That's awesome. That came out wrong. Not the dead wife part. I have been talking to the Resident Assistant in my dorm section. It helps. I get it. Good for you."

It seemed to Declan that he and his brother were finding good ways to get through their grief.

Chapter Twenty-Eight

Meanwhile, Teddy was downstairs with the dogs. She tried to kill time by watching streaming television, a favorite pastime. Unfortunately, her TV fix was not working. After thirty minutes of rewatching *Downton Abbey*, she went up to Declan's room. She wanted the binder. She needed a hug from her husband, and this was the only way to get it. She settled back onto the couch with her preferred mode of entertainment at the moment and read.

Christmas 2015

It is only fitting in a year featuring Back to the Future Day, Rocky's triumphant return in Creed, The Peanuts Movie and the Star Wars revival that the McNamara family too went throwback and revisited old stomping grounds.

On a London business trip, Colin's work colleague got him special access to his childhood home at Chicksands, a British military base. This trip doubled as a romantic getaway, with Teddy flying over for a Valentine's celebration. We saw one of her crushes, X-Men's James McAvoy, in the West End play The Ruling Class and — since we were without the kids — made it back to Babble, our favorite Mayfair nightclub from a decade ago. A day trip to the quaint college town of Cambridge rounded out the jaunt.

Like Rusty Griswold, Colin got the itch to relive a vacation from his youth with a road trip west, including a return to the real Walley World — LA's Magic Mountain amusement park. None of us were eager to experience Colin's 1982 4,500-mile family station wagon odyssey, so a flight to Phoenix shortened our drive to under 2,000 miles.

With a parental responsibility to expose our boys to landmarks on the trek, naturally, we started at the Palm Springs resort immortalized in Beverly Hills, 90210 when Tori Spelling's character, Donna Martin, was thrown down the stairs by her boyfriend. Being a good sport, Teddy reenacted the scene for our enjoyment. At San Diego's Hotel del Coronado, the boys were the ones taking a tumble, as surfing proved more challenging than last year in Hawaii. This prompted the question: What brings more pleasure —

gliding smoothly atop the ocean yourself or watching your brother violently faceplant into the waves?

All in all, our quest for fun featured a list of Americana attractions that would make Clark Griswold proud: the Grand Canyon and its glass-bottom skywalk, Hoover Dam, Meteor Crater, Sedona's Red Rocks, Montezuma Castle and Bearizona Wildlife Park, where the family fell in love with an adorable brown bear cub.

Our fondness for the little bear led to us welcoming its clone to our family in the form of a Cairn Terrier puppy. A terror to Molly with playful dogfights, the rambunctious Sally is named after Charlie Brown's little sister, a favorite of Teddy's.

A summer trip to the Midwest was filled with adventures in Chicago, Ronan's third year of basketball camp at Notre Dame and the 65th wedding anniversary of Teddy's parents in Ohio. The boys also had notable solo journeys, as Ronan went on a field trip to Washington, DC with his middle school classmates, and both Ronan and Declan embarked on their first flight without any supervision, visiting Colin's brother Aiden and his family in Colorado Springs.

More big changes came for our family when school

resumed. After four years of training and nearly 500 lessons, Declan earned his first-degree black belt in martial arts. Now at the grade level when school sports begin, Ronan started his seventh-grade basketball season with a bang, leading the team in scoring through seven games, and then a thud, as a broken foot sidelined him for six weeks. And Teddy also got into the turn-back-the-clock spirit, returning to LMC for the third time, for those of you keeping score.

As the holidays approached, we enjoyed one more family excursion, heading up to Boston to watch the Fighting Irish play football at baseball's hallowed Fenway Park. Along with reuniting with old classmates, we visited the Freedom Trail, the bar from Cheers and Harvard, which we all agreed might be a good safety school for our boys if their top choice of Notre Dame doesn't work out. Here's wishing you and your family nothing but the best this Christmas season!

Colin, Teddy, Ronan and Declan

Teddy gave Sally some extra tummy rubs in honor of her joining the family in 2015. Teddy immediately fell in love with the silly puppy when she saw her at the Washington Feed Store after picking up Ronan from Algebra Camp at his middle school. She laughed at the notion of a rising seventh grader being subjected to math camp during the summer, but Ronan seemed to take it in stride. As an activity she had done many times before, she and the boys went to the feed store "just to look at the puppies" for something to kill time during the long, hot summer. Sally was a Cairn Terrier and should have looked scruffy, like Toto from the *Wizard of Oz*. But this puppy was fluffy like a little brown bear. It was three against one, so we made her part of the family despite Colin's protests.

Teddy also reflected on what an action-packed year 2015 was. It certainly appeared to be out of a storybook and really was when you eliminate all the noise that day-to-day life presents. She realized that's really the magic of the letters. They allow you to relive what matters most without the rattle of the everyday annoyances and struggles. Teddy flipped through the remaining pages of the binder. Only five more letters were left unread, a wrenching realization.

"Would I have done anything differently if I had known it would all end so soon?" Teddy thought to herself.

The gloss over in Teddy's 2015 story was that joining LMC for the third time made her more miserable than the previous two times she worked there because this time around had her reporting to woefully incompetent people in the global marketing department. If only she could go back and not have cared about work, not have been so stressed and annoyed all the time. In reality, she really didn't care about work once she had children. It was all about the paycheck. They needed the money. It was only the checks that kept her in a game she was no longer interested in playing. Teddy believed she would have been that carefree person Colin had met so long ago in 1999 if it wasn't for the working mom role she was forced to fulfill. This read was a bittersweet experience, so Teddy decided to keep up her "one letter at a time" rule ... especially since she had actually read two today, if she counted the letter she and Dana read together.

Nearing the end of the letters, coupled with the holidays closing in, started to get Teddy down. Not only because the holidays would be hard but because she realized she had no plan for her life. She bitterly laughed at herself again about how badly she had always wanted to quit her job and just be a mom. She knew being a mom didn't mean doing nothing. She just longed for far fewer people to please in her life. Longed for less scheduling and precision. Simply living at a slower pace.

Now she had that luxury, but at the wrong time in her children's lives and her own life. Being at home with nothing to focus on except her sorrow felt like a prison. Teddy was not her mother who could entertain herself at home with countless chores and hobbies. Her mother even took up doing adult coloring books in her nineties to stay busy. That was not

Teddy. She always imagined not working as being freeing. Maybe it was, but not under these circumstances. She had to start thinking about life in 2022 and beyond. She knew she couldn't read Christmas letters forever.

Becoming a teacher was the only thought that kept popping into her head when she thought of the future. Sadly, Sue's discouragement of the idea immediately followed most instances of such thought. Was it so horrible to think about moving on? And it wasn't moving on with another man, for God's sake. It was moving on with a darn job. It was her right, wasn't it? Why did she care what Sue or anyone thought? But deep down, she did. Always fearing being viewed as "bad," would people think she was selfish for finding a new career? Was there some rule she needed to abide by regarding how much time she should spend alone in her house before finding a new life? She did not know why there was such guilt over something that was good and something she denied herself her entire adult life.

In frustration, Teddy grabbed her phone. She needed to call her mother. It had been a week since she had spoken to her elderly mother who was too frail to even make it to the funeral. The rule was a week – a call to the parents once a week. Sadly, it was still Teddy being there for her mother instead of the other way around. She noticed she had new e-mails, so she procrastinated by taking a peek. Junk, swipe to delete, junk, swipe to delete, more spam, swipe to delete, then sdesilva@smcps.org.

Teddy felt a tingle of anticipation and drew in her breath sharply. She did not immediately recognize this positive feeling, this jolt of adrenaline after living nearly two months in a state of bizarre numbness. It was a tiny spark of interest and happiness. She tapped to see what Mr. DeSilva had to say.

Subject: Declan update

Dear Mrs. McNamara,

Just writing to let you know Declan continues to do very well in class and, more importantly, during our conversations. He is sad, of course, but he seems to have strength beyond his years, too.

He told me about the Christmas letters your family writes. Declan seems to be very engaged with them. I used to write a Christmas letter, too. I have not for a few years now. Interesting commonality we have.

I will continue this sort of update with you periodically so you can feel comfortable about our interactions.

Regards,

Sam, pardon my infraction, Mr. DeSilva

His e-mail sign off gave Teddy a chuckle. This Mr. DeSilva was indeed a good guy. Teddy was so pleased that he updated her. So, what next, do I write back? Something pulled her to keep the interaction going. She began typing.

To: sdesilva@smcps.org

Subject: Thank you

Dear Mr. DeSilva,

Thank you for the update. I very much appreciate your consideration in filling me in on Declan's wellbeing.

Declan mentioned that you are a Christmas letter writer as well. My husband was the author in our family. I played the role of editor. I had the easier job.

I guess we are both in the "used to do Christmas letter club" as this year I don't see our family sending one. I guess life is full of phases.

Thank you for your support of Declan. It means a lot to me.

Regards,

Mrs. McNamara

Send.

Chapter Twenty-Nine

Teddy took a few days break from the letters and decided to focus on Thanksgiving. She spent a substantial amount of time combing through recipes, hoping to try a few new dishes. She felt a desire to make an atypical meal. Maybe it was to avoid triggering memories. She wasn't sure, but that was likely her motivation, experiencing a continued love-hate relationship with her memories. Thankfully, much more love than hate. Focusing on the good times helped her stay out of the pit of rage. She often tiptoed around when thinking about Colin's culpability in what happened.

"Who knew you could prepare potatoes in so many different ways? Hasselback potatoes, never heard of them before," she said to Lucy and Sally emphatically. The dogs just gazed up at her from their chosen places under her chair at the kitchen island.

She called to talk to Ronan to see how he felt about a menu that didn't include the traditions – cornbread stuffing, broccoli, cheese and bacon casserole, corn souffle and mashed potatoes.

"Hey, Cakey, how are you?" she asked, using his baby nickname, which was short for Baby Cakes, as she used to fondly and frequently call her first born.

"Good, Mom, how are you?" Ronan replied. Ronan was not fond of the name Cakey, so he just ignored his mother's use of it.

"Fine, just wanted to see how you are doing now that you are about a week out from coming home again."

"Everything is good. Classes are going really well, Mom. I am taking care of business. And we have our SYR this Friday. I don't have a date yet, but I am going to ask someone today."

An SYR is a dorm dance, and SYR stands for "set up your roommate," but the tradition of setting up dates for your roommates has apparently passed. This is probably a good thing because, in Teddy's era, the students jokingly referred to SYRs as "screw your roommates" because of the many bad blind dates that resulted.

"I am sure you are, and I am glad you are going to go to the dance. Those experiences are important. Curious, Ronan, would you be okay with different sides for our Thanksgiving dinner this year and maybe even trying to do a deep-fried turkey? Just kind of feeling like a changeup might be to eat and good for heads and hearts."

"Um, well, I mean, I feel bad dictating anything because I don't cook it and you do. But I love Thanksgiving just as it has always been," Ronan replied with empathy but honesty as well.

"I knew you would say that, but I don't know. I just feel like we need a change to, um, help us," Teddy continued.

"Well, to be honest, I am not sure a change in menu is going to make us forget or make this any easier, Mom. You know that, right?"

Ronan was direct and never sugarcoated his feelings or his desires. Teddy believed his ability to articulate how he felt and what he wanted in a genuine way would serve him well in adulthood.

"Yeah ... yeah, I guess you are right. Silly thought, I guess," Teddy responded, keeping her tears at bay.

Ronan could hear her crying.

"Mom, Declan and I are going to be with you. We will get through it. It won't be easy, but we will. You love to cook Thanksgiving food, and you have perfected that menu over the years. Make it, and let's enjoy it," said Ronan with mature conviction.

They both remained silent. An unfortunate, uncomfortable pause was upon them.

"What have you been doing with your days?" Ronan asked to break the intense silence.

"Well, not much really. I stopped reading the Christmas letters for a while and focused on recipe research this week. I know, I am really tearing it up with activity," Teddy joked, as she tried to bring some levity back to the conversation with her son. The last thing she was interested in was making it harder for Ronan.

"I know you are not going to go to work at LMC, but you should do something. I think you should consider teaching. You never really got your shot back in 2012 when you started subbing because you got pulled back into marketing work, but you really could do that now, Mom."

"Whoa, Ro! Are you clairvoyant? I have been thinking that I need to have a plan for 2022. Teaching is an idea that I have been giving heavy consideration. Thanks, sweetie. But don't you think I should just focus on you and Decks? I kind of feel guilty making plans for, well, me," said Teddy trailing off.

"Mom, you told me to get back to it, and it was the best advice I could have ever gotten. You made Declan stop his hiding out and get back to school. That seems to be good too, but ya know, with him, it's often hard to tell—that little brick wall of goofiness. Anyway—you have nothing to feel guilty about. We are not toddlers. I am nineteen and he's seventeen. You deserve to pick yourself up and continue living. What's been cool about you as a mom is that you do things: you work, you stay fit, you stay current. You stay in the game. Don't stop that now, even though I know it's hard."

"My God, Ronan. Such wisdom."

"Ha, well, I am trying. Look into teaching, Mom. As Nike says, 'just do it.'"

"Ok, my little angel. I will. I cannot thank you enough for this pep talk. Bye, sweets, love you."

"Love ya, Mom."

Her son had grown to be a great young man. She thought back to the joy of bringing him to Notre Dame as an actual student in August, not just for a football weekend or basketball camp. He was so excited to begin what he saw as his destiny. She hoped his father's death was not too heavily impacting his experience. Her mind drifted to the many activities of that joyous welcome weekend, but the three of them talking about another of Teddy's "ideas she had first" made her smile the most for some silly reason.

For what was probably the thirtieth time, Teddy told Colin and Ronan how she had the idea in the late '80s for what was now the Eddy Street Commons development: a trendy, mixed-used retail and living area within walking distance of campus. Teddy still believed unwaveringly that she was the first to have the idea for a shopping and restaurant area close to the college to enhance the desolate outskirts of the campus. Teddy knew they were humoring her as they just agreed and smiled, seemingly aware that there was no use in arguing with her genius and foresightedness.

From all accounts, Ronan was immersing himself in the college experience. Photos he would send from football gamedays warmed her heart. The tales he told of the many off-campus parties and bar gatherings certainly made it seem like he was not spending his days in bed grieving. Teddy wished there were far fewer stories of going out to bars – and getting thrown out of them – given Ronan was just nineteen. But what could she do? He was in college, doing what college kids do.

She was thankful once again for holding Ronan back in Pre-K. Given the extra year, Ronan would turn twenty-one the summer before his junior year. Strangely, this was actually one of the benefits she and Colin discussed back when they were painstakingly making the decision. "Less underage drinking at college," she could hear Colin saying. "And an extra year at home under our roof."

Teddy took Ronan's encouragement to heart about teaching and used his words to stamp out the guilt she was feeling from Sue's comments. All those years ago, when she decided that having a family was the "more to life" that she was seeking, she had only been half right. Looking back now, part of her lack of fulfillment was that she followed the wrong career path. The golden handcuffs of a sizable paycheck kept her working for companies she did not like, with people she nearly detested. And it was the circumstances with Colin's career, too, that kept her trapped. But now, she did have the freedom to choose. It was bittersweet, of course, as she would work in detestable jobs forever if it meant Colin was still by her side. But instead of being mad at Colin, she realized she may need to be thankful that she now had an opportunity she never thought would present itself. She was getting a career do-over, and she decided to be happy about it.

She spent the afternoon looking into the steps she

would need to go through to become a teacher. With the wonders of the internet, finding information was no challenge at all. She recalled a lot of it from the last time she entertained moving into teaching back in 2012. But, of course, many things had changed. For better or worse, it was even easier now. Ten more years of our schools being underfunded and a mass exodus of students from public schools in Houston meant even fewer people were pursuing teaching. This was a sad reality for society, with the thinnest silver lining being that Teddy's path to becoming a teacher could be more easily achieved.

When Declan got home, she was pleased to tell him about her afternoon's work. She had not had an interesting update to share with him in months. He seemed genuinely happy for her and thought teaching could be a good idea, too.

"You were so popular when you subbed. I never told you then, but my friends thought you were so cool," Declan shared.

"Really? Tell me more!" joked Teddy.

"Don't get so excited. That was elementary school cool, Mom," quipped Declan.

"Hey, have you chatted with Mr. DeSilva lately?"

"Yeah, actually talked to him today."

"About?"

"Just stuff."

"Just stuff?

"Yeah, stuff," repeated Declan. "He said he may do a Christmas letter this year. I think I told you that he and his wife used to do one, but he stopped after she died. But me talking about ours has him thinking. Kinda cool, I guess."

"Yeah, that is. Poor guy. I obviously feel his pain. Who knows, maybe I will start up the letters again someday too. If I might become a teacher in my fifties, then I guess nothing is out of the question, right?"

"Sure, Mom, you never know what is around the corner, I suppose," said Declan blandly, ensuring that he did not tip his hand about his plan for the letter.

That evening after dinner, Teddy decided her self-imposed moratorium from the Christmas letters had lasted long enough. She made some progress focusing on her life ahead over the last couple of days, so she felt deserving of indulgence in the past. She asked Declan if he wanted to read with her, knowing he had likely already read 2016. He accepted, which pleased her. It felt less like wallowing if she wasn't reading alone. Lucy and Sally flanked them on the couch, looking like two gargoyles on each arm of the deep blue couch, protecting them.

Christmas 2016

Approaching a new year gives us an opportunity to share our unique experiences from the past 12 months with family and friends. Wait a minute; Notre Dame, New Orleans, Lego, London and AAU basketball are all getting mentions yet again. Yes, this might be a familiar carol, so please proceed at your own risk as we try our best to avoid a Groundhog Day edition of the McNamara Christmas letter.

Hey, we moved in 2016, and that's not an every year thing for us! It's more of an every five years thing, as we continue to keep the realtors in the inner-loop area of Houston very busy. This new home – which stands just one-tenth of a mile away from our first place and within three miles of all of our previous houses – zoned us to our sons' preferred high school and gave Teddy an office for working from home. Moving also helped to rid us of the excess that had accumulated over the years, including reducing our boxes of kids' crafts and keepsakes by half. As Teddy noted while chucking artwork into trash bags, "This stuff sure seemed a lot cuter when they were little!"

Declan embraced the change of address, enjoying our new neighborhood for bike rides and dog walks. His new *bedroom came with two new roommates, as our terriers Molly and Sally now spend their nights beside Declan's bed. Now at Cronkite Middle School with Ronan, Declan is on the school's robotics team, constructing and operating Lego-based robots for competitions. The 12-year-old is also a fan of high-end supercars and was recently delighted when he arrived home from school to find a $300,000 McLaren parked right in front of our home. Sadly for him, it wasn't ours, but he gets great enjoyment from the consolation prize of taking a turn behind the wheel of our Mini Countryman at a nearby stadium parking lot.*

Ronan benefited from the move with a new king-size bed and close proximity to friends and neighborhood hangouts. His interests have expanded beyond sports to include house parties and Vineyard Vines fashion. Now the tallest member of our family, Ronan plays basketball for the passing-focused Crusader team – a rarity in AAU play – and Cronkite's eighth-grade team, for whom he scored a career-high 35 points in the season opener. The 14-year-old attributed his hot start to the workouts we permitted while he was grounded for getting Saturday detention. We also made him watch The Breakfast Club before serving his sentence. Paraphrasing Simple Minds, we lectured to him, "Hey! Hey! Hey! Hey! Don't you ... forget about this."

To celebrate our 15th anniversary, we headed back to New Orleans, this time venturing away from busy Bourbon Street to explore the wonders of Magazine Street. We also tortured ourselves with two in-state road trips to see Notre Dame football, as the underwhelming team stumbled its way through a Texas two-step. Work trips provided the chance to take in some fantastic shows, with Teddy enjoying School of Rock and Kinky Boots on Broadway and Colin stepping back to the '70s with Electric Light Orchestra and Supertramp concerts in London. Colin's recent business trip was an 18,000-mile odyssey to Manilla, where luxury retail surroundings and an uncomfortable December heat made him feel like he never left Houston. We'll close out the year with a getaway to the winter wonderland of Lake Louise in the Canadian Rockies.

Now you're completely caught up on every riveting detail of our fascinating family life. Someday, we may spare you from this day-by-day play-by-play. Till then, here's wishing you a very Merry Christmas!

Colin, Teddy, Ronan and Declan

"Why did Ronan get Saturday detention? I forget," asked Declan.

"Well, he and Parker, you know Parker. Well, they

played this game where they choked each other with the new ID lanyards Cronkite made you guys wear that year to see who could handle getting choked the longest," Teddy replied. "Remember?"

"Oh yeah. Idiot," Declan said, summing up the story quite eloquently. "He has a knack for crazy stuff, doesn't he?

"Yes, kind of like this golden dome climbing and Edwards Fortyhands nonsense!" Teddy exclaimed.

"Mom, I know you are still a little worried. Don't be. Well, try not to be. Ronan always finds a way to come out okay. He may not take the easiest route sometimes, but he gets there. He got to Notre Dame, didn't he? He is not gonna mess it up."

"Well, well, wise one. Thank you for the perspective. If you ever think otherwise, you have an obligation to tell me. It's not tattling! Okay?

"Okay, Mom," said Declan uncomfortably. "I am still amazed at how Dad made our daily existence seem so interesting."

"Yes, he had a gift. That's for sure. I know I certainly don't, so there will be no letter this year," Teddy said, giving Declan a tight squeeze.

"It's okay, Mom," said Declan, keeping his plan safely to himself.

Chapter Thirty

As November slowly wore on, Teddy tried to psych herself up for the holidays ahead. She resigned herself to making the traditional meal, as Ronan requested for Thanksgiving, but invited her friend Dana and her family over after politely declining her mother-in-law's invitation. A holiday meal with only the three of them without Colin would have been too much for Teddy to handle. Too soon. A small group gathering would help take the edge off. Teddy felt like this was a good compromise between doing something completely new – like taking a vacation in an attempt to ignore the holiday – and wallowing at the Thanksgiving table with just the three-pack.

Teddy realized she could not put off Sue any longer about the invitation for Thanksgiving. She had been dodging the topic every time she spoke with Sue and Richard. She bravely punched Sue's name on her phone, selfishly hoping to get Sue's voicemail. Alas, Teddy was not that lucky.

"Hi Teddy," sang Sue brightly.

"Hi Sue, how are you?"

"Oh, we're doing alright, Teddy. You? Taking care of those boys?" fired off Sue, not waiting for Teddy to respond to the first question about her wellbeing.

"Yes, they both seem to be doing pretty well, given the circumstances," said a tentative Teddy, as if awaiting an assault.

"That's wonderful to hear. See, not jumping into other things too soon is the right path, Teddy. Just take care of the precious boys."

Teddy ignored the jab and proceeded to tell Sue that they would not be able to make it for Thanksgiving. She explained that the boys wanted to be home, especially Ronan, since he had not seen his high school friends in months.

Sue curtly accepted the decline and quickly wrapped up the phone call. Teddy was relieved that she had gathered the courage to politely decline Sue and Richard's invitation but was fuming at the continued interest only in her sons and the unsolicited life advice.

Teddy was also pleased that Ronan was coming home despite nearly a day of travel for just a few days in town and being closely followed by another trip home for Christmas break in mid-December. There was talk between Teddy and Colin before their world changed of them going to Notre Dame for Thanksgiving. "That would have been nice until Colin messed that up," Teddy thought. She was becoming freer with her thoughts and emotions, allowing herself to make Colin the villain. She wasn't proud and would never admit it, but that was partly how she continued to feel.

She put the thought of what could have been for Thanksgiving out of her mind. This is what she had, and this is what she would deal with. Having her boys home felt more important than ever to her despite her abject fear of it being a horribly depressing holiday. She felt downright schizophrenic about the upcoming weekend. Her grief counselor assured her that she was coping as effectively as possible and that she was not developing any sort of true mental disorder. From day to day, Teddy's agreement or disagreement with the therapist's opinion varied wildly.

Teddy was going through the motions of being "normal." She, however, felt alone, like she did before Colin. Teddy's family had never been there for her so, of course, they were not there for her now. Nothing new. She was the servant in the family. The one who tried to please everyone, with no one concerned about taking care of or pleasing her. It's just the way it was. Teddy had grown quite used to it. It's all she ever knew from her family experience. This is much of the reason why Teddy reinvented herself with her own family: Colin, Ronan and Declan. She rarely engaged with or spoke about her family. Her children only met their uncles a handful of times because that's the way Teddy wanted it. She did a little better with her parents, but not much. As a sort of punishment for their lack of showing they cared, Teddy kept her children away from them and their austere, cold ways.

As the daughter in the relationship, she was expected to call her mother, which she did weekly. The phone call initiation power play with her parents was a game they played with all their children. Teddy supposed it was their passive-aggressive way of claiming authority. "We don't call because we know you are busy, and we do not know your schedules."

Despite their strained relationship through her adulthood, Teddy had good moments with her mother. After seeing *The Sound of Music* in the historic Palladium Theater in her hometown when Teddy was in the second grade, she and her mother read the book *The Story of the Trapp Family Singers* aloud to each other. That was a nice memory and that event sparked Teddy's love of novels.

Like her mother, her brothers never called to check on her either. Teddy's sisters-in-law texted a few times but nothing substantial. Just simple "hugs" or "thinking of you" or heart emojis type stuff. They were not close, even the one who was her maid of honor, so she did not expect much anyway.

Keeping busy was a tried-and-true coping mechanism that she was employing in her current circumstance. Teddy tried to focus on her seasonal decorating and menu preparation. She needed to do things to help her not think too much. Teddy was the only person she knew who decorated for Thanksgiving back in the early 2000s. Decorating for the holiday has become more popular, but she was a trendsetter nearly twenty years ago with her turkey plates and pumpkin-filled tablescape. It was her favorite holiday, and she always enjoyed setting a beautiful table and having the mantle decorated. In fact, Teddy decorated for every holiday, including St. Patrick's Day and a made-up season she called "Birthday Season." It ran from June first through July seventh because three of the four-pack's four birthdays fell in that timeframe: Colin, Declan and Ronan.

At the kitchen island, Teddy stared at her laptop screen. The application for the alternative certification course to become a teacher was complete. She had not yet submitted it. Thoughts were swirling. The classes did not start until January, so there was time to change her mind if she wanted to. Ronan saying "just do it" during their earlier call motivated her. She got a jolt of excitement and submitted. It felt good to push the button on the application and take a ceremonial step toward something focused on the future. Pushing the submit button was truly a triumph. She savored the private moment and felt that Colin would be proud of her. This step was not selfish, as Sue tried to paint it. It was necessary. It was even deserved.

To Teddy's surprise, Declan came bouncing downstairs with hopping footsteps and asked to read a letter. She had no idea that he had been in his room attempting to write the 2021 letter and felt stuck. His request was intended to help him get some inspiration. Of course, she was happy to oblige the request, despite being completely unaware of her son's motivation.

Christmas 2017

With our sons now teenagers and high school entering the picture, that innocent joy of their childhood Christmases seems like a distant memory. So much so that Teddy recently forced our boys to take their picture with the mall Santa in a desperate attempt to recapture the magic of years gone by.

Or maybe it was just payback for Ronan reminding her, "You know, you only have a few more holiday seasons with me here at home." Of course, some days that seems like a few too many. Let's look back at the most memorable days of the last 12 months.

We closed out last year with some fun in the snow, delighting in a week of winter adventures at Lake Louise in the Canadian Rockies. Whether this trip fell within the year timeframe to be Christmas letter-eligible caused much deliberation for Colin, who ultimately decided to live on the wild side and throw it in. The snow followed us to our next excursion, as a blizzard greeted us in Washington, DC, where we joined Declan after his school's spring break field trip. Last school year ended with both boys receiving accolades. Ronan won his team's Mr. Basketball award as its leading scorer, and Declan earned special recognition for exhibiting the outstanding qualities representative of the school's International Baccalaureate program.

Our child chauffeur duties lightened with school's end in June, so we escaped to England and Ireland for two weeks without the kids. Palaces and performances highlighted our getaway, as we treated ourselves to royal accommodations at Irish castles Ballynahinch and Dromoland after catching Phil Collins in Dublin and Robbie Williams in London.

We also witnessed a bizarre bestiality-themed West End play starring Damian Lewis, who is a favorite of Teddy's … at least until he professed his love to a goat. We returned home to learn that while we were away, Ronan had continued his ongoing mission of living out every '80s teen movie. This year, he was all about Risky Business, as cops shut down his Friday night party thrown together during his few hours home alone. Apparently, like Tom Cruise's character, our oldest son felt like sometimes you just gotta say, "What the heck?" The discovery of this party caused immediate vacation withdrawal for Colin, who quickly retreated back to London for a work trip.

Summer fun continued with our first of two trips to Notre Dame (as we also made it back in the fall to watch the Irish wallop USC, 49-14). On the August visit, Declan experienced ziplining and the Indiana Dunes, while Ronan hooped it up at ND's basketball camp for the fourth time in five years. After these good times, summer concluded with the cruddiest of endings. Ronan suffered a Lisfranc fracture in his foot, requiring surgery and 12 weeks of immobilization. His surgery happened with Hurricane Harvey closing in on Houston, as he was one of the last patients in the Texas Medical Center before flooding shut down the city. Fortunately, we made it through the storm's devastation with minimal damage.

We started our return to normal following a two-week storm-related delay to the school year. Ronan began his freshman year at Landis High School on crutches, but we were thankful that his recovery was much quicker than expected. Already back to playing for the Landis basketball team, Ronan fills the rest of his time working as a ball kid for the Houston Rockets and student reporter for our neighborhood magazine, The Take. A cross-country runner for Cronkite Middle School, Declan turned teen from head to toe, sporting a stylish new haircut and trendy Yeezy sneakers. Declan's Lego interest has also evolved, as he uses his building skills to construct robotics machines for school competitions and his artistic talents to customize minifigures with paint and clay.

All in all, our year was packed with positives ... minus the considerable midyear speed bump. Here's wishing you all the best this Christmas season!

Colin, Teddy, Ronan and Declan

"Soooo, when are you going to tell me the whole story about Ronan's party while your dad and I were away?" asked Teddy teasingly.

"You know that's for a Thanksgiving or Christmas that

is still way off in the future, Mom!"

Teddy laughed and gave Declan a hug before he bolted back upstairs.

The trip to Ireland and England was to celebrate Teddy's fiftieth birthday. She broke down in tears realizing that Colin would never make it to that age, and they would not have a trip filled with memories to celebrate him reaching that milestone. Her heart ached. She remembered how stressed and unhappy she was during the fall of 2017. Ronan's injury and the hurricane. Teddy recalled how she practically shaved her head with a short pixie haircut that did not suit her because she was in the wicked middle of menopause symptoms. Her anxiety about Ronan's injury, work, and the storm's aftermath was all too much for her. However, she realized now that all those issues should have been categorized as inconveniences. What she was experiencing now was devastation. She was embarrassed thinking back to that time. Now she knew better.

Teddy felt defeated. Her realization that Colin would never reach fifty and the feeling of being cheated out of time with him put her into wallow mode. She wondered if she would ever feel truly good again. If life was simply a collection of memories, she felt irretrievably cheated. If memories were priceless diamonds, maybe she had no right to gather more of them. But she still wanted to add to her collection. How could she not? Desperate to put her mind on something else, she decided to read a second letter. She was nearing the end anyway.

Christmas 2018

This magical Notre Dame football year has filled our household with joy and cheer! Too Seussical? Well, no Grinch will steal our Christmas ... especially since the college football playoffs don't start until four days after. Let's dive right into our year in review.

Declan is closing out middle school, wrapping up what Don Henley refers to as "the end of the innocence." Yes, the out-of-control and hypercompetitive college landscape sets its starting line as Day 1 of high school. That has truly warped us as parents. We recognize it. We are semi-embarrassed by it. But we accept it. So, we are letting Declan enjoy the final stress-free year ... of the rest of his life. During his blowoff year, he has taken up golf – the ultimate leisure activity – with he and Teddy becoming regulars at Radford Park's driving range. He loves everything about the links, except for the clothing: "That's the worst sort of attire for sports: wearing church clothes!" Declan also enjoys running cross country with his school team, sculpting Lego art for his popular Brick Pup account on Instagram and playing the videogame Fortnite, which might need to be played fortnightly (instead of nightly) when he enters the real world ... eight short months from now.

Ronan changed schools this year with a transfer to St. Michael's College Preparatory, which is living up to its rep as one of the country's top Catholic high schools. Switching from public school, he pointed out that school Mass in the auditorium does have an unexpected perk: "No kneeling. It's the coolest thing. Only sitting and standing." Maybe he thinks the grueling wear and tear from the church pews would hamper his performance for the school's basketball team. When Ronan is not driving to the hoop, he's driving himself to school, which has relieved us from being his Uber. Babysitting and petsitting gigs fund his social life and give him gas money. The next Alex P. Keaton is also in the school's Young Conservatives and Investment Clubs. Other activities include writing for The Take, as he covered the Astros for the neighborhood magazine, and working with the Rockets ball crew, as he helped the team to a franchise record and NBA-leading 65 wins last season.

Teddy has become a machine on her Peloton, energizing herself with fitness cycle workouts. This summer, she faced off against Ronan in a heated battle to see who could achieve a higher score. With both of them flying high, the only thing missing from this spirited competition was the "Theme from Rocky" playing (and, just like in the end of Rocky III, the winner will never be revealed). If these Peloton showdowns become family-wide matchups, things will get ugly quickly.

Colin stopped shaving over the summer, and we narrowed down the reason to: A) Laziness; B) Midlife crisis; C) Whim; or D) All of the above. Whatever the answer, a beard appeared. Bearing a slight resemblance to the Notre Dame Leprechaun, Colin said he'd stave off shaving until the Irish lost a game. Fortunately, that has yet to happen. If we had known Colin's scruff might positively influence our favorite team's win total, we would have tossed his razor ages ago.

Speaking of the 12-0 Irish, we made our way up to South Bend for the tone-setting, season-opening win over Michigan following summer trips to our alma mater for basketball and volunteer camps. Not wanting to miss a single snap this season, Colin even tracked down a Notre Dame game watch party at a pub near Westminster Abbey on one of his London work trips. To show our kids (and maybe ourselves) that the world doesn't revolve around ND, we also made campus visits to the University of Chicago and

UCLA, where legendary Bruins coach John Wooden's credo of "competitive greatness" resonated with Ronan ... often in the stupidest ways, as he continually tries to one-up Declan in the most trivial and ridiculous aspects of life. On the LA trip, we also ventured to Venice Beach, where Ronan inserted himself into the blacktop action on the White Men Can't Jump courts. Wearing pink Vineyard Vines shorts, he played Woody Harrelson's fish-out-of-water role to perfection.

We know that Notre Dame is the underdog in the national championship race, but we are happily road-tripping to root them on against Clemson in the Cotton Bowl – 25 years after Colin was a student trainer for the Irish in the very same bowl game. And we've stayed off the naughty list this year (for the most part), so here's hoping for a pigskin miracle (or two)! We hope you have a wonderful Christmas, too!

Colin, Teddy, Ronan and Declan

Feeling a bit better thinking about the fun they had at the Cotton Bowl, Teddy closed the binder. The letter did its job by pulling Teddy out of her grief abyss. Enough for one day. The irony, however, was not lost on her when she reflected on the worry she had when Ronan started driving. Little did she know it was her husband, not her son, whom she should have worried about dying prematurely.

Chapter Thirty-One

As Thanksgiving got closer with each day, Declan was having his own holiday anxiety in the privacy of his bedroom, which he only left to eat snacks or meals. This wasn't different behavior caused by the loss. It was just Declan and probably most teens. He was working diligently on the 2021 letter, determined to persevere and perfect it, despite its innate predicament. At times, he felt like it was coming along nicely. Then, other reads would make him frustrated and insecure. He was on an emotional seesaw about what he was producing. "Was it good enough to follow his dad's works? Was it a tribute or a lame copy? Would it help his family or hurt it?" he thought in never-ending spirals.

That evening, after dinner, Declan's mother asked if he wanted to read a letter with her. She had taken a few days off from reading them, but this chilly midweek evening made her feel like they needed a pick-me-up. Declan felt like he wanted to decline, but he didn't. On second thought, "Maybe a fresh read of a letter would inspire me again, as it had been a while since I'd read one," he thought. So, he agreed, and they read together the two-pack they were becoming. They read the 2018 letter despite Teddy reading it alone a few days prior.

Declan got some energy and inspiration from the letter, so he was pleased that he did not decline his mother's request. He worked on reflecting their summer trip to Sedona and their Easter trip to Notre Dame to buy Ronan's college supplies to await him in storage until August. While writing, an idea popped into his mind. He realized the letter needed a tribute to his father. He knew that something like that was not in keeping with the letter, but it felt that this particular letter needed that sort of thing.

"Ugh, this is so hard," he screamed inside his head. He thought back to when Christmas letter writing was simple … just letters to Santa asking for toys. This letter required so much more, especially for Declan. Talking about emotions and feelings was not high on his list. For the "let's just not talk about it" kid, this exercise was excruciating. But he was intensely determined. And Declan was fierce when he was determined. Apparently, it is the redhead in him, as he had been told many times.

The idea of letters to Santa kept creeping into Declan's mind as he was writing. It's sad that people stop writing letters to Santa when they grow up. He rationalized that it would be weird for older people to write to an imaginary figure asking for stuff and explaining how good they had been that year. However, the notion of people writing these kinds of letters at Christmas lingered in his mind.

Thinking he had put together a pretty decent draft, Declan wanted some input. But whom could he ask? He was determined to keep this a secret from his mother, so she was out. And Ronan was Ronan. He doubted his brother would be up to the task, given his salty attitude about reading the letters. Mr. DeSilva seemed to be the obvious choice. He was an English teacher who mercilessly critiqued Declan's work over the semester, so he could certainly help with this project. As a bonus, he wrote Christmas letters himself, so he would sort of get it.

Declan felt their relationship was where it needed to be for such a request, so he shot him an e-mail with the draft attached. "I hope it's decent, Chuck," Declan said, as he looked up at the large photo of Rockets star Charles Barkley above his desk. The photo tugged at Declan's heart. He and his father were just starting to connect over his newfound interest in the NBA.

He hoped he would not be waiting too long for Mr. DeSilva's critique. Thanksgiving break was nearly upon him. "Unfair," he thought, realizing that he created a deadline for himself during a break from school. But he believed it was worth it.

"Declan," shouted Mr. DeSilva across the atrium the next day at school.

"Oh, hi, Mr. DeSilva," said Declan, backtracking to where Mr. DeSilva stood.

"Have a minute?"

"Sure, I guess the lunch line can wait," said Declan.

"Let's take a seat right here. These chairs in the atrium are surprisingly comfortable," said Mr. DeSilva.

Declan hoped this was about the draft letter he had sent, but he was unsure. Mr. DeSilva looked so serious.

"It means a lot that you asked me to read your letter draft."

"I appreciate you doing it," said Declan, focusing on the ask, not the emotion Mr. DeSilva was attempting to convey.

"So … is it okay?"

"You can be very proud of yourself. It's well written. But more importantly, Declan, you beautifully expressed emotion."

"Thank you," Declan responded softly but with satisfaction.

"You hit on all the pieces of a Christmas letter, giving updates that your family and friends will appreciate. And you addressed your father's death really well. That intro paragraph took me a bit by surprise, but after rereading it a couple times, it wasn't as irreverent as I initially thought."

Declan laughed. "Yeah, you would have to know my dad to get that he would have actually loved that intro."

"What does your mother think, Declan?"

"Oh, she doesn't even know I am writing it. I want it to be a surprise for her on Thanksgiving. I realized that if I told her I was writing it, the letter would become a burden to her. Another project in the long list of projects she supported me with. So, it's a secret. I think it is the right call."

"I am impressed, Declan. Really impressed. I think she will be just thrilled."

"Thanks."

"Of course, I do have a few comments that I will send you in edit mode via e-mail," said Mr. DeSilva, slipping back into teacher mode.

"Of course you do!" said Declan, smirking. "Thank you very much for helping me. Have you decided whether you are going to write a letter this year, Mr. DeSilva?"

"No, I have not. There is a part of me that wants to. You are inspiring me. I just have not put pen to paper yet."

"Now, Mr. DeSilva, are you procrastinating?"

The two parted, feeling optimistic.

With the help of Mr. DeSilva, Declan was pleased with where the Christmas letter stood with Thanksgiving break arriving. Now less than a week out from his planned reveal, he was happy to let the pressure go and just have fun with his friends on a Friday night. He could also go to the Freshman Retreat and do his retreat leader gig without this task looming. He felt bad about leaving his mother alone, but he was looking forward to the overnight retreat. He liked his leadership partner and expected to have a good time.

Retreats by grade level were an important part of his high school's culture. Declan always came away amazed at what his peers dealt with at home. For an affluent school, there were still lots of problems. It seems that so-called privilege doesn't inoculate you from all the bad things in life, despite what the media conveys. Declan's new circumstances were certainly a testament to that. "Life is just hard, and it's hard for everyone in different ways," he thought as he drove the familiar route to the Whataburger, where he was meeting his friends to start off some Friday night fun.

Chapter Thirty-Two

Although Teddy was nervous about being alone overnight in the house for the first time since the horrible *it* happened, Teddy could not bring herself to stop Declan from participating in the Freshman Retreat. He had come a long way in developing his social and leadership skills. His volunteering to be a retreat leader was a huge sign of his maturation. And Teddy hadn't lost her edge for college admissions fodder. These were the types of things any college Declan applied to would want to see. So, she kept her apprehension to herself. Life as a mother doing the right things for your child, not what you yourself actually want or need.

Thankfully, he would be away only one night. The

retreat was not at the school's retreat center at a posh ranch an hour outside of Houston, but rather, the freshman and their leaders had the joy of sleeping on the floor in various classrooms around the campus. One could say it was intended as a bonding experience. It felt better to Teddy that Declan would be just a mere five miles away. When she kissed his cheek Saturday morning as he headed out the door, she held him a little longer than normal. Miraculously, Declan didn't stiffen up or pull away, seemingly knowing his leaving for the night would be hard for his mother.

Teddy lounged on the couch, drinking her morning tea as she planned the day ahead. She knew she needed to keep herself busy. Shopping seemed like the obvious activity to kill time and check a few tasks off her list. Sometimes, life's treadmill of mindless and often pointless activities is exactly what you need.

First, she tackled grocery shopping. She got all the nonperishable items she needed for her meal. Ronan verbalized his excitement over her cornbread stuffing and bacon, cheese and broccoli casserole on their last call, stating that the dining hall food was not all that bad, just repetitive. Like his mother, Ronan loved the side dishes more than the turkey. Teddy's cornbread stuffing was what she believed to be her best dish. She had curated this recipe over the years, tweaking and making adjustments based on other recipes she read. She believed the addition of water chestnuts, of all things, took the dish from good to great. Every year, she just loved the crunch that the atypical ingredient provided in her dish. As she shopped, she was proud that she was hosting her sons and her friends. She felt she was making strides. She was weaning herself off the hours of sleep she had embraced to make the days go by faster in less conscious pain.

And, she had applied to the alternative certification teaching program. She had something to work towards. She believed that to be progress as well, despite having moments where she thought she should just be home with Declan instead of off taking night and weekend classes come January. It was hard for her to believe how one sentence from her mother-in-law was rooted in her psyche. But maybe she shouldn't completely blame Sue. Teddy realized she needed to own some of her anxiety. Maybe it was guilt. Maybe it was fear. She did not know.

Teddy had been thinking about the teaching program more and more over the past weeks. It was amazing to her that she could be ready to apply for a full-time teaching job over the summer for the 2022-2023 school year if she started courses in January. The ease and rapidity of becoming a teacher was good for her needs. It did make her wonder again about the sheer desperation there is for teachers if it's so easy to become one. "How many marginally qualified teachers were out there?" she wondered, feeling continued concern with the state of education in America.

When she finished unpacking all the groceries, she called Ronan. She forgot he was in pregame mode for today's ND football game. When he answered, she immediately heard all the ruckus around him. He was in one of the many tailgating lots surrounding the stadium on campus. She could picture the hundreds of tailgate gatherings with flags and balloons flying against the blue fall sky to help invitees find their gatherings. They talked briefly and agreed to talk the next day. Teddy was pleased to hear the joy in her son's voice. She, however, couldn't believe that she forgot today was a Notre Dame gameday. That would never have happened with Colin around.

Teddy decided to put off the mall for a few hours and watch the game, which would start in about forty-five minutes. She hadn't watched any ND football the entire season. In the previous weeks, she had not been ready to watch without Colin. For no particular reason, today, she felt like she could. So, she did.

It certainly wasn't as much fun watching alone, of course, but it wasn't horrible either. She persevered and was glad. It felt somewhat good. She realized while watching the game that ND and its beloved football games were not exclusively in her past with Colin. It was the future. Ronan was there and seemed to be thriving. And who knew, maybe Declan would go there too. Regardless, she felt good, not guilty, thinking about the future and taking enjoyment in the present.

With the energy the football game gave her, she went to the Houston Emporium, a gigantic retail mecca that was part tourist attraction for suburbanites and part Rodeo Drive with countless upscale stores. Of the hundreds of establishments, Teddy only went to a precious few. The place was always manic on the weekends, and the Saturday before Thanksgiving was no exception.

As she approached the third athletic shoe store on her list of stops, she passed the Santa photo display. The memories of taking the boys when they were little on the Wednesday evening before Thanksgiving gushed into her mind. The tradition started with Ronan at six months old, as that time fit in well with his sleeping and eating schedule. It just became a tradition after that.

Teddy was one for schedules and traditions. She used to joke that if the Pope came to their house during naptime to see the kids, he would just have to wait until her sons awoke naturally. Apparently, even mall Santas were required to work around her infants' nap schedules. One year for Christmas when the boys were in late elementary school, Colin got Teddy a stylized gold Christmas tree with photo frames for ornaments. He put the boys' Santa photos in the ornament frames. It was one of Teddy's prized possessions. A treasure of memories marking the boys' year-over-year growth and changes.

Colin's love for Christmas was infectious. Their Christmas tree was another of his triumphs. They collected ornaments throughout their entire relationship. They had unique ornaments with each representing a memory or having a personal association. The tree was simply amazing for both its beauty and its originality. There were sentimental ornaments, homemade ornaments by Ronan and Declan, funny ornaments like the symbol that Prince created to replace his name and the *Die Hard* ornament of Bruce Willis' John McClane in an air duct as well as ornaments Teddy made with her mother as a child of Snow White and Seven Dwarfs.

When they met, Teddy had created what she thought was an absolutely gorgeous tree with a burgundy and gold color scheme. It featured a metallic ribbon, gold bulbs of varying sizes and many burgundy magnolia flowers with gold edging. She was excited to show Colin her magazine-worthy tree. Teddy smiled as she thought about how unimpressed Colin was with the tree, saying, "It's pretty, but it feels kind of fake. Like something you would find in the lobby of a five-star hotel." Teddy was slightly offended, but she took it in stride and went along with Colin's vision of collecting ornaments that were meaningful to them, and she was certainly glad now that she did. The tree was another collection of memories for which she was deeply thankful.

Teddy was relieved to make it home from shopping. After several hours of fighting the crowds, she decided it was time to fight with the Christmas tree. Their tree was a quite large artificial model that had to be put together limb by limb. It was a time-consuming task that Colin normally handled. Teddy usually only did the lights on the tree. Colin was a bit of an ogre when it came to ornaments. Only Colin could touch them. So, there was no family tree trimming. It was Colin and his twelve boxes of ornaments on a project that filled a couple of late nights leading up to Thanksgiving.

Teddy wanted to get the tree set up, so it was ready for the upcoming holiday. She would break Colin's tradition of solo decorating by doing it with the boys on Thanksgiving and Black Friday. She had to start somewhere with new traditions, she figured. This was a tradition she had been wanting to break for years. "Now I can," thought Teddy wistfully.

She was proud of herself for making it through the day alone. She stayed busy and was exhausted, so she headed to bed early. No reason to push it by staying up and potentially freaking out with loneliness.

***

At the retreat, Declan was engaged in many conversations and reflections with his group of freshmen. The Christmas letter and the intersection with letters to Santa kept creeping into his thoughts. With his letter nearly done, he was putting the finishing touches on the tribute section about his dad. That's when it hit him. So many people at the school, both friends and teachers, helped him after his father died. He wanted to write a Christmas letter to each of them to express what they meant to him. "Well, it wouldn't exactly be a Christmas letter or a letter to Santa. It would be a new concoction entirely," he thought with a bit of pride bubbling within. He was sure that people would appreciate getting something like that from him. He was learning the value of sharing feelings, and this was a way to do just that in a nonverbal way, which felt more comfortable to him.

Chapter Thirty-Three

Waiting for Declan to come home from the retreat on Sunday afternoon was grating on Teddy. She was proud that she had made it through the day before, including the very tough and lonely evening, but she was ready for her son's company, well, more accurately, him just being in the same building as she was. She lived in the real world and knew he would retreat to his room for most of his time at home. Her cousin, who lives in Vancouver, called, so she was able to kill a bit of her evening alone with a nice conversation.

The two laughed about some of their childhood memories of Christmas when her family would visit Ohio and the summers when Teddy and her parents would go to Vancouver. There were some funny tales the two women shared because they were much like sisters, with each of them having siblings with wide age gaps, Teddy's brothers being much older, and Angela's brother and sister being six and eight years younger. When children, the pair couldn't wait to see each other, but predictably, fights would ensue within thirty minutes of togetherness. They laughed about the matching pajamas Teddy's mother made them each Christmas and the clay fight they had in the lake at Angela's parents' summer cottage.

In hindsight, Teddy should have done a Sunday brunch or something to pass the time with Dana. Teddy, however, didn't like to rely on others. She didn't want them to think she was using them to get through this time. She was more comfortable grinding through on her own. It was her way.

She decided to call Ronan to see how things were going with him and make sure he was set for his trip home.

"Hey, Rony," Teddy said when he picked up.

"Hey, Mom," Ronan replied.

"How was the game and the tailgating yesterday?

"Oh, it was a good time, Mom. The games have been the highlight, as you know from experience."

"Yes, I do. I watched the game yesterday, too. The first

one of the season for me. It was somewhat sad, but it was okay. It felt good. How are you doing?" Teddy continued.

"Wow. That's great to hear, Mom. Did you see me on TV?" joked Ronan. "And I am fine, Mom."

"Ha! I wish I could have seen you on TV. That would be so cool, and better than seeing you on social media! Got ya! Ready to come home?"

"Yes, ready for a break. I've been hitting it hard, Mom. My grades going into finals look really good," Ronan said with pride, letting his mother's shot about his social media fame pass.

"That's wonderful. I am really happy for you and proud. Feels like you are at the right place indeed."

"Mom, really ... I am. I have always loved Notre Dame, as you know, but the people here have been so great to me during this time. I don't think I've told you about my Resident Assistant, but after fall break, he shared about losing his father in high school to cancer. His passing was not unexpected, but the diagnosis was a horrible shock. So, he gets it. It really helped to have someone in my hallway that understood what I was going through. You may have noticed at the break, I was not really myself, kinda lost and negative. My RA said his getting into ND was a tribute to his dad. That's kinda when I decided I was going to double down on work and get good grades for Dad. He helped me so much with the application and essay writing process to get me in here. You both did. My RA's story made me realize that the best thing I could do is finish what we all started really well."

"Oh, Ronan, although sad for both of you, it's wonderful that you were put in each other's paths," said Teddy. "That's how God works."

"I don't know if I ever told you this, but at first, I kinda felt like ND was tarnished due to Dad's, um, death. I was kind of upset that my dream was being tainted in a way. My RA helped me see that Dad would hate it if I felt like that. That he had somehow hurt my ND experience. So, I decided to hunker down on academics. That's why I have been working so hard. To show Dad, and I guess me and you, that it's not all ruined."

"I get it, Ronan. I do. Not letting this tarnish our lives is a struggle. Your RA sounds wise. What's his name?"

"Marcus. He's from Detroit and is a finance major too. He is just one of many guys who have helped me put things on the right track, Mom. I'm so glad that I am here. Thank you. I probably don't thank you enough for getting me here."

"Oh, Cakey, you gonna make me cry. I love you," responded Teddy in one of the many funny voices she used with regularity with the dogs and the boys, her heart welling up with sadness, appreciation and joy all at the same time.

"What are you doing today, Mom? Doing okay without Deck?" asked Ronan.

"Yes, I made it. He should be home in a few hours. I admit I was just feeling lonely, so I called you," Teddy shared.

"That's fine, Mom. I am happy to talk for a while."

"Are you ready to decorate the tree?"

"Oh yeah, I guess we will have to do it," Ronan said without continuing his thought, "because Dad's not here."

"Yep, it's on us. We finally get to do the tree together," she laughed, leaving unsaid, "because your dad never let us touch his ornaments for fear of breaking any and died due to a damn stolen pint glass."

"I guess it will be a new family tradition," said Ronan. "Dad sure was protective of his ornaments."

"Yes, yes, he was," said Teddy. "You still really don't realize how precious they are. Like the letters, they tell a story of our lives together. And many of them were actually very expensive, not just valuable from a sentimental standpoint."

"Yeah, yeah, I get it. I've heard the story of the signed Craig Biggio Astros jersey ornament you massively overpaid for at a school auction many times," kidded Ronan. "How much did you guys have to drink that night? I mean, seriously, you're not even Astros fans."

"Rudebox!" responded Teddy, referencing the title of an obscure Robbie Williams song that she and Colin used to joke about. "It is a neat ornament at least, and it'll always remind us of those silly Catholic school galas."

"I get it. Looking forward to the decorating, Mom."

"You know I've been reading Christmas letters with Declan. Would you be interested in reading one with me? I could read it out loud on the phone."

"Um, sure," said Ronan hesitantly.

Elated, Teddy ran to get the binder and flipped it open to the second to the last page. The realization that the letter reading was almost over gave her a chill.

"Oh, 2019, this was quite the year, Ronan."

Christmas 2019

With both boys now in high school, parenting is packed with mixed emotions. We find ourselves nostalgic about our sons' early childhood but also a little eager for them to matriculate onward. It's kind of like a good movie that's going a bit long, as we glance down every few minutes to check our watches. Our world has become topsy-turvy, with Declan and Ronan now taller than us and driving us around. Only our terriers, Molly and Sally, truly depend on us, demanding a steady diet of walks and couch time.

Around this time last year, we were Cotton Bowl-bound to see undefeated Notre Dame in the playoffs. Colin's good friend O'Malley – the matchmaker integral to our first meeting 20 years ago – hosted us in a lavish Jerry World suite for the big game. Friendly encounters with Notre Dame President Father Jenkins and Pro Football Hall of Famer Jerome Bettis were pregame highlights, as the Irish title hopes ended with a loss to eventual national champion Clemson.

This year, Colin's law firm job expanded; he now has an unwieldy nine-word title and global responsibilities. The new role led to additional international travel, with three trips to London and one to Berlin. In his never-ending pursuit of fun on work trips, Colin visited the Berlin Wall, cruised down the River Spree and even found an '80s music festival on his German excursion.

Soon after, we were off to London for our family vacation. UK highlights included a Chelsea FC stadium tour, Borough Market and the London Eye. At Hampton Court Palace – home to a 300-year-old garden maze that got the boys' competitive juices flowing – we saw Tears for Fears perform in its courtyard, marking our sons' first concert since they were in diapers watching the Wiggles 15 years ago.

A few days in England were followed by a week in Italy. Perched above the Spanish Steps on our first day in Rome, we enjoyed Aperol Spritzes, with "Spritz O'Clock" becoming an instant family tradition. We were thorough in our checklist of Rome's top attractions, visiting the Colosseum (ranking as Ronan's second favorite stadium on the trip, behind Chelsea's), the Pantheon (serving as another fantastic setting for Spritz O'Clock), St. Peter's Basilica (featuring a tour under the church of the excavations that house St. Peter's bones) and the Vatican Museum's Sistine Chapel (giving Michelangelo's painted ceiling a solid 30 seconds of attention after feeling like lab rats working our way through the longest, most decorated maze).

We also ventured outside of Rome for two day trips. First, we journeyed to Florence, known for its museums. Naturally, the one we led off with was the Museo Salvatore Ferragamo, so Teddy could absorb all the important history of the fashion designer. After that, we visited the Uffizi Gallery, the Duomo with its 463 steps, Ponte Vecchio and Michelangelo's sculpture of David. Our second getaway *stood out as Teddy's favorite day of the vacation, as we hired a driver to take us along the Amalfi Coast. We stopped and shopped in the gorgeous waterfront towns of Ravello, Amalfi and Maiori. By the end of the scenic drive, Teddy decided that these heavenly surroundings would be our retirement destination, as well as spots for both boys' weddings. She needed an extended Spritz O'Clock to help her get over leaving this place of such incredible beauty.*

Following Italy, we had an overnight in Windsor, staying at the castle used in the Rocky Horror Picture Show and other movies. At Heathrow, we were on the same flight as Texans Pro Bowl quarterback Deshaun Watson, adding to the long list of athletes Ronan has met. At 6-foot-3, our oldest is now taller than many of the pros he comes across. Other summer bright spots included a few days in Boston to check out Boston College, a two-week away camp near Dallas for Declan and AAU hoops tournaments at Texas A&M, Rice and Dallas for Ronan.

With school back in full swing, Teddy doesn't have to worry about dropoffs and pickups for the first time in forever. Instead, Declan and Ronan ride on their own in a sleek black Ford Explorer, which Ronan declared their best Christmas present ever (possibly forgetting about the Thomas the Tank Engine set they received when he was two).

Declan, currently in possession of a learner's permit, is excited for next year when it will truly become a shared vehicle. On their daily commutes, the boys talk about the NBA, video games and countless other topics much more interesting than what they had to suffer through with us as parents. Enjoying her morning tea, Teddy loves sending the boys off to school, especially on Mass days when they wear the traditional high school/college formal outfit: blue blazer, tie and khakis.

St. Michael's continues to impress us with strong academics accompanied by spiritual growth through community service and class retreats. Ronan was even elected class Pope in Theology class, an accolade he'll need to weave into next year's applications to Catholic colleges. Both boys earned spots on Knights sports teams, with Declan making the school golf team and Ronan playing basketball for the varsity squad. Additionally, Declan has joined his older brother as a student reporter for our neighborhood magazine, The Take.

We hope that we won't be just dreaming of a white Christmas this year, as we'll be enjoying the holidays in the Colorado Rockies with family and friends. Wherever you celebrate the season, may your days be merry and bright.

Colin, Teddy, Ronan and Declan

"Man, that was a great year, Mom," said Ronan. "I get it more now why you guys have been reading these. That trip to England and Italy was something. Amalfi was just crazy amazing. That driver taking all those hairpin turns and the views that were out of movies."

"Yes, overall, reading the letters has been good. There have been moments when reliving the past hurt more than it helped. We had such a wonderful life, didn't we? And of course, I will always remember Amalfi and Spritz O'Clock. All if it," Teddy said, leaving out that she had declared on the trip that she wanted the boys to return to spread her ashes there when the time came.

"Yes, Mom, we did. I am so sorry this happened to you," said Ronan, in an exhaling whisper.

"It happened to all of us, and I am sorry too."

"Well, Mom, I cannot wait to see you on Tuesday night and to decorate the tree, eat tons of your awesome food and watch the dog show, okay?"

"Yes, okay, honey. Love you!"

"Bye, Mom. See you in a few days."

Teddy flopped back on the couch and looked at her phone with the faint hope of something to help her kill time until Declan arrived home. New e-mail. More junk, probably. Amongst the typical junk was an e-mail Mr. DeSilva sent yesterday that she had missed.

Tap to open. A tiny spark went through her which made her bristle.

"What is going on with me?" she said to the girls who were next to her on the couch.

Subject: Another Declan Update

Dear Mrs. McNamara,

Declan is really opening up to me. We had many conversations over the last couple of weeks about his past but, more importantly, his future. Despite his loss, he is focused on making the best of things. He is nervous but excited about the prospect of going to college. He has increasing interest in Notre Dame, as I am sure you already know. His grades and activities, if they stay as they are, should give him such an opportunity.

Emotionally, I have been impressed by his strength. He is not in denial, but he is also not using his father's passing to start bad habits, which is very common in both youths and adults.

I am certainly hoping he goes to Notre Dame. Like you and your husband, I went there too. I was in the class of '83. I sure hope ND beats Wake Forest tomorrow. It should be a good game.

Happy Thanksgiving,

Mr. DeSilva

Teddy stared at the screen. He went to Notre Dame. Mr. DeSilva is a Notre Dame boy? She felt flushed, then ashamed. She forced herself to dismiss the thought of the undeniably handsome and kind Mr. DeSilva being a Notre Dame graduate. "Who cared if he went to Notre Dame anyway, "she mentally scolded herself. That was her ideal man criteria from long ago. She was not in the market for a man and never would be. She had a rule. If ever divorced or widowed, no more men. One and done was her philosophy.

Teddy, however, was glad to hear that Declan was doing well. That is what mattered.

She crafted a polite reply to Mr. DeSilva, keeping it strictly friendly and professional. She rationalized that it would be rude not to acknowledge his e-mail.

To: sdesilva@smcps.org

Subject: Thank you

Dear Mr. DeSilva,

Thank you for the continued updates about Declan. They are

much appreciated. That is wonderful news about his increasing interest in Notre Dame. It makes me very happy.

Always nice to know a fellow Domer. Go Irish.

Happy Thanksgiving,

Mrs. McNamara

Send.

The Tuesday before Thanksgiving arrived. Teddy had some energy in her step as a result. Ronan was on his flight from Chicago, and she was surprisingly optimistic about Thanksgiving. Ronan sent her a photo of the car that ferried him to Chicago. It was a stretch Escalade limousine packed with twelve college kids eager to make the ninety-minute trek to O'Hare to get home for the break.

"Boy, how life has changed for these college kids," she mused.

Despite all of her angst about the holidays, Thanksgiving was here. The start of it all. Thanksgiving was her favorite holiday, and she was determined to be strong for herself and for her sons. She was locked in with mental goals set.

She and Declan had used his two additional days off from school prior to Ronan coming home to get ready. That meant buying lots of junk food and getting all the ornament boxes out from under the stairs, which was a Harry Potter-like space stuffed with nothing but holiday décor. Had they lived in this house when the boys were younger, Teddy could imagine using this under-the-stairs area as a hideout for the boys.

Teddy only bumped her head twice while excavating the twelve meticulously packed ornament boxes from their storage spot. That meant she only cursed her beloved Colin twice, as well. This was typically his job, so Teddy felt okay with cursing him with each head bump she endured from the precarious storage spot. Teddy decided to replace the Wednesday before Thanksgiving mall Santa photo tradition with tree trimming. 2021 was the year for new things, whether she wanted it to be or not.

Declan and Teddy made the long journey to the airport to get Ronan in the late afternoon. "It felt good to be together," thought Teddy as she drove with Ronan and his bags securely in the Explorer. She felt foolish for thinking that as soon as she got home when, both boys immediately retreated to their rooms!

Chapter Thirty-Four

Declan decided not to share the letter with Ronan prior to the big reveal he planned for Thanksgiving Day. He felt good about the letter and decided that was all that mattered. Now that "the" letter was done, Declan started to think more seriously about the idea of writing letters to friends and faculty who helped him out during this extraordinary semester. He decided he would give it a try. He took the same "just do it" philosophy with his family letter, and it felt like he had achieved his goal, so why not try this?

He started on a letter to his best friend, Aaron. Aaron didn't go to his high school, but they had been best friends since middle school. Aaron got into a more prestigious high school, so they separated after eighth grade but remained best friends. Aaron was always there for him throughout these last few months. He did a good job of treating Declan normally, not pitying him or acting like Declan might break if he said the wrong thing. Aaron just got Declan. Always did and thankfully really did during this most difficult experience.

The structure of this idea that he had concocted in his mind blended a family Christmas letter with a letter to Santa. He felt like a little walk down memory lane was needed in keeping with the traditional Christmas letter, along with a heavy dose of thanking Aaron for all that their friendship meant. Unlike a Santa letter where you ask for things, this letter would be acknowledging and thanking the recipient for the gifts they had given the writer over the last year. In essence, acknowledging their good behavior that, of course, Santa saw as he was compiling his "Nice List."

Declan thought this was a sound concept, so he began writing Aaron's letter. He outlined inside jokes they shared while playing video games as well as various triumphs on the basketball court at Sundown Park in the neighborhood. Declan then moved on to thank Aaron for being a friend who helped him in a bleak time by just being himself and treating Declan like normal, too, not a victim or some sort of damaged goods. He closed with a joke, saying, "Santa will be copied on this letter, so he is sure to know what list to put you on."

He sat back and reread the letter. He liked it. It was

shorter than the traditional Christmas letter, but he thought it worked. Declan believed that people would be happy to receive these, so he kept writing to others. And if they weren't well received, writing the letters strangely felt good to him. He hated to think "therapeutic," but yes, they probably were just that. He enjoyed deeply thinking about the year and the memories with each person. Ultimately, he had drafted seven letters by the time he was done. He had written the afternoon away, and it was now dark.

Ronan barged into his room after apparently just waking from a nap, which meant he was moody.

"What ya doing, slimy?" asked Ronan, not really interested in the answer, and flexing his shirtless biceps in Declan's face.

"Writing letters," said Declan apprehensively.

"The letter?"

"Yes, and some others," replied Declan.

"What others?"

"I decided to write letters to a few friends and teachers that helped me this year," Declan responded.

"Oh, interesting. That's cool, bro," said Ronan, to Declan's amazement. Not getting told he was stupid was a triumph Declan relished at that given moment.

"Thanks."

"Deckhead, I was thinking about how much the ornaments mean to Mom and how much the letters do, too. What do you think about my having ornaments made that have a picture of each letter printed on them?" asked Ronan somewhat apprehensively.

"I think that is a really good idea. See ... you can have a good idea every so often," said Declan pleased with his jab of his older brother. "Do you think you can find a place to do that?"

"Sure, everything's makable on the internet," replied Ronan energetically. "I will go look into it now and see what I can find."

But before leaving Declan's room, Ronan playfully lunged at him, and they started to wrestle. It had been a long time since they had engaged in one of their silly wrestling bouts, during the summer probably. With Ronan being nearly forty pounds heavier than Declan, these were never fair fights. More like brotherly hazing.

Later that day as they ate dinner at the kitchen island, just the three-pack, Declan thought about how he and his brother were poised with good ways to help their mother through the first holiday without their dad. This pleased him, especially since Ronan seemed to be out of his funk.

The meal was lighthearted, probably the best vibe in their house in months. Teddy made one of Ronan's favorites, butter cheese pizza. It was her mother's recipe – butter and garlic as the sauce and parmesan and mozzarella as the only toppings. It was a simple delight, and she felt good making it for her son that fall day.

Teddy expressed excitement about the tree decorating the next day as she outlined how she saw the next day unfolding. She was seemingly determined to make "Thanksgiving Eve" a time of joy like it had been back when Declan and Ronan were small and geared up to chat with Santa in their matching little festive outfits. The brothers knew better than to give any hint of resistance to her plans.

Chapter Thirty-Five

Teddy had the Christmas music playing and the boxes of ornaments all set out by the time the sleepy and cranky teenagers made their first appearance a little before noon. Knowing that they would sleep the morning away, Teddy had a brunch feast ready to go with eggs, bacon and Belgian waffles. Declan loved waffles, and Ronan was a bacon-eating machine. Knowing this would be an all-afternoon activity, Teddy wanted the boys to be well fed. She was hoping with three people, it would go faster than when Colin solely trimmed the tree. That was a multiday affair!

It felt strange to do the tree as Colin never let anyone touch a thing. The boys were certainly on their A-game, as there was no complaining at all. They seemed to genuinely enjoy looking at the ornaments and talking about the memories associated with them.

Ronan seemed particularly into the Notre Dame ornaments that Teddy had collected when the school started producing them back in the '90s. He had never paid much attention to them in the past. Being on the beloved campus seemed to have piqued his interest in them. His favorite seemed to be the colorful replica of the painting inside the Golden Dome featuring angels in heaven.

"I need to go into the main building and look at the ceiling when I get back. I never realized how beautiful the paintings are," said Ronan who was not known for his art appreciation. The Bud Light can ornament and the Aperol Spritz ornament also gave him good laughs. Those favorites did not surprise Teddy. She knew her son.

Declan seemed to appreciate the ornaments of toys like Legos but, most of all, the ornaments featuring their dogs, Molly, who had passed away in 2020, Lucy and Sally. Declan always had much more interest in the dogs than his brother. Looking at a photo ornament of Molly that Declan was holding made Teddy remember how the poor dog endured little Declan smooshing down her head with his hand in what he thought was a gesture of love.

Teddy loved the ornaments from their many fantastic trips over the years. From London to Italy to Hawaii, they had quite a collection of memories that made their Christmas tree a tribute to their family's good times together. Santa on a turtle from Hawaii, a ceramic lemon from Amalfi, the tree was a treasure. Despite the bittersweet nature of this particular tree-trimming task, Teddy was more happy than sad. At least she could say that she and Colin savored life together. It was a rich, full life. The letters and the ornaments were definitive proof of that important fact. Her memory collection was a pretty darn good one.

There was one Christmas letter left to read. Teddy hoped all afternoon that the boys would indulge her and read it together. As they were winding down the tree decorating, which took nearly four hours even with three people, Teddy tossed out her idea. She figured they would not give her too much resistance, and they did not.

Her sons' only request was to stop playing the pop Christmas music that had been in the background all afternoon. Teddy decided she could give in on that one point. She, however, still remained dismayed that her boys never appreciated the music of her era, especially Christmas music. In her mind, two of the greatest albums ever were the *Very Special Christmas I and II* released in the late '80s and early

'90s. And her husband's pop music expertise brought in so many other wonderful Christmas songs that had been released over the years. Who couldn't enjoy Billy Idol's "Yellin' at the Christmas Tree?" Her sons, apparently.

Where had she gone wrong with their musical taste development? Teddy blamed rap. Ronan started out so strong. He loved Queen and watched a video of Freddie Mercury performing at Wembley Stadium in the '80s hundreds of times when he was one and two years old. He called Mercury "the man wearing white" and sang hits like "Another One Bites the Dust" in his little babyish voice. Another favorite as a youngster was Van Morrison's "Brown Eyed Girl." How had he dropped so far, now preferring rap? This was a mystery she would likely never solve.

The three-pack was exhausted and happy to take a seat on the puffy couch in the family room. The tree was lit, giving the room that warm, cozy feeling that Teddy loved so much. The small tabletop tree with their youthful Santa photos was also turned on. Both trees were complete, making Teddy feel as if she were on stable ground.

Christmas 2020

Our family dinners cover a variety of topics. At the start of this year, one touched on a pick-me-up survey that pinpointed the exact age when people reach their low point in happiness. The "survey says" (best read in Richard Dawson's or Steve Harvey's Family Feud voice) that happiness hits an all-time low for men at 47.2 years old. With Colin just months from the point known by researchers (and possibly named by JRR Tolkien) as the "Chasm of Despair," he scoffed and stated something like, "Whatever, I've never been happier!" He may or may not have strutted away singing, "Ain't nothin' gonna break-a-my-stride ..."

Soon after, 2020 broke-a our strides, wrecked-a our plans and kicked-a our butts. (A recent TikTok resurgence saves this 1983 song from being the most outdated reference in McNamara letter history). While we're not blaming the pandemic on Colin's rebuff, it certainly didn't help. At least this unfortunate shakeup spares you from our typical Christmas letter of blathering on about trips to Notre Dame, London, etc. Who could have predicted grocery store outings would be 2020's big adventures? Besides that blasted Nostradamus-like happiness survey, of course.

We experienced loss early this year, with Teddy's father passing away at 92 years old. We also said goodbye to our oldest dog, Molly. Confident that the lockdown would give a puppy plenty of housetraining time, we got a replacement Westie within weeks. Sally's new companion,

Lucy, was an easy name to select in keeping with our tribute to Peanuts.

With a full house of remote workers and learners from mid-March until school's end, no one could have guessed that our kids would beat us back to the office. Amazingly, our neighbor offered them summer internships at his company, BioGen, one of Forbes' next billion-dollar startups. We found it hilarious when Declan brought work home on his first day while Ronan talked about his "onslaught of emails and people wanting to meet."

Declan and Ronan's internships epitomized 2020. First, George Floyd's funeral caused some disruption, with the national event being just two miles away from their office and forcing a temporary closure. A few days later, the boys' in-office experience ended entirely. A company COVID-19 scare followed by the dreaded deep nasal pokes led to us reuniting as a work-from-home family. We felt parental joy in listening to Ronan's negotiations with vendors based in the Netherlands and checking in on Declan as he programmed coding projects in Excel.

It took 15 years and socially distancing for Teddy to finally get on social media. With 25 loyal followers on Instagram, she is well on her way to being a Kardashian-esque influencer. Fortunately, our teenage sons are giving her counsel as to what she can and can't post, which has helped avoid any unwanted controversy to this point.

This year's big trip was an hour-away getaway, renting a Galveston house as a momentary diversion from our Groundhog Day existence. Of course, our pool has been a lockdown lifesaver, with splash brothers Ronan and Declan enjoying pool basketball as a daily activity for much of the year.

This fall, the boys returned to St. Michael's with new safety measures (and a whole lot of Plexiglas) in place. Hanging out on campus with friends has brought a bit of normalcy back to their lives. Along with driving down the fairways on the golf team, Declan is now driving to school with a license in hand. Recently, the boys met with the school's board of directors about the "Men for Elders" alumni outreach program they created. In this presentation, Ronan and Declan shared how they lifted the spirits of the school's oldest graduates with phone conversations during lockdown.

Watching Notre Dame march to its third undefeated regular season in nine years mostly served as a weekly reminder of the looming admissions office decision for Ronan's application. We are thankful, blessed and relieved that Santa came early this Christmas. Ronan has been accepted by his top two choices, Notre Dame and Georgetown. Oddsmakers forecast him making a LeBron-like decision to "take his talents to South ~~Beach~~ Bend."

In this most unusual year, we hope that you are managing as best as possible. We wish you and your family a healthy and happy holidays!

Colin, Teddy, Ronan and Declan

"What a year, right?" said Teddy.

"Yeah, who knew that year was really nothing to complain about?" Ronan replied with tears in his eyes.

They sat in silence with their arms around each other.

Chapter Thirty-Six

As they worked away decorating the tree, Ronan committed himself to creating Christmas Letter ornaments. He was sure they would bring so much happiness to his mom. He just hoped he could pull it off in time for Christmas. He planned to sneak away with the binder at some point that day so he could take pictures of each letter. For most of his childhood, taking this binder for a little while would go unnoticed. But it had now become an extension of Teddy, accompanying her nearly all of the time. He was toying with the idea of using his dad's professional camera but wasn't sure if getting it out of its place in the living room credenza would cause too much commotion to keep this all a secret from his mother. The fancy camera that his mom bought for his dad was intended to allow

Colin to take action shots of Ronan's basketball games. The camera was one of his dad's prized possessions. Ronan thought about all those basketball games his dad attended with the camera in hand.

After they read the 2020 letter together, Ronan took the opportunity to whisk the Christmas Letter binder with him to his room. If his mom asked, Ronan would say that he had decided that he too wanted to read all of the letters. He forewent using his dad's fancy camera, opting to ensure the surprise by just using his phone's camera. His phone was a snazzy new model that his parents got him in May as a graduation present. Its camera was terrific. He thought back fondly on the excitement of graduation season with all the parties and gifts. Things were so positive back then.

Ronan had never really looked at the binder before. He had no idea it included letters from his grandparents reflecting his father's childhood. Sentimentality wasn't Ronan's forte, like most kids his age. Before he started snapping pictures, he looked through the binder in its entirety. He was moved by the chronicling that he had previously dismissed as boring. He now understood Declan's motivation to carry on their father's tradition. He was curious how his brother had done. He genuinely hoped for the best and that this would turn out to be a good thing for his mom.

The role reversal of him and his brother doing caring things for their mother was not lost on him. He and Declan were lucky. Both of their parents did so much for them, big and small. The vacations, the nice house, an outstanding education that would prepare them for anything, the frequent home-cooked meals, pool basketball and sports viewing as well as discussions about everything and anything.

Ronan looked around his room, which could double as a Notre Dame and NBA museum, given the number of photos and memorabilia looking back at him from the walls and shelves. Ronan had photos with more than twenty NBA stars after games his father took him to. These were just a few of the treasures Ronan knew he was fortunate to experience and were his motivation to do something meaningful for his mom now.

He enjoyed going through each year, starting in 1999 when his parents met and taking a clear photo of the front and back of each letter. The letter's backsides featured photos. Ronan was shocked that the photos from the early years were black and white. He figured color printing was very expensive twenty years ago, so his frugal father accepted black and white copies. It made it feel like those photos were forty years old, not twenty. The nineteen-year-old was not able to fathom that digital cameras were a new technology the year he was born.

Looking at photos of him and his brother growing up in this family brought a feeling of sentimentality that Ronan didn't know he possessed.

Next, Ronan had to upload each photo to the vendor site that he decided to use. He was pleased with the ceramic rectangle that would carry the front and back of each letter. They may be a little big at three by five inches but making them any smaller would make them impossible to read with indiscernible photos. The mocked-up design for each looked nice since each letter was printed on different holiday stationery each year.

His submitted order said delivery would be December sixteenth, the day he was scheduled to return home for Christmas break. Ronan was thrilled with the timing but wondered if he would be able to keep this a secret. He was so pleased that he figured out a way to get in the holiday spirit for his mother that he was bursting.

Declan came into Ronan's room just as Ronan was finishing his project.

"What's up?" said Ronan.

Declan, who was waiting for an insult or an order to get out, paused and then said, "Nothing, just wanted to see what you are doing."

"Just finished something I was working on," Ronan said casually. "So, are you reading the letter tomorrow?"

"Yes, I am ready, at least I think I am," Declan responded. "I just hope she likes it and that this is a positive thing."

"After reading one with you guys today, I realize that they are a good thing. Although they may make you sad, on the one hand, I also feel that connection to Dad because of the way they are written. He captured our memories, the story of our lives," said Ronan softly, trailing off.

"All right, thanks. I appreciate the support. I've kinda felt alone on this. It helps that you see what I see in doing this."

"Yeah, sorry I've been down on all this letter stuff. I can read it for you and give my thoughts if you want. I know I haven't been helpful. It's just a weird time. It's hard to know what is right. But for what it's worth, bro, it takes guts to take this on, and I am proud of you."

Declan seemed to be blown away by his brother's words. He didn't say anything in reply. He just held his brother's gaze. No more words were needed.

Chapter Thirty-Seven

On Thanksgiving morning, Declan found his mother busily cooking. She seemed happy. He knew the kitchen was a happy place for her. She always said she enjoyed making the Thanksgiving meal. The parades were on in the background, and Declan knew she was looking forward to the National Dog Show that came on afterward. The entire family always hoped a Westie or a Cairn would at least win the terrier category, if not the grand prize, as those breeds seemed to always be overlooked. It was a typical Thanksgiving, barring one massive omission.

Originally, Declan envisioned reading the letter after dinner. But because they were having his mom's friends over, Declan changed his plans to a morning reading because reading the letter with only the three-pack was simply how it needed to be. He kept almost asking his mother to sit down for a minute, but then his nerves overtook him, and he said nothing while sitting at the kitchen island, paralyzed with nerves. After several aborted attempts in his mind, Declan finally spoke up.

"Hey, Mom, when you have a good time for a break, let me know. I want to show you something," he said tentatively.

"Oh, okay, Declanator. Give me two minutes to finish chopping this onion," said Teddy using another of Declan's nicknames of her own making.

"Okay, I will get Ronan. I want him with us, too."

The three sat on the couch in the family room just off the kitchen. Declan asked to sit in the middle. He pulled out a sheet of paper with typing on one side. Teddy was not sure what this paper was. Declan started to speak in explanation.

"Mom, reading the Christmas letters really helped me during this time, and I think it helped you too. I really never paid that much attention to them, but looking at the binder was really meaningful to me. It's our family history, and I don't want it to end this year just because Dad is not with us … because I think he's still here. He's here in all of us, and I hope this letter shows that."

Teddy was already getting tears in her eyes, but she seemed to be doing her best to stay composed. Declan launched into reading the letter out loud in his deep voice.

Christmas 2021

Colin was always into pop music, and he love-hated bad cover versions of songs. We hope that he is looking down from Heaven love-hating this bad cover version of our family Christmas letter. Of course, he'll surely be disappointed that we didn't go with a "Papa Got Run Over by a Reindeer" parody for the letter, but it's way too soon, and we're missing him way too much.

Here are our highlights: the good and the bad.

Not to go all Old Testament on you, but, like the dove bringing the olive branch to Noah, 2021 opened with its own sign of hope: a return to in-person sporting events. After cheering on the Rockets in their New Year's Eve home opener, we drove to Dallas for the relocated Rose Bowl on New Year's Day. Reuniting with ND friends at Jerry World made us optimistic about the end of lockdowns, even if it didn't bring an end to Notre Dame playoff letdowns.

Before we could get too excited about the possibility of better days ahead, the February freeze fiasco left us without power for several days. A month later, a very COVIDy spring break meant canceling trip plans and staying put at home ... yet again.

Fortunately, the Easter Bunny brought us vaccinations and a much-needed vacation to Notre Dame. We celebrated Easter Mass at the Basilica and stocked up on supplies for Ronan's freshman year. Once vaccines were in full effect, we replaced social distancing with socializing. Who could have guessed how much we would miss school dances and parent galas?

Summer provided another opportunity for escape, so we relaxed in Arizona for a week at Sedona's Enchantment Resort. Highlights included an off-road Jeep adventure through the Red Rock wilderness and a Lakers/Suns playoff game for Declan's birthday.

In August, we brought Ronan to Notre Dame, where his dorm room gives him a view of both the Golden Dome and Teddy's old dorm. He has quickly adjusted to college and its freedoms. "Ronan McNamara's Day Off" in Chicago included a Cubs game at Wrigley and a night on the town. As Ferris Bueller once said, "Life moves pretty fast ..."

Declan adjusted quickly to being the only child left in the roost, although no Ronan on St. Michael's commutes means much quieter rides. Now a junior, Declan's social life, high school golf and rec league hoops fill his calendar.

And then, of course, there was the incident that stole our beloved Colin from us entirely too soon. He was a wonderful father, husband, friend and boss, so we were told by the outpouring of sentiment we received in September. He will be missed, and this letter lives on as a tribute to him. The Christmas letter was one of the special traditions Colin built with and for his family. Like many things, it was a labor of love for those he loved so much. We hope he knows just how much we love him.

During this holiday season of peace, love and joy, we wish you a merry Christmas and, hopefully, an even better new year. Thank you for the love and support you've shown during this difficult time.

All our love,

The McNamara Family

Teddy was stunned. She sat motionless with tears streaming down her face. Happy tears. Proud tears. Thankful tears.

"Declan," his mother exclaimed once she regained her composure. "Your letter could not be more perfect. Your father must be so proud right now. I know I am ... whatever beyond proud is! And thankful. What an amazing act of remembrance. My little Declan."

"Yeah, Declan," said a teary-eyed Ronan. "I think you nailed it. I am impressed at how you captured the humor and wit Dad had, especially since you are not that funny. But seriously, bro, what you did is amazing. I am proud of you, too."

"It was really hard to write," admitted Declan. "I am not going to lie. It's like, what do you put in it ... then you're like, what do I leave out? How do you make it not sound like an activity list? And then writing about Dad, that just sucked."

"Yeah, when I read them, they made me think of so many silly stories that didn't make the cut," replied Ronan.

"Like what?" inquired Teddy.

"I have one," said Declan," I don't know why Dad left out all of Ronan's crying when we would have confetti egg fights at Easter."

"Oh, okay, that's how you're going to play this," said Ronan.

The brotherly competitive juices started to flow.

"Or how about when I picked Adrian Peterson and Chris Johnson in that fantasy draft when you were in the fourth grade, and you ran off screaming and crying?"

continued Declan, who rarely had the upper hand on sibling insults. "Or how about the Easter egg hunt when you got the big golden egg and were so proud of yourself only to be pranked by Dad? Inside it contained no money or candy but a note that carried your favorite line at the time: 'not really though.' You know I am just roastin' and toastin' you, right, Ronan?"

"Roastin' and toastin'" was a phrase Ronan made up in his late middle school years when he started to learn the fine art of "the burn," as these insults were referred to in the '80s.

Ronan had either matured or was simply stunned, as he didn't come back with retaliatory insults against his brother. They all laughed and hugged. Declan was thrilled that the letter worked. It was a good thing. Teddy suggested the three of them should select the stationery tomorrow, go through the photos, and do the layout this afternoon.

"Your dad always handled production, and since that's my contribution to this project, I don't want to be late getting these out!"

Declan thought, "Yep, that's my mom, always turning things into a project with roles, responsibilities and timelines."

Ronan chimed in, telling them both about the

ornaments. The timing seemingly felt right.

"I was going to make this a surprise, but I feel like showing you now is the right thing. I've made Christmas tree ornaments out of every letter since 1999. They will arrive on December sixteenth. I have realized how much the letters, and the ornaments mean to you and to us, Mom. I hope you like them."

Ronan got his laptop and took over the middle spot on the couch to show his mom and Declan each ornament mockup.

They marveled at how cool this new collection for their tree would be. They all seemed to realize at that moment that although life would never be the same, they would still have special moments and special memories.

They sat there together, giving thanks for each other without uttering a word.

Chapter Thirty-Eight

The three-pack's Thanksgiving weekend was very good, considering the life adjustment they were in the midst of making. Teddy couldn't have been prouder of her boys' resiliency and her own, in fact. After Ronan was put back on a plane for Chicago to return to college, yet again, Teddy decided that she was going to pursue teaching. Like her sons, she had to begin new things while carrying on the memory of her husband. She called Dana to share the news.

"Hey there, is this a good time? Sorry to call you at work," opened Teddy.

"It's fine, Teddy. Are you okay?" asked Dana.

"Yes, thanks again for coming to Thanksgiving. It really helped to have more people around for the holiday. And I really appreciate you having two dinners – mine and your sisters. I bet you are sick of turkey!"

"It was very nice, Teddy. We enjoyed ourselves. It was nice to see the kids together again."

"Emily sure seems to be doing well. College life seems to be agreeing with her," added Teddy.

"Yes, she does. I'm really pleased. She seems to like the people and her classes much more than she did in high school. Ronan and Declan are doing so well, too, Teddy. What they did with the letter and the ornaments is just amazing. I still get misty thinking about it."

"It really is shocking how resilient they are. That's why I am calling. They inspired me to take the leap into teaching. I never told you, but I signed up for those alternative certification courses about a month ago. The program where you take a few classes, then a few tests, then voila, you are a teacher. I never told you because I was so unsure about really doing it, said Teddy.

"This is a wonderful thing! But what is making you continue to feel unsure?"

"Well, the guilt, I guess. I felt like I should just focus on the boys and make sure they were doing alright through all of this. I didn't feel like I should make plans for myself. I guess it's kind of like my rule—you know, my rule about if I ever got divorced or ... um, you know ... whatever ... I would never remarry. I guess it is kind of the same philosophy. I should just focus on the boys."

"Teddy! You and your rules! I know they come from a good place, and they give you structure, but rules are meant to be broken. You broke that silly five-year older, five-year younger thing and that brought you more than two decades with Colin."

"Yes, well, my mother-in-law kind of started the guilt. I mentioned the teaching idea to her, and she promptly put me in my place, saying Colin left me in a good place financially, so I should focus on the boys, not a job."

"I can see how that would sting. I cannot believe you did not tell me about that."

"Yes, well, you know me. I am a solo problem solver! I did talk to Mr. DeSilva about teaching when I met with him to ensure he was not a weirdo."

"I assume he was supportive. By the way, you said he was not a nerd. But you never painted a picture for me. What's he like?"

"You will never believe this, but he's extremely attractive in a sort of Mark Consuelos, a.k.a. Mr. Kelly Ripa, kind of way. Decidedly not a nerd. And I recently learned he went to Notre Dame! He was a few years ahead of me. I guess that puts him closer to sixty than my original guess of mid-fifties."

"Mr. Kelly Ripa, whoa … How did you find out about this ND thing?"

"He e-mails me from time to time to give me updates about his chats with Declan. And in his last note he talked about how Declan does indeed want to go to Notre Dame and that he is rooting for that because he went there too. Can you believe that?"

"No, I cannot believe there is a hottie in your life who also went to ND. Lightning striking twice!"

"Oh please, it's not like that. Seriously, my husband just died a couple months ago, Dana, and you know my rule about men if I am ever divorced or widowed. Not for me. Over it. One and done. Be serious!"

"Sorry, probably in bad taste, but we gotta start joking again, Teddy. But back to safer subjects, this teaching thing is a no-brainer. You will be terrific, and moving on is what Colin would want. Remember, moving on is not forgetting. It's not moving away from your past or your love. It's living, and it's the only option," said Dana emphatically.

"You don't think it's too soon? I don't want to rush things and end up in a disaster," asked Teddy pensively.

"It's not too soon if you are feeling interested in it. And what could be the disaster? If you try it and don't like it, you just stop. There is no potential disaster. Colin would be thrilled that you can actually pursue something you really always wanted to do."

"Yes, I did spend countless hours as a child playing at my chalkboard teaching my imaginary students, wearing my mother's high heels. Okay, then, I am going to do it! I cannot believe it. I have a plan, a horizon. Feels like forever since I felt this feeling of purpose."

"Well then, I truly do think it's the right thing. Sorry, but I gotta run. Late for a Zoom. Hugs! Go for it!" sang Dana happily as she hung up.

Chapter Thirty-Nine

Declan was so happy with the response his mom and Ronan had to his Christmas letter. This validation motivated him to finish up the other letters he started. He wondered if people would think the letters strange. He pushed that thought out of his head because he had this inner drive telling him to share his feelings.

The Christmas letters seemed to have unlocked something deep within him. He realized that sharing yourself with others was really a gift and even a responsibility. During his free period, he spent time refining the seven letters he started before the break. By the period's end, he felt like they were ready to go. He would see what stationery his mom selected for the family letter and potentially use that for his "bespoke" Christmas letters. He just hoped she didn't pick out something weird. They ended up not selecting the stationery as a group while Ronan was home. Ronan's busy social life seeing high school friends over his weekend home didn't allow for much shopping time.

When he arrived home from golf practice, Declan saw three stationery options on the kitchen counter. The first featured Rudolph, the version from the Rankin/Bass 1960s TV special his mother loved so much, the second a typical snowy house scene and the third snowflakes. In Declan's mind, Rudolph was the winner. He thought his dad would be proud of the theme tie-in to his opening paragraph's attempt at morbid humor.

"So, what do you think?" asked Teddy when she entered the kitchen.

"Rudolph, no competition, Mom."

"Yeah, I kind of thought it was the obvious choice, but I didn't want to only get that one. Since we are going with the reindeer joke in the opening, it certainly fits," said Teddy. "I think your father would approve of the irreverent joke ... ugh, now onto production."

His mother spent the evening finalizing the photographs on the back and going through the address list.

Declan and his mother always knew this was a big project, but they were finding out firsthand just what a labor of love this was.

Declan could tell his mother was gratified that they were carrying on the letter. Looking at the photographs from the last year tugged terribly at both of them. Ronan saw the visible devastation looking at the last photograph of his father with Ronan at the Notre Dame move-in weekend. Declan could almost hear his mother's thoughts of "had she only known it would be the last photo."

Impressively, his mother said, "At least your father's last photograph was at a place he loved the most."

"Yeah, Mom. That is a really good point. That's good that you can take something sad and look at it from a positive perspective. Both my grief counselor and Mr. DeSilva have talked about that as a, what do they call it, a coping mechanism."

"Yes, I guess it's what we've got to do. You and Ronan have certainly done it, and you are inspiring me. You guys are just THE best kiddos," she said, reaching out to give Declan a squeeze.

The pair struggled with whether to put in a photo of the newly reduced three-pack taken at Thanksgiving by Dana.

Declan suggested they not, with his mother agreeing. They had concluded they were most comfortable with signing the letter as "The McNamara family" rather than listing their names which would require the omission of Colin. The letter was a testament that the three of them were coping and thankful. Photographic and salutation evidence of their loss was not needed, and Declan was sure none of the recipients were ready for a family image without his father.

Ronan okayed the final photo layout for the letter's backside via text, and Teddy tore out of the house to get copies made.

Meanwhile, Declan took the ten sheets of stationery he skimmed off the top of the pile to their little home printer. He hoped the letters would print properly. This printer was not fancy and struggled to print more than a few pages at a time. Nonetheless, he did a test page, and it seemed to work. He adjusted the spacing a bit on each letter's page so the type font filled up the page. All and all, he was pleased with how they looked.

He did his best to do a crisp accordion fold on each. As he folded each letter, he reread them. Aaron's letter was about him treating Declan normally, which meant so much. Zach, a friend at St. Mike's, was about how he helped him get notes and makeup work during his skipping school days. Declan was pleased that Zach had become such a good friend. It took Declan a while to make friends in high school, but Zach was definitely a quality guy. Next was the letter to Juan, his golfing partner. Prior to his dad's death, he and Juan were just casual friends, nothing deep. But afterward, Juan made extra efforts to talk to Declan while on the course. He persevered in getting Declan to open up about his feelings. Although Declan didn't like the prying at first, he came to realize that Juan's concern and empathy helped him deal with the loss of his dad and come out of his shell in other social settings.

Josh was his final letter to a friend. Josh was in an interesting situation. He actually cheated off of Declan their freshman year without Declan's knowledge. When Declan learned about this, he decided Josh was definitely not his kind of person. And so for two years, Declan steered clear of him. But after the accident, Josh and Declan were paired randomly by a teacher for a Theology project. Declan was very upset about this pairing but had no choice. Working with Josh really showed Declan that people could change. Josh worked hard, and he and Declan became good friends and now frequently played video games and basketball together.

Dr. Fields was an amazing teacher and made AP Physics a great experience. She also dealt with Declan's situation with the right touch for Declan. She reached out to

Declan via e-mail every week to check in so as not to ask Declan how he was doing in front of the other students. Her sensitivity meant so much to Declan because he never wanted attention drawn to himself.

Mr. Z in the Learning Resource Center also meant so much to him this year. They worked together for the last six months after Declan was diagnosed with a learning difference. Mr. Z focused on things called executive functions, but what really made the most difference to him was how he gave usable tips about how to be more social. His parents were always on him about that, but for some reason, Mr. Z's encouragement and tactics made a difference in his ability and willingness to socialize.

Lastly, Mr. DeSilva's letter. Strangely, Declan thought of Mr. DeSilva as almost a friend now, and Declan was decidedly not one of those guys who befriended teachers. Mr. DeSilva's chats, although not completely welcome in the beginning, really helped him cope. And he could never thank him enough for helping him finalize the Christmas letter. For that, Mr. DeSilva would never be forgotten.

Declan tucked each letter into its corresponding envelope. Although the family Christmas Letter was delivered by mail, Declan planned to hand deliver these on St. Nicholas Day. His mom always made St. Nicholas Day a fun holiday by making everyone in the family put their shoes outside their bedroom doors the night before, so they woke to goodies like video games, t-shirts or new Christmas pajamas spilling out of their shoes. St. Nicholas Day is a longstanding tradition in Italian households. Declan wanted to deliver the letters on that day as a small homage to his mother.

That evening, Declan and his mother started the envelope-stuffing project. Putting together more than one hundred letters would take a few days. They were in no rush. As they folded, stuffed, labeled and stamped each letter, Declan considered telling his mom about his other letters but decided against it. For no real reason, he just wasn't ready to share.

On December sixth, St. Nicholas Day, outside of his door that morning were new Christmas pajamas featuring Rudolph the Red-Nosed Reindeer from the Rankin/Bass special. "The tradition continued," thought Declan when he opened his door that morning and saw them, smiling at his mom's nod to the Christmas letter stationery.

Traditions really were important. He got it. He never really gave them any thought before, but this year he got it. He was sure his mom sent a set to Ronan, too, but he texted to find out. And, yes, Ronan had a matching set of Rudolph pajamas delivered the day before! Exactly what a nineteen-year-old boy who lives in a dorm is willing to sport!

At school, Declan personally delivered each letter but asked each person to read it later. The pressure of watching each person read it in front of him was too much to handle. As the day wore on, he heard from every recipient, and there was genuine happiness in each of their voices. Everyone loved the thought, the effort, especially the line about Santa being copied. The letters were a hit, and Declan felt good about what he had done. In fact, each person who got a letter thought the idea was fantastic. Each saying in their own way, "I should do this."

Chapter Forty

Mid-December was upon the three-pack, a mere few days prior to the start of Christmas break for both Ronan and Declan. Friends and family's response to Declan's letter was euphoric. No one, except Dana and Mr. DeSilva, who was added to the list, knew it was Declan's work until they contacted Teddy, telling her how pleased they were that *she* carried on the tradition. She was proud every time she got to tell recipients that it was her son *Declan* who picked up the torch and carried on Colin's legacy.

Her son had blossomed, and Teddy couldn't have been happier for herself and, of course, for Declan. She always knew he would sprout, grow wings, whatever trite euphemism you prefer. But as her youngest, she was always torn between him staying young – as she jokingly used to plead with him to "stay baby" – and growing up, as one naturally should. This Christmas letter was a clear sign that he was a young man who would be a positive part of the world.

Meanwhile, at school, Christmas letters shared among students and faculty seemed to take a life of their own. More and more people were giving and receiving bespoke Christmas letters, Declan McNamara's heartfelt creation. This simple gesture of kindness had evolved into its own sort of movement. The typically low-key Declan had become a bit of a celebrity on campus because of it. Unknown to Declan, he was even going to be mentioned by the school president, Father Jones, in the school's Christmas mass homily.

His mother was personally invited to attend the mass, which parents were typically not allowed to attend due to space limitations. His mother received a call from Father Jones's assistant two days prior. Given that she always wanted to attend a student mass, she didn't ask why. She simply accepted, assuming the school was just being kind, given what had happened to her family just a few months earlier. Teddy was always pleased with the choice of this school academically, but over the years, she grew to appreciate the community of caring that came with it.

The students were gathered for their final mass of the

semester. The mass began like any other with the various rituals of a Catholic Mass. Boys were sitting and standing as the mass progressed. The homily was always the most meaningful part of the mass for Teddy and for most people, assuming the priest made relatable remarks to the congregation about the Bible readings and their lives. In this case, Father Jones's homily told the story of Declan's Christmas letters. Declan was stunned but also extremely glad that his mother was there to hear the story.

Father Jones described the letters as "the true spirit of Christmas. The giving of oneself was what Jesus was brought to this earth to encourage among us. Expressing gratitude towards people in your life is a valuable gift."

Father Jones went on to say that "it's the small gestures that make life better and brighter" for everyone. Father even appreciated Declan's humor in mentioning that each letter noted that Santa was getting a copy to ensure he would know which list to assign the person. He challenged the St. Michael's community to find ways to give of themselves, not just during the holidays but throughout the year. He promised the impact would be positive and would be noticeable, just as Declan's letters begot more letters until the St. Michael's campus was afloat in comradery and good feelings. A positive and noticeable transformation had occurred, with some fondly referring to it as "a Christmas miracle."

Chapter Forty-One

Teddy sat in the auditorium where the school masses took place, surrounded by twelve hundred boys in their Catholic schoolboy uniform of khaki pants and blue blazers in quiet awe. She couldn't believe her little Declan had done this. She was so proud of the family letter he wrote and now this, another unexpected act of love and growth. She always loved Declan's sweet little heart. He was growing up and becoming such a wonderful person. Both boys were. Ronan's ornaments arrived the day before and were such a lovely tribute to Colin and to their family. She was truly blessed.

Although a major chapter of her life's collection of memories was complete, Teddy understood that there were more chapters to be written and many more memories to come. The key was to be open to creating them.

After Mass, Declan waited for his mother outside the auditorium. He decided being late to class was okay, given the circumstances. When he saw his mom, her eyes were filled with tears, happy tears.

"You made a 'thing,' Declan!" she exclaimed, hugging him tightly with a reference to how the family would often look for projects – "things" – in which to get involved. "It's such a great idea, and from the sounds of it from the homily, it's truly a trend. You're like your mama, an idea person, but in your case, you acted upon your idea, which is the most important part. Or should I put it in today's terms? You are an influencer! Have you thought of a name for your invention?"

"No, I didn't really think of it as an invention," said Declan shyly.

"How about calling them 'CC Santa Letters'?" suggested Teddy. "Because ... you are kind of writing to the recipient about what they meant to you, and you say that Santa is getting a copy. Get it? You know, CC means carbon copy, which is from ancient times—even before me, Declan— if someone was to get a copy of a letter, it was done with something called carbon paper. Anyway ..."

"Yes, I get it, Mom. I know about CCs from email. I

guess that works."

They laughed together at the strange turn of events. No one, including Declan, would have ever thought he would be a trendsetter. As they were walking through the tree-filled campus, Ronan came running up out of breath.

Both Declan and Teddy were shocked. Ronan wasn't due to arrive until later in the day.

"What are you doing here? How did you get here?" blurted Teddy, hugging him closely. "I'm so happy to see you!"

"Well, Mom, Father Jones called me and told me about what Declan created and told me he was featuring it in his Christmas mass homily and asked if I could get home for it. I tried getting on an earlier flight via standby, but it looks like I just missed it," Ronan explained.

"You did, but you tried. That's what matters," said Declan.

The three of them sat on a bench in the quad, soaking up the seventy-degree December day and the beauty of the campus. They silently held hands, appreciating that they were together. Christmas was going to be okay. They were going to be okay. The Christmas letters saved them. Teddy was sure of it.

"Thank you, Colin, my love, as always. I appreciate you and all that you do for our family," she said in her head.

Teddy was gratified that they seemed to be doing more than simply going on. They, especially her boys, were moving ahead, living, but not forgetting.

Chapter Forty-Two

Declan turned and saw Mr. DeSilva approaching in a slight jog.

"Hi, Mr. DeSilva," said Declan.

"I am so glad I caught up with you," said Mr. DeSilva, slightly out of breath. "Hi everyone."

"Hey, Mr. DeSilva," said Ronan. "Remember me?"

"Of course, I remember you. It's only been a few months since you left our little campus for the big leagues at Notre Dame. I am not senile just yet."

"How are you, Mr. DeSilva?" inquired Teddy.

"I am doing well. Thank you. That is why I ran to talk with all of you. I want to share some news. Talking with

Declan over the last couple of months, seeing him have the strength to carry on your family's Christmas letter tradition and then receiving his personal Christmas letter motivated me to start up my Christmas letter again. My wife was the main author, making this quite a challenge. But I was inspired. So, thank you, Declan. When I started talking to you about your loss, I thought I was the one helping you. As it turns out, you helped me just as much. I cannot thank you enough. Getting to know you and your mother has been a bright spot this year."

"That's great, Mr. DeSilva," responded Declan.

"It sounds like Declan has been influencing a lot of people here at school. Who would have thought my quiet little brother ..." Ronan commented.

"Well, that is just lovely to hear, Mr. DeSilva. Moving ahead. It's what we must do. I've come to appreciate that it's just that ... it's moving ahead, not moving on or forgetting," said Teddy.

"Well put," replied Mr. DeSilva. "Speaking of moving ahead. Have you decided whether you are going to take teaching classes?"

"Yes, I am signed up and plan to start in January. I just may be a teacher by the next school year, if you can believe it," exclaimed Teddy.

"I can, and I think you will be great. And I am happy to help you if the need arises."

"Thank you. That is a kind offer, Mr. DeSilva."

"Bye, McNamaras. Have a Merry Christmas," said Mr. DeSilva as he started to turn away.

"Merry Christmas," said Teddy, catching his eyes just before he turned fully away.

"Mom," said Declan. "Why don't we invite him over for Christmas Day?"

"Mr. DeSilva? Oh, I am sure he has plans," rebutted a shocked Teddy.

"No, Mom, I know he does not. He doesn't have much family. I think we should invite him. You'd want someone to invite you if *you* were alone, right?

"Well, yes. You are very sweet, Declan. Ronan, how do you feel about this?" inquired Teddy.

"Mom, I don't know how to tell you this, but you two have a vibe. I know that's gross, and I cannot believe I just said that, but I saw it. And he's a nice man who clearly deserves some kindness, so it's a no-brainer," said Ronan.

"Well, go run after him, one of you," said Teddy, flustered but excited.

Part Three

Is *moving ahead* forgetting?

November 2022

Chapter Forty-Three

"Sam, what do you think of me assigning my tenth grader's CC Santa letters?" inquired Teddy, as she nestled deeper into Mr. DeSilva's chest while they lay on his couch.

This early November day was the first day with a bit of a chill in the air in Houston.

"It's still funny to me that you are now calling me Sam. There were so many months of Mr. DeSilva—at least eight, correct?

"Look, don't hassle me about my rules. You seem to make me break many of them. First, the teacher's name rule, then the dating after divorce/death rule, not to mention that you are six years older than I am, breaking my five years younger/older rule. Clearly, you are trouble, Mr. Samuel DeSilva, making a good girl like me break all my good rules."

They shared a good laugh.

"Yes, I think that would be a wonderful assignment. I may have to borrow that for my students."

Although Teddy and Sam decided after months of mere friendship to move ahead and officially date, they agreed, however, that they were never moving on from the first spouses. Just moving ahead with a different part of life.

***

"Okay, ladies and gentlemen, I have an unusual assignment for you this holiday season," Teddy explained to her tenth grade Literature class. "I realize we normally read books and write about various aspects of those works. This assignment will be original works by you, not an analysis of others. So, it should be a nice change of pace."

Teddy went on to explain the Christmas letters that her late husband wrote and how her son carried on the tradition after his father died last year.

"That's awful," said Olivia, one of her notoriously talkative students.

"Yes and no," Teddy replied. "Yes, his death was terrible, but my son taking on the tradition means the world to me. It's what made me realize that life was going to go on. But it wasn't just the Christmas letters that gave me hope for the future. My son also wrote personal letters to people who meant a lot to him over the last year. The letters talked about their time together over the year, like a normal Christmas letter, but also thanked them for things that meant a lot to him over the year. He ended each letter saying, 'Santa will be copied on this letter, so he is sure to know what list to put you on.' So, it's sort of a Christmas letter and a letter to Santa combined."

"My son wrote seven letters last year for friends and teachers at his school, and it took off," Teddy continued. "People at his school were writing letters left and right to friends, teachers and parents. It became a 'thing.' So, your assignment is to pick three people and write what I call 'CC Santa Letters' as I just described. My goal is to make what my son started an even bigger 'thing' to honor my sons and late husband. Because these letters are personal, I will not read them, but I encourage you to put in effort for those three special people and be sure to actually give out the letters."

"My son hesitated about giving them to each recipient last year, but he was so glad that he did," Teddy concluded. "Telling people how you feel and showing appreciation is lifechanging. Oh, and every grade for this assignment will be an A. Merry Christmas."

***

Colin saw it all from the heavens. His sons were growing and thriving, and his wife was charting a new path he knew she deserved. They were living, continuing to build a collection of memories. He wanted nothing more than for them all to live. He understood "moving ahead" and "going on" or whatever sensitive term was given to people coping and living after the death of a loved one did not mean he was forgotten. Colin was thankful and content. He indeed had friendship, love and loyalty from his family, and nothing could change that.

Acknowledgments

Thanks to my many friends who were readers along the way and encouraged me to pursue this story.

Without my husband Dan's wit and commitment to producing Christmas letters each year, this book would not have been possible, so thank you, and I love you.

Thank you to my sons Kevin and Carter for enriching my life with so many precious moments of joy, laughter and love.

Special acknowledgement goes to Anna Bierhaus for her developmental editing efforts and to Daniel Forero for the beautiful cover art.

Thank you to the University of Notre Dame for being a defining part of my life for more than thirty years.

Thank you, God, for always being with me and giving me lightning bolts of clarity when I have needed them most and for always being with me, even when I don't realize it.

About The Author

Life in Christmas Letters is Theresa McKenna's first novel and is based upon the Christmas letters that her husband has written for more than twenty-five years.

The story is semiautobiographical and taps into Theresa's upbringing by first-generation Italian American parents, the lifelong impact of attending the University of Notre Dame and her feelings about being a working mother.

Theresa is a retired marketing professional who lives in Houston, Texas, with her husband. Her two sons are college students at Notre Dame.